# Private Military and Security Companies

Over the past twenty years, private military and security companies (PMSCs) have become significant elements of national security arrangements, assuming many of the functions that have traditionally been undertaken by state armies. Given the centrality of control over the use of coercive force to the functioning and identity of the modern state, and to international order, these developments are clearly of great practical and conceptual interest.

This edited volume provides an interdisciplinary overview of PMSCs: what they are, why they have emerged in their current form, how they operate, their current and likely future military, political, social and economic impact, and the moral and legal constraints that do and should apply to their operation. The book is divided into three sections, focusing first upon normative issues raised by the development of PMSCs, then upon state regulation and policy towards PMSCs, and examining finally the impact of PMSCs on civil–military relations. Bringing theory and empirical research into mutually illuminating contact, the book includes contributions from experts in international relations, political theory, international and corporate law, and economics, and also breaks important new ground by including philosophical discussions of PMSCs.

Students of PMSCs, international security and international relations will find much of interest in this book.

**Andrew Alexandra** is Senior Research Fellow at the Centre for Applied Philosophy and Public Ethics at the University of Melbourne

**Deane-Peter Baker** is Senior Lecturer in Philosophy and Ethics at the University of KwaZulu-Natal in South Africa, and is also Director of the University of KwaZulu-Natal Strategic Studies Group.

**Marina Caparini** is Senior Fellow, Research Division, at the Geneva Centre for the Democratic Control of Armed Forces.

# Cass Military Studies

# Private Military and Security Companies

Ethics, policies and civil–military relations

Edited by
Andrew Alexandra,
Deane-Peter Baker and
Marina Caparini

 Routledge
Taylor & Francis Group

LONDON AND NEW YORK

First published 2008
by Routledge
2 Park Square, Milton Park, Abingdon, Oxon OX14 4RN

Simultaneously published in the USA and Canada
by Routledge
270 Madison Ave, New York, NY 10016

*Routledge is an imprint of the Taylor & Francis Group,
an informa business*

Typeset in Palatino by
Newgen Imaging Systems (P) Ltd, Chennai, India
Printed and bound in Great Britain by
Biddles Digital, King's Lynn

*British Library Cataloguing in Publication Data*
A catalogue record for this book is available
from the British Library

*Library of Congress Cataloging in Publication Data*
A catalog record for this book has been requested

ISBN10: 0–415–43275–8 (hbk)
ISBN10: 0–203–93083–5 (ebk)

ISBN13: 978–0–415–43275–7 (hbk)
ISBN13: 978–0–203–93083–0 (ebk)

# Contents

# Contributors

**Andrew Alexandra** is Senior Research Fellow at the Centre for Applied Philosophy and Public Ethics at the University of Melbourne. He is the co-author of *Police Ethics* (Allen and Unwin, 2nd edn, 2006) and *Reason, Values and Institutions* (Tertiary Press, 2002), and editor of the *Australian Journal of Professional and Applied Ethics*.

**Deane-Peter Baker** is Senior Lecturer in the School of Philosophy and Ethics at the University of KwaZulu-Natal. He is also Director of the University of KwaZulu-Natal's Strategic Studies Group and is currently Chairman of the Ethics Society of South Africa. He is Consultant to the South African National Defence Force and is the South Africa coordinator for the Privatized Military Operations Industry Study conducted annually by the Industrial College of the Armed Forces, National Defense University, Washington DC.

**Jurgen Brauer** is Professor of Economics at the James M. Hull College of Business at Augusta State University, Augusta, GA, USA. He is Co-editor of *The Economics of Peace and Security Journal* (with J. Paul Dunne), and co-edits Routledge's Defence and Peace Economics monograph series (with Keith Hartley). His latest book (with Hubert van Tuyll), on economics of military history, is forthcoming with the University of Chicago Press, in 2008.

**Doug Brooks** is President of the International Peace Operations Association (IPOA), a non-governmental, non-profit, non-partisan association of service companies dedicated to improving international peacekeeping efforts through greater privatization. He is a specialist on African security issues and has written extensively on the regulation and constructive utilization of the private sector for international stabilization, peacekeeping and humanitarian missions, especially in Africa. He has testified before the US Congress and the South African Parliament and is a frequent contributor to international news programmes.

**Marina Caparini** is Senior Fellow in the Research Division of the Geneva Centre for the Democratic Control of Armed Forces (DCAF).

Her research focuses on oversight and accountability of the security sector. Recent publications include 'Domestic Regulation: Licensing Regimes for the Export of Military Goods and Services' in Simon Chesterman and Chia Lehnardt (eds), *From Mercenaries to Market: The Rise and Regulation of Private Military Companies* (Oxford: OUP, 2007); and 'Applying a Security Governance Perspective to the Privatisation of Security' in *Private Actors and Security Governance*, A. Bryden and M. Caparini (eds), (LIT Verlag, 2006).

**Matan Chorev** is a graduate of the Fletcher School of Law and Diplomacy, Tufts University. He is Co-founder of the New Initiative for Middle East Peace (NIMEP), a project of the Tufts Institute for Global Leadership. He is a past Research Associate at the International Peace Operations Association (IPOA) and Rosenthal Fellow at the Office of the Deputy Assistant Secretary of Defense for Policy Planning.

**Dominick Donald** is Senior Analyst with AEGIS, a British private security company. He served in the British Army, worked as Programme Officer for the UN in New York, wrote leaders (editorials) for *The Times* and was Contributing Editor at *Red Herring Magazine* before joining AEGIS at its inception in 2002. He has a PhD in War Studies from King's College London, has contributed to several academic journals and is the author of the Whitehall Paper, *After the Bubble: British Private Security Companies after Iraq* (RUSI, 2006).

**Adedeji Ebo** is Senior Fellow and Head of Africa Programme at the Geneva Centre for the Democratic Control of Armed Forces (DCAF), Switzerland. He was previously Associate Professor and Head of Department of Political Science and Defence Studies at the Nigerian Defence Academy, Kaduna, Nigeria.

**Mervyn Frost** joined the Department of War Studies at King's College, University of London in 2003 as Professor of International Relations in the Centre for International Relations. His academic qualifications include BA (Stellenbosch), MA (Stellenbosch), BPhil (Oxford), and DPhil (Stellenbosch). He was educated at the University of Stellenbosch and subsequently, as a Rhodes Scholar, he studied Politics at Oxford. His major publications are: *Towards a Normative Theory of International Relations* (Cambridge University Press, 1986), *Ethics in International Relations* (Cambridge University Press, 1996) and *Constituting Human Rights: Global Civil Society and the Society of Democratic States* (London: Routledge, 2002).

**Emanuela-Chiara Gillard** is Legal Adviser in the Legal Division of the International Committee of the Red Cross, where she is responsible, inter alia, for legal issues raised by displacement, the protection of civilians, women and children in armed conflict, occupation, multi-national forces and private military/security companies. In 2003 and 2004 she spent several months in the field as legal adviser to the ICRC's operations in Iraq. Prior to joining the ICRC in 2000, Ms Gillard was Legal Adviser at the United Nations Compensation Commission, in charge of government claims for losses arising from Iraq's invasion and occupation of Kuwait. Ms Gillard is a solicitor of the Supreme Court of England and Wales and holds BA and LLM degrees from the University of Cambridge.

**Asa Kasher** is Emeritus Professor of Philosophy at Tel Aviv University, where he was Laura Schwarz-Kipp Professor of Professional Ethics and Philosophy of Practice. He is also a senior research associate at the IDF College of National Defense and Vice-Chair of the Jerusalem Centre for Ethics. He played a major role in writing the IDF first Code of Ethics and guidelines of the Military Ethics of Fighting Terrorism. He won the national highest Prize of Israel for his contributions to philosophy.

**Christopher Kinsey** is Lecturer in International Security in the Defence Studies Department, King's College, London. He works at the United Kingdom's Joint Services Command and Staff College lecturing to officers of all nationalities. Prior to taking up this lecturership he was an ESRC post-doctoral fellow at the Department of International Politics, Aberystwyth University. He researches the impact of private security on international politics. He is the author of *Corporate Soldiers and International Security* (London: Routledge, 2006).

**Elke Krahmann** is Senior Lecturer in International Relations at the University of Bristol. She has previously been a DAAD fellow at the Center for European Studies at Harvard University. Her publications include *New Threats and New Actors in International Security* (ed.) (Palgrave, 2005) and *Multilevel Networks in European Foreign Policy* (Ashgate, 2003). Currently she is working on a monograph on the privatization of the armed forces in Europe and North America.

**Joseph Runzo** is Professor of Philosophy and Religious Studies at Chapman University, Life Member of Clare Hall, Cambridge University and Executive Director of the Global Ethics and Religion Forum, an international educational non-profit organization. Joseph Runzo has written ten books and he is currently directing an inter-national project to revise Just War theory and military ethics for the twenty-first century. His most recent articles include, 'War and the Role of Religion in Global Civil Society' in *Civil Society, Religion and Global Governance* (London: Routledge, 2007).

**Christopher Spearin** is Assistant Professor in the Department of Defence Studies at the Canadian Forces College. His research concerns change in militaries, global security governance, non-state actors, mercenaries, the privatization of security and Canadian foreign and defence policy. His work has been published in a variety of forums, including *Canadian Foreign Policy, Canadian Military Journal, International Peacekeeping, Journal of Conflict Studies, Civil Wars, World Defence Systems, Contemporary Security Policy, International Journal, International Politics* and *Parameters*.

**Uwe Steinhoff** is Senior Research Associate in the Oxford Leverhulme Programme on the Changing Character of War. Before going to Oxford, he taught philosophy at Humboldt University, Berlin. He is the author of *Effiziente Ethik: Über Rationalität, Selbstformung, Politik und Postmoderne* (Mentis, 2006), *Kritik der kommunikativen Rationalität: Eine Darstellung und Kritik der kommunikationstheoretischen Philosophie von Jürgen Habermas und Karl-Otto Apel* (Mentis, 2006) and *Moralisch korrektes Töten: Zur Ethik des Krieges und des Terrorismus* (Melzer, Neu-Isenburg 2006). The latter book is forthcoming in English as *On the Ethics of War and Terrorism* (Oxford University Press, 2007).

**Jessica Wolfendale** is Australian Research Council Postdoctoral Research Fellow at the Centre for Applied Philosophy and Public Ethics. She has published on military ethics, the ethics of torture, and moral philosophy, and is the author of *'Torture and the Military Profession'*, forthcoming from Palgrave MacMillan.

**Herbert Wulf** was the Founding Director of the Bonn International Center for Conversion. He is now Chief Technical Advisor to UNDP, Pyongyang on Arms Control in North Korea and Visiting Scholar at the Australian Centre for Peace and Conflict Studies, University of Queensland, Brisbane. His research interests concern the defence industry peacekeeping, development policy and international relations.

# Acknowledgements

This volume is the culmination of a programme of research that began with an international interdisciplinary conference held in South Africa in 2005. The conference was sponsored by the School of Philosophy and Ethics and the Unilever Ethics Centre at the University of KwaZulu-Natal, the Australian Research Council Special Research Centre for Applied Philosophy and Public Ethics and the Geneva Centre for the Democratic Control of Armed Forces. The editors would like to extend their thanks to these organizations for their support, without which this project would never have gotten off the ground.

# Introduction
## The ethics and governance of private military and security companies

*Andrew Alexandra, Deane-Peter Baker*
*and Marina Caparini*

The emergence and astonishing growth of private military and security companies (PMSCs) is clearly one of the most noteworthy developments in national and international security arrangements of the past three decades. PMSCs can provide a range of services commercially, up to and including military force, which have long been the preserve of national defence forces and other state security structures. PMSCs differ in two fundamental, and related, ways from such forces: (1) their commercial orientation and (2) their capacity to offer their services to a range of different clients, including non-state actors. These facts about PMSCs appear to bring them into conflict with the norms which have long been at the heart of moral theorizing about, and legal regulation of, organized coercive force, such as the monopoly of the state over such force, the citizen army as the paradigmatic form for its organization, the illegitimacy of mercenary military forces and so on.

These apparent conflicts have provoked a range of different responses. Some argue that once the true nature of PMSCs is understood, or the rationale for the norms fully spelt out, it will be evident that the conflict is *merely* apparent. Others take it that the conflict is real, though they differ about what follows from that. Some think that if the right kinds of adjustment to the organization or regulation of PMSCs are made, the conflict will disappear. Others think that, in the light of contemporary realities, the conflict will not disappear, but that changes do need to be made to the norms which we accept as governing the activities of PMSCs. Finally, there are those who believe that given the reality of the conflict, PMSCs should be forbidden, or at least tightly circumscribed in their activities.

The essays in this collection exemplify this range of responses to the challenges presented by PMSCs in their different functions and contexts of operation. Before considering the details of these responses, it is perhaps worth pointing to two (apparently) novel features of the context within which the debates about PMSCs are occurring, and a set of the implicitly accepted presumptions which govern those debates. The first source of novelty is the fluid geo-political era following the end of the

Cold War. In the developed world, the collapse of the Soviet system removed the threat which had been the main *raison d'être* of the military forces of Western states. At the same time, the crumbling of the main ideological alternative to the capitalist system contributed to the growing influence of neo-liberalism, marked by the trend towards the privatization of a range of services previously provided by the state. The increasing role of PMSCs is merely one example of that trend. In the developing world, the end of the bi-polar international order removed the incentive that the sole remaining great power had to gain influence over the rulers of small states by providing them with the resources they need to secure themselves against usurpation. Consequently, in fragile states, particularly in Africa, where governments possess only tenuous legitimacy and limited coercive power, state and non-state actors alike have been forced to look for other providers of security. Finally, the dissolution of a tight-knit international order of states has stimulated 'new wars' involving non-state actors, such as religious or ethnic-based organizations. These new wars can affect developed and developing states alike, and seem to require flexible and rapid responses of a kind which traditional armies find difficult to provide.

The changes in the geo-political order pointed to above have thrown into doubt the capacity of state armies to provide the needed force – or at least to do so as effectively as PMSCs, or without the supplementation by PMSCs – in certain circumstances. The second source of novelty is relevant to the assessment of the legitimacy of PMSCs as providers of the needed force. As commercial enterprises PMSCs may in a straight-forwardly technical sense be considered mercenary organizations. However, they differ from the traditional mercenary forces in their corporate structure, which means that they are at least notionally capable of being constrained by various forms of national and international regulations and accountable to the interests of stockholders and other interested parties. Mercenary military organizations have, of course, long been seen as morally and legally illegitimate. However, it is arguable that the corporate structure of PMSCs removes (many of) the reasons for that status.

While there is much disagreement among the contributors to this collection about the nature and meaning of the developments pointed to above for the assessment of PMSCs, there is broad consensus about the basic structure of the evaluative framework which is to be used for that assessment. Indeed, that consensus has become so firm that it generally 'goes without saying'. It is, however, worth briefly making it explicit, in order to clarify the points at which disagreement arises. All the contributors draw on what might be thought of as a broadly liberal view of justified (political) violence. According to this view, violence is not justified either as an end in itself, or as a means to an end. Notwithstanding, violence, or the threat of violence, can become justified (and in some cases obligatory) in as much as it is necessary as a means to deter or prevent the violation of rights, or to rectify such violations if they nevertheless occur. This view has obvious implications for the evaluation of the use of coercive force by military institutions – rendering it illegitimate in the case of invasion, but justified as a response to such invasion, say. It also has implications for the structure of such institutions. If, for example, it is true that state armies are less likely to be used for unjustified military adventures than private forces, that is a powerful reason to prefer state armies. In any case, much of the disagreement between contributors to this collection regarding the desirability of PMSCs relative to state forces, the forms of regulation that should be put into place to control them and the like, stems from their differing assessments about how compatible they are with the liberal view.

The chapters in the first section of this collection focus on a range of ethical issues that are raised by PMSCs, especially in relation to their capacity to provide military force. There is a long and rich tradition of theory dealing with the ethics of war and related matters: philosophical discussion of these matters has been particularly lively over the past thirty-five years or so, following the publication of Michael Walzer's *Just and Unjust Wars*. It is a striking feature of that discussion, however, that it has had very little to say about the ethics of mercenary military fighting in general, and even less about the ethics of PMSCs specifically. There appears to have been a tendency to accept the popular and legal assessment of mercenaries as morally reprehensible, if not completely unacceptable.

As indicated above, PMSCs are mercenary organizations, though whether they are, so to speak, *just* mercenary organizations is controversial. However, if mercenary organizations are *per se* morally unacceptable, then so must PMSCs be. In order to see whether mercenary organizations are *per se* morally unacceptable, we must examine the reasoning behind the moral opprobrium attached to them. The first step in doing so is to attempt to specify what it is that is meant by 'mercenary'.

In his chapter 'What are mercenaries?' Uwe Steinhoff sets out to provide a satisfactory understanding of the term 'mercenary', first by presenting a satisfactory definition of 'mercenary' as it applies to individual fighters, then by looking at the supposed differences between 'traditional' mercenary groups and modern PMSCs. Steinhoff considers what he describes as a typical definition, consonant with the recent international agreements, given by Francoise Hampson, according to which

> Mercenaries appear to have three essential characteristics. They are foreign, motivated principally by financial gain and use force, but not as regular members of the armed forces of a State.[1]

The characteristics which distinguish a mercenary from a regular soldier, on this sort of account, can be specified in terms of affiliation, motivation and organizational incorporation. Though a mercenary, so understood, will not be morally admirable and may even be essentially morally disreputable – they are, after all, 'primarily motivated' by financial gain to engage in activities which might include killing their fellow human beings – they are not by definition morally beyond the pale, since it is at least consistent with this definition that a mercenary accepts certain moral-side constraints such that they will not, for example, fight in a clearly unjust war. Steinhoff points to a number of apparent counter-examples to Hampson's definition, where someone we would generally count as a mercenary lacks one or more of these distinguishing characteristics. Steinhoff offers his own definition, which has it that

> A *mercenary* is a person who is contracted to provide military services to groups other than his own (in terms of nation, ethnic group, class, etc.) and is ready to deliver this service even if this involves taking part in hostilities. Which groups are relevant depends on the nature of the conflict.[2]

Again, this does not make a mercenary morally beyond the pale by definition, and it is a narrower definition than that offered by Hampson, since it does not make either motivation or organizational incorporation an essential feature of a mercenary. To this extent it offers a smaller target for counter-examples. On the other hand, there are worries that such a narrow definition will still not reach to some paradigm cases of mercenaries, such as an amoral fighter who offers their services to the highest bidder – which, as it happens, is their own state. The broader methodological issue here concerns the nature of definition. Perhaps 'mercenary' is better understood as a family resemblance term – where any particular use of the term will have some (but not necessarily all) characteristics in common with any other – rather than something that can be defined in terms of necessary and sufficient conditions.

Even if the moral illegitimacy of individual mercenary soldiers is not established by definitional fiat, it remains an open question whether mercenary *organizations*, in particular PMSCs, are or could be morally acceptable. In the second strand of his paper Steinhoff takes issue with the argument that PMSCs differ from traditional mercenary forces in ways that allow for a meaningful moral distinction to be made between them. The implication would seem to be that PMSCs and traditional mercenary forces morally stand or fall together.

Deane-Peter Baker also focuses on the moral status of individual mercenary soldiers in his chapter 'Of "mercenaries" and prostitutes: can private warriors be ethical?' The very term 'mercenary' is morally pejorative. It implies actions or attitudes inappropriately motivated by considerations of personal financial gain. While such motivations are unexceptional in commercial transactions, they are obviously objectionable in, say, conjugal relations. Baker considers whether the motivations of regular soldiers differ from those of mercenaries in ways that mean that while regular soldiers are morally admirable (or at least morally acceptable) the mercenary soldier – *qua* mercenary soldier – is 'morally reprehensible'. In certain situations, the mere presence of financial consideration among an agent's motivational set is thought to be sufficient to taint the action so motivated. However, as Baker points out, the presence of such a motivation can hardly be what morally distinguishes regular from mercenary soldiers, since modern standing armies are 'professional' – that is, they provide a paid job for their members. Perhaps, then, the relevant difference between mercenaries and regular soldiers rests on the relationship they have with the state for which they fight? Regular soldiers will (now) typically be citizens of that state, and hence are fighting in defence of their homeland, while mercenaries need not be citizens of the state which employs them. Still, surely the relevant question concerns the justice of the cause for which soldiers fight, and there is no reason to think that mercenaries cannot take that into account, or that citizens always will.

Even if Baker's arguments are cogent, the most that they establish is that PMSCs cannot be objected to simply on the basis that they use mercenary soldiers. They do not show, as Baker notes, that there may not be other, consequentialist, reasons to prefer to maintain public armed forces as the sole, or at least principal, providers of military force. Mervyn Frost's analysis picks up from Baker's by examining the individuals that start-up private military companies in their social context. He points out that these individuals are actors within specific sorts of social practices, and that these practices have ethical norms embedded in them. In the first instance, the private warrior is a *civilian*, that is, a member of global civil society. As a member of global civil society, he is also a rights-holder: he has the right, for example, to own property, make contracts and so on. As such, the individual has the right to start a company of whatever sort he chooses, so long as in doing so he does not violate the rights of his fellow members of the global civil society. An important proviso is that such a company must be open to scrutiny to ensure that no rights violations are taking place. Qua civilian, Frost argues, there is no reason to think that there is anything special about the private warrior that would make his company unethical, so long as no rights violations take place. In addition to being a civilian, the founder and owner of a private military company is also a *citizen* – that is, he takes his place within the society of sovereign states. This fact, Frost points out, places significant restrictions on the activities that the individual concerned can undertake. A set of ethical values is expressed in the law of the state of which the individual is a member, as well as in the laws and norms that regulate the society of sovereign states. Of course a company that violates one of these laws or norms should expect to face punishment, but again Frost contends that there is nothing special about the private military company in this regard, and that there is an ethical space within the constraints imposed by the society of sovereign states within which PMSCs can exist.

It is of course true that much of the ethical concern over the existence of private military companies has to do with the *sort* of service they provide. Are there, Frost asks, some functions – such as the employment of armed force – that states ought not to privatize? While there are clearly important differences between private warriors and soldiers of the state (such as those raised by Jessica Wolfendale in her contribution to this volume), Frost argues that the key perspective on this is that of the citizen, who, he argues, will not care as much about who defends the nation as he or she will care that the nation is in fact defended. One wonders here whether Frost's position gives sufficient attention to the importance of national identity on the issue of national security. Trust and 'ownership' are important issues when it comes to as emotive a topic as defending the state and the communities it represents. Nonetheless the challenge of the final section of Frost's chapter is an important one. Accepting that there are practical problems that may result in ethical problems, Frost nonetheless contends that there is no conceptual difference between the outsourcing of military functions and the outsourcing of any other state function. If the service is provided more efficiently, and the state is able to retain indirect control (through regulation) over the company providing the service, then at least on this basis it appears that privatizing military functions is indeed ethical.

In perhaps the most wide-ranging chapter of the first section, Joseph Runzo is at pains to show that the phenomenon of the private military company exists within the broad context of a shift in the focus of contemporary warfare towards discretionary operations directed against terrorism or in support of humanitarian objectives (and sometimes both). The ethics of war, exemplified by Just War Theory, evolves along with the evolution of warfare itself, Runzo argues, and his chapter is an attempt to articulate a revised version of Just War Theory that accounts for the contemporary conflict environment. Before doing so, however, he puts forward what he believes to be two significant problems with the employment of private military companies in contemporary conflicts. First, he is troubled by the thought that 'the personnel of a PMC neither systematically studies military law and Just War Theory nor operates under the purview of military law.' While this has most certainly been true in the past, one wonders whether this is really an intrinsic problem with the private military and security company. Indeed, at the time of writing, the contractors in Iraq with contracts from the the US military are coming to terms with the implications of new legislation that brings them under the Uniform Code of Military Justice of the US armed forces.

One wonders also to what extent it is true that the personnel of these firms lack the necessary grasp of military law and Just War Theory. Given that PMSCs tend to employ those with military or law enforcement backgrounds, it seems likely that there is in fact a fair degree of proficiency in these matters among private warriors. Added to this is the fact that the industry is increasingly taking self-regulatory steps to ensure that its members act ethically on the battlefield. For example, the International Peace Operations Association, one of the largest associations of PMSCs, has in conjunction with American University recently launched a training programme aimed at 'field managers and independent contractors' which has the stated goal of serving

> as a mechanism by which the IPOA Code of Conduct and other standards can be operationalized by contractors active in conflict and post-conflict environments around the world. Participants will be trained in essential areas such as international humanitarian law, NGO/IO interaction, cultural, gender and religious sensitivities and learn how to operationalize field guidelines, increase productivity levels and to improve interaction with other actors.[3]

The second problem with using PMSCs in conflict zones, which concerns Runzo, is that, while they may provide some short-term military advantage, they are not suited to the long-term endeavour of building peace because 'they are not in the business of reconciliation.' This is of course a problem that is regularly pointed out about military forces in general, and it's hard to see here how this is a significant problem with PMSCs in particular. In a later chapter, Brooks and Chorev argue the contrary point that, because PMSCs tend to employ a significant proportion of local personnel, this reduces their intrusiveness, which, if true, might be argued as an advantage for PMSCs over regular military forces in building peace.

Drawing on a wide range of religious and other sources, Runzo moves on to outline a global honour ethic for the contemporary warrior and an accordingly adjusted contemporary version of Just War Theory. Both of these, he argues, leave little room for the private warrior. The contractor, Runzo contends, is less likely to be free of the ropes of materialism (and so will face death with regret rather than resolution), more likely to dehumanize the enemy, and has a greater propensity to use weapons to kill rather than to defend peace. In this regard Runzo is clearly in sharp disagreement with Baker.

Christopher Kinsey examines how the concept of corporate social responsibility (CSR) applies to the private security industry. He suggests that if PMSCs want to be viewed as socially responsible and enjoy public legitimacy, not only as individual firms but more broadly as an industry, they must seek to implement high standards in several distinct aspects of their working practices. Although he notes a recent case in which a prominent PMSC's lack of CSR had tragic consequences for some of its employees, Kinsey finds that ethical considerations are increasingly being taken into account by the sector, and in several cases firms have voluntarily gone beyond contractual commitments to ensure the well-being of individuals and organizations affected by their activities. Kinsey underscores that the attitude of senior managers is vital in influencing corporate culture and the extent to which CSR is accepted within the company. Another characteristic of PMSCs' corporate social responsibility that emerges is the element of contingency planning, which may make some PMSC bids less competitive on a purely cost-efficiency basis in the tendering process, but which tends to allow greater flexibility for the company in responding to any unexpected developments without being rigidly tied to minimalizing its costs. Kinsey also notes the responsibility of the client to ensure that PMSCs whose services they have contracted act within the law and adhere to any social or ethical policies they espouse.

The second section of the book deals mainly with laws and policies concerning the use of private military and security companies. Authors explore the various ways that the commercial military and security industry impacts upon states, their efforts to employ and harness the activities of private actors, as well as mechanisms to control and regulate them. Andrew Alexandra sets the PMSC trend firmly in the domain of state security, and more specifically in the context of the security dilemma: traditionally states acquire more arms and develop more powerful armies for self-protection, but in doing so create insecurity among other states. In the same way, a state's resort to the use of PMSCs increases its capacities and fosters insecurity among its neighbours. Moreover, due to their nature as corporate entities existing in a competitive environment, PMSCs will have an interest in generating more business. Such firms also seek to wield political influence, an issue linked to the power of the defence industry and the phenomenon of the revolving door, or the employment of senior former officials to assist in lobbying for business. Alexandra also remarks on the interest of PMSCs in greater efficiency and effectiveness in their 'methods of production'; 'greater productive efficiency' may imply, for example, the resort to 'cheaper labour' as reflected in the recruitment of third-country nationals from less-developed states and paying them 'the market rate' which is much less than that for employees from more-developed states. This might also imply reducing vetting or training of employees, under-equipping or under-insuring in the interest of cutting costs.

Alexandra puts the spotlight on the relationship between state political authority and the institutional actors mandated to provide security. Political control must be exercised without political interference. But similarly, constraints must exist to restrain executives who may find it easier to deploy private military firms than armed forces to pursue and further national interests. This would not only be encouraged by PMSCs, but would also stimulate insecurity among other states, further driving the dynamic of resorting to private military firms. Alexandra maintains that just as there are other state agencies that are insulated from direct political control in order to lessen the possibility of political misuse (he gives the example of central banks but one could also point to intelligence agencies and police as state institutions in various democratic states where there has been a deliberate effort to insulate them from direct political control), so should the institutions providing for the state's defence be insulated from political manipulation and the other factors that contribute to the security dilemma. In a role analogous to insurance companies, PMSCs could fulfil the role of primary providers of security for states in an international security insurance market, providing security whilst seeking to minimize the risk of having to provide it.

In his chapter 'Private military companies: markets, ethics, economics' Jurgen Brauer focuses on the question of the relative economic efficiency of PMSCs and public providers. Given the attractiveness of theft over honest toil, productive market economies require coercive force agencies (paid for by devices such as taxes) to deter potential property-right violations, and to enforce rectification if such violations do occur. If protective agencies are too large, relative to the need for them, they impose a dead-weight cost on the economy. On the other hand, if they are too small, or too slow or ineffective in the deployment of force when it is needed, productive economic activity will be disrupted. According to Brauer, economic theory provides us with no a priori reason for preferring either public or private agencies as providers of coercive capacity. The basic question is not whether states should purchase coercive capacity from private or public providers, but rather how regulatory frameworks should be structured so as to ensure that it is provided in ways which generate the most economically efficient outcomes. If, as some claim, public provision is inadequate in a range of situations, private provision becomes attractive. However, until recently, the regulatory framework for military force, at least, has focused almost entirely on public provision, with private provision being discouraged or even forbidden. Properly framed and enforced regulation can actually be to the advantage of PMSCs, since it allows potential clients to feel confident that they will conform to the conditions of their contract.

Brooks and Chorev draw our attention to the inescapable ethical dimension of policy by way of a provocative argument to the effect that idealistic and utopian policies which sideline or undermine the private provision of peacekeeping-related services are in fact implicit in the deaths of the victims of humanitarian catastrophes. Arguing that successful peace operations require a level of competence and capability generally only found in Western militaries, Brooks and Chorev point out that Western armed forces have shown little interest in the messy business of peace-keeping. This capability gap, however, can be filled by the private sector, according to Brooks and Chorev. Contractors, it is argued, offer the cost-effectiveness, qualitative enhancements and surge capacity that are necessary to make peace-support operations successful, thereby saving lives. Like many of the contributors to this book, Brooks and Chorev emphasize the need to ensure the responsible use of the private sector, and, indeed, go further by outlining some of the controls that are already in place as well as offering suggestions for other means of control.

Dominick Donald addresses the rapidly evolving dimension of private intelligence services provided by the US and the UK firms to both government and commercial clients. The US government in particular has become a large consumer of private intelligence since the advent of the war on terror, turning to private security companies to provide substantial numbers of translators and interpreters, and more controversially interrogators, in Iraq and Afghanistan. Private security companies are also used to sift through huge quantities of raw data, often using technical programmes and information technology. Private intelligence is also being offered to commercial clients, often as political or business risk analysis for the firms that operate in difficult environments or who are considering working with new partners. Donald notes an ongoing shift in the intelligence market which is seeing a convergence of the needs of government and commercial clients. In the context of the global war on terror and the potential use of economic targets against Western interests, both governments and businesses are concerned with political risk. Donald notes a key development in the role of private firms in providing strategic level input as states struggle to build up their intelligence capabilities as a part of their counter-terrorism efforts.

While Donald's analysis points to the widening scope of the privatization of functions previously considered the monopoly of the state, Ade Ebo calls attention to the need to broaden our analytical focus beyond purely commercial actors to view other non-state actors who are involved in providing military and security services. Focusing particularly on West Africa, Ebo recalls that the state has never fully enjoyed the monopoly of legitimate force. Citizens have consequently sought security from the non-state actors, and he further describes security governance in West Africa as a landscape of actors including armed opposition groups, international non-governmental organizations, mercenaries, foreign PMSCs, local private security companies, criminal networks and key individuals and groups in civil society. In view of the experience in West Africa, Ebo suggests the need to re-evaluate traditional Weberian assumptions about the centrality of the state in security governance. It is not clear, however, whether his closing recommendations in the chapter are aimed at strengthening the state authority, or expanding the multiplicity of local actors (as opposed to foreign PMSCs) who are involved in security provision and governance.

The following two chapters turn to regulation of private military and security companies. Emanuela-Chiara Gillard examines PMSCs operating in situations of armed conflict from the perspective of international humanitarian law (IHL). Contrary to the common claim that PMSCs exist in a legal vacuum, IHL is clear on various issues concerning PMSC employees. However, certain ambiguities continue to exist in IHL, and combined with the complexities of the circumstances involving PMSC employees, require that the precise application of IHL to PMSC employees needs to be determined on a case-by-case basis. Gillard's chapter underscores that multiple actors, state and non-state, have obligations to ensure respect for IHL. Fundamentally, states that hire PMSCs remain responsible for meeting their obligations under IHL, as well as ensuring that any PMSCs acting on their behalf respect IHL. Gillard proposes several measures that private military and security companies can take to ensure that their staff respect IHL, including adequate vetting, training in principles of IHL, clear guidelines with regard to procedures and rules of engagement, and mechanisms for investigating alleged violations of IHL by employees. Yet, although states remain responsible for investigating and prosecuting serious violations of IHL committed by PMSC employees they have hired, several factors have hindered the state enforcement of IHL, including the practice of granting immunity to PMSC employees in conflict zones, the non-functioning of local courts in those areas, the lack of will or capacity of the hiring state to exercise extraterritorial jurisdiction over the PMSC staff, or difficulties in collecting the evidence and witnesses for effective prosecution of individuals. Finally, Gillard notes that in addition to the states that hire PMSCs, 'states of nationality' of the PMSC can help ensure respect for IHL by introducing a licensing or regulatory system, and 'host states' where PMSCs perform services could similarly introduce registration or licensing systems.

Turning from the international to the national level, Marina Caparini examines certain aspects of the US regulatory approach governing commercial military and security services. As the key source state of PMSCs, various US laws exist that can, at least in theory, be used to prosecute security contractors for serious crimes committed overseas. In practice, however, she argues that there has been lack of legal clarity, a rapidly shifting regulatory landscape and perhaps most importantly, an enforcement gap resulting from practical and political disincentives for prosecuting security contractors alleged to have committed crimes abroad.

The third section of the book turns more specifically to the impact that private military companies are having on state armed forces, and on the broader dimension of civil–military relations, the relationship between civilians – represented both by political leadership and the citizenry – and those agents entrusted with the authority to use force externally on behalf of the state; traditionally those agents have been the state armed forces but increasingly in some countries private military and security companies are employed to use force on behalf of the state.

Herbert Wulf considers two current trends that are affecting the state monopoly of force: first, the trend towards outsourcing state military functions to PMSCs, and second, the increasing use of state armed forces abroad. Both incur problems with accountability and democratic control. Wulf notes that the inexorable privatization of security through outsourcing is worrying because it involves the transformation of security from a public good into a private good or commercial product. The corollary of this is that only those who can afford it will benefit from it. The implicit criticism is that privatization of security undermines the social compact in which the sovereign (state) agrees to provide order and security for the collectivity in return for the acquiescence of the public. The impact of PMSC profit motive and risk-avoidance behaviour on their involvement in conflict is unknown: does it lead them to prolong a conflict since their services will continue to be needed, or does it lead them to avoid engagement in situations likely to cause damage or loss of personnel and materiel? Wulf also notes that military outsourcing to PMSCs adds further complications to the already delicate balance of contemporary civil–military relations. Mirroring this lack of parliamentary control of international military interventions is the lack of parliamentary control and oversight of PMSCs, whether at the domestic or international level – and both undermine the state (public) monopoly of force.

Christopher Spearin makes a crucial distinction between the capacities of the weak and the powerful states to shape the global market for private security. The United States in particular possesses the capacity to structure the market and the behaviour of many PMSCs. He observes that the new American 'way of war' – featuring an emphasis on high technology and special forces as well as eschewing reliance on military allies and willingness to undertake independent measures, even indeed preventative war – reinforces the US reliance on private security companies. Further, that PMSCs tethered to the hegemonic US geo-strategic interests and foreign policy have less need to assert their legitimacy or innovate in developing business opportunities in the way that Executive Outcomes or Sandline did because their main client, the US government, satisfies many of their needs for contracts. The US government market is so significant for the US-based PMSCs that it informally, but very effectively, promotes their compliance with US interests and is the major factor shaping the structures of the PMSCs and of the market for the industry more broadly. Spearin notes that, at the same time, humanitarian non-governmental organizations (NGOs) are similarly constrained by their growing reliance on states for funding, and their traditional reluctance to engage proactively with PMSCs despite the growing threats of violence targeting their employees. Both PMSCs and humanitarian NGOs, then, are non-state actors that are profoundly affected by the gravitational pull of the most powerful states.

In her chapter 'The military and the community: comparing national military forces and private military companies', Jessica Wolfendale accepts that there is no intrinsic moral difference between national military forces and mercenary forces, but claims that allowing mercenary organizations such as PMCs to become the principal providers of military force would have politically undesirable effects. Wolfendale points out that the main purpose of military forces is to protect their nation, which she characterizes as 'the community of citizens'. However, they are directed by, and answerable to, not the nation as such, but rather 'the state' – the corporate organization which rules over the nation. Though the state itself is supposed to act as an agent of the nation, notoriously this does not always happen. Such failures become particularly problematic when the state is using its armed forces against, or irrespective of, the wishes of the community. However, the community is less likely to know, or care, about such a failure, or be in a position to do much about it even if it does care about whether the state uses a PMC or a national army, given the connection between the community and the national military.

Consequentialist arguments like this, of course, depend on the factual support for their strength. Since we have no meaningful contrast class with nations which use national armies – that is, modern nations which have depended on PMCs as their primary provider of military force – Wolfendale's argument is not conclusive but at most suggestive Moreover, if we are to assess the relative merits of national armies versus PMCs on consequential grounds, we need to consider *all* the likely consequences of preferring one to the other, including their military effectiveness, rapidity of response and cost. And, of course, these consequences may vary from place to place or time to time.

Asa Kasher addresses certain ethical problems that could arise from the 'organizational interface' between a state military force and a private military company that is contracted to provide support to it. His analysis derives from the observation that each has a distinct type of ethics that influences the goals, attitudes, values and behaviour of the organization and its members. One potential ethical problem that could arise from their interaction concerns the sharing of lessons learnt from combat, specifically, the withholding of information by PMSC employees even when that information concerns the firm's contracted interaction with the military force. Due to the competitive relationship that exists among PMSCs as commercial entities, there might similarly be an unwillingness to share information in debriefings where there is the possibility that company information will be distributed to other private firms performing outsourced duties for the military force. Given the difference between the ethics of a state military and those of a profit-oriented private military company, organizational interaction necessarily includes the interaction of organizational ethics. In Kasher's view, the interaction between a state military and PMSC personnel through outsourced training, logistics, intelligence collection or combat functions will result in the erosion of ethical standards of the military force. For that reason, he countenances a highly restrictive form of civil–military relations in the form of state military interaction with only the tangible products of PMSCs, that is, materiel and equipment.

Finally, Elke Krahmann argues that the recent emergence of the military contractor working for a private company under contract for a government at home and abroad heralds the development of a new, post-modern model of the soldier. In contrast to the more traditional models of the citizen–soldier and the military professional, the military entrepreneur provides military services out of self-interest and financial rewards rather than a sense of loyalty or duty to the state. Krahmann notes that the 'new model soldier' will have an important impact on the nature of the citizen–state relationship; whereas democratic values were explicitly inculcated among members of many Western state armed forces through the idea of the democratic control of the armed forces, democratic values are largely irrelevant for private military contractors.

The contemporary PMSC phenomenon has in many respects taken academics, analysts and military practitioners by surprise. Who would have thought, ten years ago, that a situation would arise in which contractors employed and deployed by the US government in support of military operations in the US military's biggest current deployment (Iraq) would actually outnumber the US troops in theatre?[4] The rapid development of the industry, its pervasive presence on the ground supporting the US-led interventions in both Afghanistan and Iraq, and the extensive degree to which the US government relies on PMSCs generally in its foreign policy, including the war on terror, have much broader significance than their impact on US foreign and security policy. The perspectives represented in this volume make clear that the debate over the appropriate role of private military and security companies in contemporary warfare is by no means resolved. Participants in the debate – academics, practitioners, policy makers and civil society as well as members of the industry itself – continue to debate how such firms should be called and defined, their legitimate scope of activity and whether there are functions that inherently should be performed by the state, the impact that privatization and outsourcing functions to PMSCs can and should have on the state, and the rights and duties of such firms vis-à-vis the clients they work for and the people they employ, and of course on society more broadly.

While no single volume can hope to address every aspect of this complex new phenomenon on the contemporary battlefield, it is our belief that the chapters contained in this book add a useful and wide-ranging set of perspectives to the literature currently available on this topic. In particular, we hope that the closer examination of the ethical dimensions of private military and security companies and some of the implications of their use contributes to moving beyond the often-superficial and Manichean categorizations that have tended to characterize public debate on these issues.

## Notes

1 Uwe Steinhoff, 'What are Mercenaries?', Ch. 1, pp. 19–20.
2 Uwe Steinhoff, 'What are Mercenaries?', Ch. 1, p. 28.
3 'Humanitarian Conduct and Enhanced Operations: Specialized Training for Field Managers and Independent Contractors', Peacebuilding and Development Institute website. www.american.edu/sis/peacebuilding/security/traininginfo.htm, accessed 27 March 2007.
4 T. Christian Miller, 'Private Contractors Outnumber U.S. Troops in Iraq', *Los Angeles Times*, 4 July 2007.

# Part I
# Ethics

# 1   What are mercenaries?

*Uwe Steinhoff*

The private sale of military services to foreign parties has become a huge industry. From 1994 to 2002, the US Defence Department entered into over 3,000 contracts with military firms, with an estimated value of $300 billion.[1] Around 50,000 – the exact numbers are unknown – privately employed armed men are presently working in Iraq. Iraq is only exceptional with regard to the quantity. Private military firms have provided services in over 110 countries.[2] These military services include logistics, advice and even combat. Private military firms or companies (PMFs or PMCs) are working for NGOs, for the UN, for states, for rebels, for criminal organizations and for multinational corporations. The co-operation with the latter is often used to secure enormously lucrative mining licenses in weak states. Some critics have therefore spoken of an armed corporate imperialism. Certain strong states, on the other hand, apparently host PMFs in order to promote national arms sales and to use these firms as proxies that enable them to pursue certain foreign policies while simultaneously dissociating themselves from them. The PMFs and their employees, in turn, dissociate themselves from mercenaries. Allegedly, they and their employees are something different, respectable and legitimate.

Given the extreme and growing importance of the PMF and mercenary phenomenon, it is necessary to philosophically examine it in order to determine its ethical ramifications. The first step, obviously, would consist in providing an adequate definition of the term 'mercenary'. Precisely this is attempted in this chapter. It will be argued that the common, legal definitions of 'mercenary' are too narrow, and a broader and more adequate definition will be offered: A mercenary is a person who sells the service of taking part in hostilities to groups other than his own (in terms of nation, ethnic group, class and so on) and is ready to deliver this service. In the light of this definition PMFs are mercenary organizations. Besides, it shall also be demonstrated that the differences between the 'new' PMFs and older forms of mercenary organizations have been extremely exaggerated.

What is a mercenary? A typical answer, given by Francoise J. Hampson, goes like this: Mercenaries appear to have three essential characteristics.

They are foreign, motivated principally by financial gain and use force, but not as regular members of the armed forces of a State.[3] Hampson further explains

> The first element distinguishes mercenaries from members of the indigenous population who may take up arms for reasons of monetary gain. The second characteristic would exclude volunteers who fought for ideological reasons or out of a sense of adventure. The final element distinguishes mercenaries from the armed forces of a State involved in a conflict within another State and from foreigners serving as an integral part of the armed forces of a State, such as the French Foreign Legion and the Gurkha regiments in the British army. It also excludes individuals who train or advise the armed forces of a State, on condition that they do not themselves use force.[4]

This account corresponds more or less to the one given by Article 47 of the 1977 Additional Protocols to the Geneva Convention and to the ones given by most encyclopaedias.

However, there are serious problems with it. Let us consider the first element first: Why should members of the 'indigenous' population not be mercenaries? What, by the way, does 'indigenous' mean? The San Francisco streetcar men who prepared to strike in April 1902, for example, saw themselves as 'defending family and home against a corporation that had mobilized the "offscourings of society" against them, thousands of strikebreaking *mercenaries* form eastern city slums, ready for shipment across the continent, who resembled the Hessians that Washington and their forebears had fought in the Revolution.'[5] Indeed, there is a certain resemblance, and there is also a certain resemblance between the business of recruiting strike-breakers at the American East Coast in order to transport them to the West Coast to corporations willing to pay for their services on the one hand and the business of recruiting fighting men in Europe or the United States in order to transport them to African states or to corporations extracting resources there on the other. Of course, the strike-breakers from the East Coast are not indigenous to the West Coast, but they are no *foreigners*, either. They are Americans. Should the nationality really play such an important role for the definition of 'mercenary'? Old Athens sometimes hired soldiers from other city–states. These soldiers were not citizens of Athens, and fighting for Athens for financial gain they were certainly mercenaries. But they were not foreign. They were Greek. Another example is the Free Companies, 'vagabond bands of mercenary soldiers who, as the feudal system declined, flourished in late medieval Europe.'[6] These companies are in the literature on mercenaries rightfully considered as paradigmatic examples of the trade. If nationality were a decisive element, however, many of the members of these bands couldn't be mercenaries at all. Fra Moriales Great Company, for instance, which operated in Italy, was joined by many Italians. It seems to be completely counterintuitive, though, to claim that their Swiss comrades were mercenaries, while they, the Italians, fighting at their side for exactly the same reasons, namely for financial gain and out of adventurism, were not. Yet another example can be taken from modern conflicts. Why shouldn't a group of armed Bosnian Muslims hired by Bosnian Croats to fight Bosnian Serb troops not be considered mercenaries if they do what they are hired for? The same holds for ethnic or tribal rivalries within African states. What all this suggests is that, yes, mercenaries do not belong to the group on behalf of which they are fighting, but, no, these groups do not have to be defined in terms of nationality.[7]

The second criterion is even more problematic. If one looks at what are considered paradigmatic examples of mercenaries, for example, the men of the Free companies or 'Mad' Mike Hoare's and Bob Denard's men in the Congo in the 1960s or 'Colonel' Callan in Angola in the 1970s, it becomes very clear that these men, or at least a very significant part of them, were *not* motivated principally by financial gain (which does not mean that they were not at all motivated by financial gain), but by adventurism or a love for war and fighting.[8] As Anthony Mockler states:

> Here then is the real mark of the mercenary – a devotion to war for its own sake. By this the mercenary can be distinguished from the professional soldier whose mark is generally a devotion to the external trappings of the military profession rather than to the actual fighting.[9]

However, Mockler seems to draw the wrong conclusion here. It is true that the fact that someone is not principally motivated by financial gain does not mean that he is not a mercenary, for certain clear and paradigmatic examples of mercenaries were not so motivated. But from this does not follow that those of Hoare's men who would not have fought if they had received the same amount of money for a less dangerous and exciting job weren't mercenaries. Of course they were. In other words, we should simply drop the requirement of being principally motivated by financial gain, instead of substituting it by adventurism or a love for war.

But don't we have at least to distinguish the mercenary from the ideologically motivated volunteer? After all, this seems to be a morally relevant distinction:

> The mercenary's loyalty is only governed by his contract, not by any greater or permanent cause or duty. Unlike other soldiers, they are neither serving country, nor protecting family or home, nor fighting for a greater force that they believe in.[10]

This is a common characterization of the mercenary, but is it a correct one? Although the mercenary is usually depicted as someone who fights for the highest bidder, this, again, does not go well with paradigmatic examples of mercenaries. In fact, many critics of mercenaries, foremost Machiavelli, claim that mercenaries are very reluctant to fight their kind. 'Dogs don't eat dogs', these critics say. But the two criticisms are obviously not compatible. Moreover, it is also a fact that mercenary leaders like Hoare and Denard have rarely (if ever) fought wars that did not have the approval of the governments of their home countries. And then there are mercenaries like the famous Count von Rosen who are so selective about the wars they fight in that they can hardly be distinguished from ideologically motivated volunteers. Thus, there are not only two options, the man ready to fight for the highest bidder and the man who would only fight for his own country.

What are we to make of this? The financial motive, to be sure, should remain part of the definition of 'mercenary'. Someone who fights for free or for relatively small pay in war after war is a *pure* adventurer or a war junkie, not a mercenary. On the other hand, the financial motive does not need to override or dominate all others, not even moral or ideological ones. Mercenaries who fight exclusively in wars that meet certain moral or ideological preconditions are not only conceivable but also real. The conclusion to be drawn is that a mercenary has to fulfil the requirement of being ready to fight for groups other than his own (in terms of nation, ethnic group, class and so on), provided that he receives a reasonable payment for it. That he be ready to fight for *any* group, provided he gets a reasonable remuneration, is *not* required.

Hampson's final element has two parts: the actual use of force and the 'irregularity'requirement. What does 'actual use of force mean'? Well, a mere advisor does not shoot a gun, but so rarely do generals. Nevertheless, generals 'take part in the hostilities', as the expression in the laws of war goes. They do this by giving direct commands (for example, to shoot at the enemy, which is more or less equivalent to pulling the trigger themselves); they are part of the 'chain of command'. The war effort, however, is not only borne by these chains of commands but also by contractual arrangements. The workers in an ammunition factory are not under a military command, they do not receive 'orders' in the military sense, and for disobeying their superiors they do not end up in front of a court martial. All the same, ammunition factories and their staff are seen in the laws of war as legitimate targets, because they are, obviously, part of the war effort. In the technical sense in which the expression 'taking part in the hostilities' figures in the laws of war, they do, of course, not take part in the hostilities, because the chain of command is not present (which does not mean that the ammunition *factory* is not a legitimate target according to the laws of war). In a common sense interpretation of the expression, however, they do. But this also holds true, and not less obviously so, for military advisors, especially if their advice is decisive. As long as no armed conflict is going on, a hired foreign trainer or advisor of an army is not taking part in the hostilities, for the simple fact that there are no hostilities. But if there are hostilities, his training or advice is a part of them. Thus, while it makes sense to say that the general, although he is not firing a gun, is still actually *using* force by giving direct commands, whereas the worker in the ammunition factory and the military advisor are not, it is far less plausible to say that the latter two, unlike the former, do not *take part* in the hostilities. They do. Since, moreover, their contribution to the war effort is often far more dangerous to the enemy then a front soldier's banging away with his rifle, it is also far more important from a moral point of view. Therefore, the requirement for the actual use of force should be substituted by the requirement of taking part in the hostilities.

Do mercenaries have *actually* to take part in hostilities? To begin with, it is important to see that mercenarism is a trade, a business, and not a label for a skill or one's training or education. While someone who has enjoyed an apprenticeship as a plumber or has passed his examinations as a lawyer might be called a plumber or a lawyer, this is not necessarily the job he is doing. He might be a taxi driver. Therefore, it is better to compare 'mercenary' to job descriptions like 'day labourer', 'taxi driver' or 'university lecturer'. Most often they are compared to prostitutes ('the whores of war'). A prostitute, of course, is still a prostitute while s/he is not having sex with a customer. On the other hand, someone's mere readiness to have sex for money is not sufficient for being a prostitute. Even if someone offers their sex services on the market, s/he is only a would-be prostitute as long as no one has actually used the service. The prostitute has to be 'baptized', so to say. Further, an initial baptism is not enough if there are no 'follow-ups'. This is, by the way, not different with other jobs. A babysitter has to work in reasonable intervals as such, otherwise she is out of business – she is not a babysitter any more. On the other hand, isn't it sufficient for a prostitute to *sell* the service? Let us say a person has decided to become a prostitute and offers their service at the market. Someone hires him or her and gives him or her the money. At the last moment, however, the customer loses his courage and flees. Is the hired and paid person a prostitute now, although s/he has not actually provided the service? Wasn't it enough to sell it? It seems it was. Although the person in the end did not have to deliver thier sexual services, s/he has prostituted himself or herself s/he has sold his/her sexual services. In the case of mercenaries it is probably even clearer that they do not actually have to deliver. For example, the men who were sent by the private military company Executive Outcomes to Papua-New Guinea in order to fight for its government against the rebels on Bogainville were never used for this purpose since the government changed its mind. However, one likely would consider them *all* as mercenaries, even those of them who had never before worked as mercenaries. The same holds true for those men who were sent to fight with Colonel Callan in Angola but never saw action. Thus, it doesn't seem necessary to take actually part in hostilities in order to be a mercenary. It is sufficient to sell the service of taking part in the hostilities and to be ready to take part in the hostilities. The second condition, readiness, excludes frauds, who pose as mercenaries, but would desert their employer before actually delivering the service they were hired for.

Let us now turn to the second part of Hampson's final element. Must the French Foreign Legion really be excluded? This seems odd. In fact, most people 'in the street', if asked for a paradigmatic example for mercenaries, would probably come up with the French Foreign Legion first. Therefore, instead of excluding such forces from the category of mercenaries, it is far more plausible to distinguish different sub-categories. There is a difference between the French Foreign Legion and the bands of mercenaries who operated in the Congo in the 1960s, but this is much more an organizational difference than one concerning the elements that are so organized – the mercenaries. Besides, nothing hinders a state to simply make a band of mercenaries it employs part of its own armed forces (that was actually done by Papua-New Guinea in the case of the men of Executive Outcomes). Why such an act – such a trick, one is tempted to say – should suddenly turn a mercenary force into regular soldiers is anything but clear. It is, moreover, particularly mysterious where the moral significance of such a 'transformation' lies.

Peter Warren Singer, however, thinks that another transformation is extremely important, also for definitional matters – namely the '*corporatization* of military service provision'.[11] Given the extreme importance of such firms, Singer's claim deserves closer scrutiny.

The sub-chapter in which Singer tries to explain where the difference between PMFs and older forms of private military service provision lies is titled: 'Privatized Military Industry: More Than Just Mercenaries'.[12] Now, while it is, no doubt, true that PMFs are more than mercenaries, one should not forget that Michael Hoare, *the* mercenary, was more than a mercenary, too. He also was a father, for example. In other words, that someone or something is more than a mercenary does not mean that he is not a mercenary. Of course, PMFs are not mercenaries. But the bands of the Congo mercenaries or the medieval Free Companies were not mercenaries, either. An *organization* of mercenaries is not a mercenary. Nevertheless, it is still an organization of *mercenaries* – be it in the form of a loose band, in the medieval form of companies or in the modern form of corporations. In fact, Singer himself admits that '[m]any PMF employees have been mercenaries both before and after their employ'. But he adds that 'their processes, relationships, and impact within local conflicts were completely different.'[13] The same, however, obviously also holds true for mercenary bands or medieval Free Companies. Thus, if entering one of these latter organizations doesn't turn a mercenary into a non-mercenary, entering the former organization doesn't do this, either.

This does not mean, to say it again, that there are no differences between PMFs and other forms of mercenary organizations. It means, however, that these differences remain within the category of mercenarism. Besides, Singer seems to exaggerate the differences to quite a degree. He declares

> Several distinguishing characteristics follow from this corporatiza-
> tion.... PMFs are ordered along pre-existing corporate lines, usually
> with a clear executive hierarchy that includes board of directors and
> share-holdings. This creates a tested, efficient, and more permanent
> structure that can compete and survive in the global marketplace.[14]

First, Singer himself notes earlier in his text that 'past military entities often mirrored, or in some cases even initiated, the development of the prevailing business form in general society'.[15] So they were often ordered along the lines of pre-existing business forms. Where is the difference? Of course, a corporation is not a (free) company, but if the transformation from loose bands to companies or from companies to loose bands doesn't transform the mercenaries who are organized in these entities to some-thing else, then nothing of this sort will happen with the transformation to a corporation, either. Besides, some of the free companies lasted for several decades, the Grand Catalan Company even for more than sixty years. Bob Denard's and Mike Hoare's mercenary bands or networks also lasted for several decades. So here, indeed, we have a difference, but not the one Singer is looking for. For in terms of testedness, efficiency and permanence at least the Free Companies – and perhaps even the merce-nary bands[16] – seem to have some advantage over the PMCs. The second implication is that this new private military actor is driven by business profit rather than individual profit. PMFs function as registered trade units, not as personal black-market ventures for individual profit or adventure.[17] Corporations aren't persons or living creatures. If they have drives, these drives are constituted by the drives of the persons who make up the corporations. These persons typically want to make profit. Although the management, if promoting its company in public, will, of course, boast with the business profit, everyone in the company, including the management, is working there for his private profit. Or, to put it in other words, 'the company's' being driven by business profit *is* its being driven by private profit. Besides, if it were true that a corporation can be driven by 'business profit' in a way that is not reducible to its individ-ual member's being driven by private profit, it is hard to see why this should be different with loose bands of mercenaries, let alone with Free Companies. The difference between 'registered trade units' and 'black-market venture' is no explanation.

> The third distinguishing characteristic of the privatized military
> industry is that the arena they compete on is the open global market.

> That is, ... PMFs are considered legal entities bound to their employers by recognized contracts and in many cases at least nominally to their home states by laws requiring registration, periodic reporting, and licensing of foreign contracts. ... This status differentiates them not only from mercenaries, who had to hide from the law, but also from past entities, such as the charter companies, that did not coexist with any state law, but rather made their own laws.[18]

Denard's and Hoare's men or the British and French Congo mercenaries in general did not, apart, perhaps, from rare circumstances, have to hide from the law of their own countries.[19] The same is true for many older mercenary entities. Second, charter companies like the East Indian Company did not make their own laws, at least not literally. Metaphorically, perhaps, but this also seems to hold true for many PMFs, as Singer himself points out.[20] Yes, the Congo mercenaries, to take this paradigmatic example again, were not subjected to registration, periodic reporting and licensing – at least not nominally. In fact, however, they practically always acted with the approval of their government. But even if they hadn't – an only *nominal* requirement to do so in the case of PMFs doesn't seem to make a big difference. Besides, there is nothing in the meaning of 'mercenary' which makes it incompatible with registration, reporting and licensing.

A fourth difference Singer notes is real, namely that the PMFs offer more military services to a wider variety of clients than traditional mercenaries did. However, it shouldn't be forgotten that the same holds for modern physicians, lawyers, carpenters and bakers as compared to traditional ones, but this does not mean that they are not physicians, lawyers, carpenters and bakers any more.

The fifth difference Singer notes is this:

> Unlike the black market, word-of-mouth recruiting forms used earlier (such as the veiled classified ads ... ), public application processes are used by most PMFs, and they work from established databases that attempt to cover the available employee pool. Firms screen potential employees for valued skill-sets and tailor their staff to specific mission needs. ... While mercenary units operate as collections of individuals, the personnel within PMFs ... are specifically grouped so as to operate with a set doctrine and greater cohesion of activity and discipline.[21]

All this is at best a quantitative difference, not a qualitative one. First, surely the men within the Free Companies, too, were 'specifically grouped so as to operate with a set doctrine and greater cohesion of activity and discipline.'[22] Second, by posting, as Singer says, '*thinly* veiled classified ads in newspapers'[23] in order to find men for his operations in the Congo in the 1960s, Hoare's recruiting process was much more public than the one used by Executive Outcomes, whose 'original recruitment was mainly word-of-mouth', as Singer himself notes. He even adds that 'this also provided a check on personnel quality'.[24] So why does he deplore in the case of 'traditional' mercenaries what he deems efficient in the case of PMFs? Incidentally, there is no evidence that word-of-mouth ever ceased to be the primary way of recruitment for EO. Nor is there such evidence for any other PMF, at least not for the ones engaging in actual combat. Moreover, even the case of a military advisor firm such as MPRI, which praises itself for its good contacts to the US Armed Forces, will hardly be different. That a company's website says 'Join us!' says very little about the actual recruitment process.

Admittedly, when the recruitment is done too publicly it 'often pulls in a true mixed-bag of soldier.'[25] And this indeed happened when Hoare went public by using newspapers. It shouldn't be forgotten, however, that EO trained in Sierra Leone 'a separate unit of army troops to operate with them' and 'also organized and trained units of a local tribal militia known as "Kamajors"'.[26] It is a moot point to argue whether these troops were technically part of EO, for the important point is that EO operated with them, which throws some doubt on the actual degree to which it operated 'with a set doctrine and greater cohesion of activity and discipline.' Moreover, Hoare's admitted recruitment of a high proportion of 'alcoholics, drunks, booze artists, bums and layabouts'[27] might be far less bizarre both from a military and moral perspective than EO's recruitment of the Kamajors, who believed in 'the magical ability of certain shirts to repel bullets, and some openly practice cannibalism, eating the heads and hearts of enemies killed in action.'[28] On the other hand, that a mercenary leader will, if he sees no other way, hire almost anyone (as, it seems, will PMFs), does not mean that he will not in most cases and preferably 'work from established databases that attempt to cover the available employee pool', to use Singer's phrase. Throughout their career, Hoare and Denard had a certain pool of reliable employees they hired again and again. The fact that their 'established databases' were in the form of memories or paper instead of electronic files is hardly relevant for distinguishing PMFs from mercenaries.

The final difference Singer sees lies in the relations of PMFs outside the industry:

> In addition to the contractual arrangements made with their customers, many are tightly linked with greater financial holdings and conglomerates....Such ties provide a whole new level of both legitimacy and connections for PMFs. In addition, they allow the firms greater access to financial capital and also to have on call other corporate resources. The only previous entities that came close to this breadth of resources were the charter companies. However, as noted

previously, their ultimate focus was on trade in goods, rather than provision of military services. In addition, charter companies only operated outside of state controls, rather than working with states.[29]

It is doubtlessly true that big PMFs have far better connections than the Congo mercenaries of the 1960s had. The case with small PMFs, however, is quite different – and this means that we have again no general difference to the Congo mercenaries. Second, it is a very bold claim – and one Singer doesn't justify at all – that the connection to financial holdings and conglomerates makes the PMFs more legitimate. In fact, it is even bold to claim that these connections at least make them *appear* more legitimate. Thanks to the strong influence of movements critical of globalization and, of course, of Multinational Corporations (MNCs), the latter are often looked at with suspicion, resentment or moral disdain. Therefore, the connection between (non-military) MNCs and PMFs will not so much boost the reputation of the latter but impair the reputation of the former. Third, it is an exaggeration to say that charter companies worked outside of state control. In the end, the state, a least the home state, retained the final say. Fourth, Singer's own analysis shows clearly that the ultimate focus of many PMFs, too, is on trade in goods, for example, in goods like diamonds or oil. Often they are paid – not officially, but actually – with licenses for resource extraction.[30]

To conclude, mercenarism is an age-old phenomenon that already existed before nations in the modern sense and before states. It can occur in many historic forms, like loose mercenary bands, internationally operating PMFs, nationally operating strike-breaking agencies, medieval Free Companies, Foreign Legions and so on. While these forms may differ from one another, they also bear significant resemblances and are recognizable as aspects of the same overall phenomenon. As a result of the above analysis, the following definition is hence suggested here:

> A *mercenary* is a person who is contracted to provide military services to groups other than his own (in terms of nation, ethnic group, class, etc.) and is ready to deliver this service even if this involves taking part in hostilities. Which groups are relevant depends on the nature of the conflict.

## Notes

1 'Military Contractors', http://topsy.org/contractors.html, accessed on 11 February 2005. This website, in turn, takes this information from Peter W. Singer, 'Peacekeepers, Inc.', *Policy Review*, 2003, Vol. 119, p. 59, available under http://proquest.umi.com, accessed 11 February 2005.
2 'Military Contractors'; Thomas Catan, 'Private Military Companies Seek an Image Change', *Financial Times*, 01 December 2004, retrieved from http://corpswatch.org/article.php?id = 11725 on 11 February 2005; 'Making a

Killing: The Business of War', www.public-i.org/report.aspx?aid= 177&sid=100, accessed on 11 Feburary 2005.
3 Françoise J. Hampson, 'Mercenaries: Diagnosis Before Proscription', *Netherlands Yearbook of International Law*, 1991, Vol. 22, pp. 5f.
4 Ibid.
5 Stephen H. Norwood, *Strikebreaking & Intimidation: Mercenaries and Masculinity in Twentieth-Century America*, Chapel Hill and London: The University of North Carolina Press, 2002, p. 2. My emphasis.
6 Anthony Mockler, *The New Mercenaries*, London: Corgi Books, 1986, p. 25.
7 T. Lynch and A.J. Walsh, 'The Good Mercenary?', *The Journal of Political Philosophy*, 2000, Vol. 8(2), pp. 133–53, pp. 140f. and 149ff.
8 Ibid, esp. pp. 34f. Petra Hagelstam, 'Soldiers of Fortune in Bosnia – The Casagrande Incident', *The Finnish Yearbook of International Law*, 1997, Vol. 8, pp. 259–84, contains a description of a mercenary who called himself 'Casagrande' and fought in Bosnia which is illustrative for the point in question. See also Norwood, *Strikebreaking & Intimidation: Mercenaries and Masculinity in Twentieth-Century America* and Peter W. Singer, 'War, Profits, and the Vacuum of Law: Privatized Military Firms and International Law', *Columbia Journal of Transnational Law*, 2004, Vol. 42(2), p. 41.
9 Mockler, *The New Mercenaries*, p. 36.
10 Singer, 'War, Profits and the Vacuum of Law', p. 41.
11 Ibid., p. 45.
12 Ibid., p. 44.
13 Ibid., p. 46.
14 Ibid., p. 45.
15 Ibid., p. 19
16 At least if we can believe the description of Mockler, which, in any case, seems to be one of the more objective, less ideologically motivated ones.
17 Singer, 'War, Profits and the Vacuum of Law', p. 46.
18 Ibid.
19 Cf. Guy Arnold , *Mercenaries: The Scourge of the Third World*, New York: St. Martin's Press, 1999, esp. ch. 14. See also Mockler, *The New Mercenaries*.
20 Singer, 'War, Profits and the Vacuum of Law', esp. ch. 10, 11, 13 and 14.
21 Ibid., pp. 46ff.
22 Ibid., p. 47.
23 Ibid., p. 42. My emphasis. The public character of this form of recruitment lies in that only very dumb or naive people could misunderstand them and in that probably far more people read them than the websites of PMFs.
24 Ibid., p. 103.
25 Ibid., p. 42.
26 Ibid., p. 113.
27 Hoare, as cited by Mockler, *The New Mercenaries*, as cited by Singer, 'War, Profits and the Vacuum of Law', p. 42.
28 Singer, 'War, Profits and the Vacuum of Law', p. 113.
29 Ibid., p. 47.
30 Ibid., esp. pp. 166–8. Cf. also Arnold, *Mercenaries: The Scourge of the Third World*, esp. ch. 11.

# 2 Of 'mercenaries' and prostitutes

## Can private warriors be ethical?

*Deane-Peter Baker*

Of all the parts of the modern world it is unquestionably Africa that has been most affected by the practice of mercenarism. Indeed, most of our era's most infamous mercenaries – 'Mad' Mike Hoare, 'Black' Jack Schramm and Bob Denard, to name a few – have plied their trade almost exclusively on African soil. The recent attempted toppling of the government of Equatorial Guinea by a group of mostly ex-South African Defence Force (SADF) personnel has been a poignant reminder that mercenarism remains very much on the African agenda. An even more pervasive presence of the private warrior in African armed conflicts has been in his recent role as the employee of the private military company, the mercenary band's more sophisticated cousin.[1]

Private military companies (PMCs), with their claim to be legitimate military service providers, are for the first time challenging the view that such groups are intrinsically, politically and ethically unacceptable. There is an increasingly vocal lobby that argues that the private provision of military services is simply a facet of a global trend, one not generally considered to be inherently ethically problematic, namely the move towards outsourcing what were traditionally government functions. Advocates of PMCs argue further that the private military industry can often perform vital military tasks – particularly in cases of humanitarian intervention – far more efficiently and in a more cost-effective fashion than traditional UN or coalition forces. There now exists a growing body of scholarly literature dedicated to debating the question of what role, if any, the private military industry can legitimately have in the context of 'new' wars and humanitarian interventions. While the debate goes on, the industry is increasing its market share of conflict zones through involvement in such conflicts as the US-led occupation of Iraq and Afghanistan and the recent African Union (AU) intervention in Sudan.

Despite the demand for legitimacy that is being made by the private military industry, the fact remains that in modern times soldiers-for-hire have been almost universally considered to be morally reprehensible. Surprisingly, however, there has been very little scholarly exploration of just what it is that so tarnishes the character of the private warrior. A recent search of the main database of the philosophical work, *The Philosophers' Index*, revealed no publications on the topic of private military companies, and only two journal articles over the past decade on mercenaries in general. It is generally assumed that there is something deeply immoral about mercenarism, to the extent that 'mercenary' is unquestionably one of the more offensive descriptions we can give of a fellow human being. But what, exactly, is it about this kind of activity that validates such moral censure? On closer inspection it becomes clear that there are really two main questions here. First, there is the question of whether or not mercenary activity is bad for the world – if so, then clearly the warrior of good conscience ought not to become a mercenary. Second, there is the question of whether there is something intrinsically morally problematic about the warrior-for-hire, something that would make it wrong to become a mercenary even in a possible world in which the employment of mercenaries led to overwhelmingly good consequences for that world. Most of the ethics-related discussion of the private military industry has been around the first of these questions, and so in the interests of exploring new ground, it is the second of these questions that shall be the focus of this chapter.

Another restriction on the scope of this chapter must also be acknowledged from the beginning. The political debate over whether military functions can be ethically outsourced to the private sector exists almost exclusively against the background of the broadly liberal political principles that underpin international law. In order to remain relevant to that debate, therefore, I shall restrict the scope of my analysis by taking that same broadly liberal background as given. Thus, there may well be good arguments for or against mercenarism that emerge from within the principles of certain religious viewpoints or philosophical traditions, but those arguments fall only within the scope of my discussion insofar as they overlap with the contemporary international debate on this topic.

In what follows I shall draw on the two papers on the ethics of mercenaries that were mentioned above, one authored by Anthony Coady[2] and the other by Tony Lynch and A.J. Walsh.[3] Following these authors I begin by considering the relevant arguments against mercenarism that were put forward by Niccolo Machiavelli. I will then turn to a consideration of the analogy that is supposed to hold between the mercenary and the prostitute, in order to assess whether or not this analogy stands up to close scrutiny.

Of course, one of the relevant issues in investigating just what is wrong with being a mercenary, is the definition of just what it is to be a mercenary. Given the limited space I have available, however, plunging headlong into a conceptual analysis of the concept of 'mercenary' is not possible here. Thankfully, it is also not necessary, as I am able to defer to the analysis of this concept carried out by Uwe Steinhoff in his chapter in this book. I shall, therefore, adopt the definition that emerges from Steinhoff's investigation, which reads as follows:

> A *mercenary* is a person who is contracted to provide military services to groups other than his own (in terms of nation, ethnic group, class, etc.) and is ready to deliver this service even if this involves taking part in hostilities. Which groups are relevant depends on the nature of the conflict.[4]

It will be noted that this definition is unusual in not defining mercenarism in terms of the motive for monetary gain, or something similar. Certainly, for most people, it is this that immediately springs to mind as the key characteristic of the mercenary warrior. But as Steinhoff points out:

> If one looks at what are considered paradigmatic examples of mercenaries, for example the men of the Free companies or 'Mad' Mike Hoare's and Bob Denard's men in the Congo in the 1960s or 'Colonel' Callan in Angola in the 1970s, it becomes very clear that these men, or at least a very significant number of them, were *not* motivated principally by financial gain (which does not mean that they were not at all motivated by financial gain), but [rather] by adventurism or a love for war and fighting.[5]

Of course money is not irrelevant here, hence the idea of contract in Steinhoff's definition. As Steinhoff puts it:

> The financial motive, to be sure, should remain part of the definition of 'mercenary'. Someone who fights for free or for relatively small pay in war after war is a *pure* adventurer or a war junkie, not a mercenary. On the other hand, the financial motive does not need to override or dominate all others, not even moral or ideological ones. Mercenaries who fight exclusively in wars that meet certain moral or ideological preconditions are not only conceivable but real.[6,7]

Before beginning our investigation proper, one final, and fairly important flag needs to be raised. I am not here attempting to analyse every single possible way the mercenary might be considered to be bad. Obviously, for example, if any kind of voluntary involvement in a situation of armed conflict were considered to be morally reprehensible, then this would be a good reason for not being a mercenary. It would, of course, also be a good reason not to volunteer to be a member of a national militia. That sort of issue is beyond what I can attempt in this chapter. What I am interested in here is what, if anything, negatively distinguishes the ethical status of the private warrior from that of an enlisted soldier, sailor or airman in the armed forces of some nation. With those constraints in place, we can now begin.

## Machiavelli and the mercenary warrior

Both Coady and Lynch and Walsh take as central the objections to mercenarism raised by Niccolo Machiavelli in his famous work, *The Prince*.[8] Following Coady, Lynch and Walsh, it seems that these are effectively threefold:

1   Mercenaries are not sufficiently bloodthirsty.
2   Mercenaries cannot be trusted because of the temptations of political power.
3   There exists some motive or motives appropriate to engaging in war that mercenaries necessarily lack, or else mercenaries are motivated by some factor that is inappropriate to engaging in war.

The first of these points need not detain us long. For it is quite clear that, even if the empirically questionable claim that mercenaries lack the killing instinct necessary for war were true, this in no way constitutes a moral failing on the part of the private warrior. 'Lack of bloodlust' is not high on any list of moral vices I've ever seen. But perhaps the point is rather one about effectiveness – the claim that the soldier for hire cannot be relied upon to do what is necessary in a battle when the crunch comes, because he is too squeamish perhaps. Again, however, it is evident that this cannot be the moral failing we are looking for. For while we might cast moral aspersions on such a private warrior, those aspersions would be in the family of such terms as 'feeble', 'pathetic' or 'hopeless'. But these are quite clearly not the moral failings we are looking for in trying to discover just what is morally wrong with being a mercenary. Indeed, this very characteristic might just as easily be considered to be an ethically positive one. A more positive version of Machiavelli's claim, as Coady points out, is that the mercenary may be less prone to the passions that lead the national or ethnic zealot soldier to demonize the enemy and seek their total destruction. In this case, it must be the soldier who fights for his country or creed who is more deserving of our moral censure than the warrior-for-hire.

The second point is even more easily dealt with. For it is quite clear that the temptation to grab power over a nation by force is at least as strong for national military forces as it is for mercenaries. In fact, it could well be argued that mercenaries are more reliable in this respect, given that they are usually foreign and therefore have less incentive to try to gain power over the nation that has contracted their services. Regardless of how true this latter empirical point is, it seems clear that there is nothing about being a mercenary that makes one more susceptible to being tempted by the lure of political power that is not also a factor for a member of a national military force or its equivalent.

The question of motives, however, is a weightier one, and requires more of our attention. The most common version of this objection is that there is something wrong with fighting for money. As pointed out above, it is a central feature of the definition of a mercenary that he be contracted to provide military services – he is not simply a volunteer, and mercenarism has an inescapable commercial dimension to it. As Lynch and Walsh point out, however, the objection cannot simply be that money is in itself a morally questionable motivator for action. For while a case could perhaps be made for this, it would also apply to such a wide range of human activities that it offers little help in discerning what singles out mercenarism as especially problematic. Perhaps, therefore, the problem is being motivated by money above all else. Lynch and Walsh helpfully suggest that we label such a person a *lucrepath*. Certainly, we do find something deeply objectionable about someone for whom the accumulation of money is always the overriding consideration. By this thinking, as Lynch and Walsh put it, 'Those criticizing mercenaries for taking blood money are then accusing them of being lucrepaths...it is not that they do things for money, but that money is the *sole* or the *dominant* consideration in their practical deliberations.'[9]

As Steinhoff's discussion makes clear, and as Lynch and Walsh themselves point out, there is no particular reason to think that mercenaries *must* be lucrepaths, or even that they *usually* are. Certainly, there is no connection of a logical kind between being a lucrepath on the one hand and, on the other, a person who is 'contracted to provide military services to groups other than his own' and who is 'ready to deliver this service even if this involves taking part in hostilities'. Steinhoff's discussion points out that there is good reason to doubt whether the pecuniary motive is the overriding one for most private warriors; indeed it is far more likely that, like the soldier of a national militia, their motives are mixed. An additional point here[10] is that there seems little reason to think that a soldier of a national militia could not be a lucrepath (though, admittedly, not an especially successful one), and if this is so, then lucrepathology cannot be a useful way of distinguishing between the moral standing of all mercenaries, on the one hand, and the set of all members of national military forces on the other.

Perhaps then, the question of appropriate motives is not that mercenaries are united by having a particular morally reprehensible motive, but rather that they lack a particular motive that is necessary for good moral standing when it comes to fighting and killing. What might such a motive be? Coady, as do Lynch and Walsh, identifies the main candidate here as that of just cause and right intention, as defined by Just War theory.[11] As Lynch and Walsh put it, '*Ex hypothesi*, killing in warfare is justifiable only when the soldier in question is motivated amongst other things by a just cause. Justifiable killing motives must not only be non-lucrepathic, but also, following Aquinas, must include just cause and right intention.'[12] Immediately, however, Lynch and Walsh point out the obvious that it is far from clear that this consideration is one that distinguishes the vile mercenary from the righteous citizen soldier. For it would be bizarre to claim that every member of a national military were so motivated, and equally doubtful that a private warrior could not be motivated in this way when entering into some or all of his contracts. As Coady points out, we can easily imagine a group of private warriors working together as 'Just Warriors Inc', who take remuneration for their services but who only offer those services in support of just causes. Indeed, many established private military companies at least pay lip service to exactly this ideal,[13] and there is no conceptual reason why private warriors of this kind could not exist.[14]

There is one further version of the 'improper motives' objection to mercenaries that may yet provide a basis for appropriate moral censure, and here again it is the lack of a motivational element that is important. Here I am referring to the idea that the private warrior is not motivated to fight by a close association with the population on whose behalf he is deploying his military skills, what Lynch and Walsh refer to as 'strong group identification'.[15] The problem with the mercenary, by this inter-pretation, is that he is a *foreigner* fighting for a group of people he cannot possibly care deeply about. The corollary of this is that it is a moral principle that one ought only to be willing to fight, kill and possibly die for the people with whom one identifies in a close and personal way. But why should this be so? Of course it is not difficult to imagine an argument to the effect that there exists some sort of moral requirement on us to be willing to fight to defend the social group to which we, in some sense, belong, at least where the relevant conditions of a Just War are met. But it does not follow from this that there are no other circumstances in which a warrior might legitimately practise his deadly trade. Take the soldiers of many nations who were deployed to the Middle East in 1990 and 1991 to eject Saddam Hussein's forces from occupied Kuwait – were they guilty of some serious moral failing? And what of the UN peacekeepers who are deployed to and sometimes fight in distant parts of the world, far from their home nations and societies? Quite clearly there are circumstances in which a warrior may ethically be involved in an armed conflict even where his identification with the group for whose benefit he fights is no more specific than his identification with the humanity in general. Furthermore, as we have already seen, there seems to be no reason to suppose that a soldier-for-hire might not, on principle, offer his services only to the group or groups with whom he strongly identifies. Unless this somehow means he is no longer a mercenary, then clearly this consideration is unhelpful in singling out the private warrior for moral condemnation. As Lynch and Walsh point out, 'such considerations are *external* to the practice of mercenarism.'[16]

Before turning to an examination of the supposed analogy between prostitutes and mercenaries, there is one final possibility that remains to be considered under the 'improper motives' rubric. And that is the thought that it is not any one of the above considerations that accounts for the badness of being a mercenary, but that it is instead the presence of any or *all* of these motivational factors. So perhaps what matters is holding a very strong (though not lucrepathic) pecuniary motive *plus* not being motivated by such ideals as just cause and right intention *plus* the lack of a strong identification with the group for whom the mercenary is employed to fight. Perhaps, but I don't think so. First, it is hard to see what it is about this combination of these factors that should lead us to a conclusion different to that reached by a consideration of each factor individually. And second, it is again not clear that this combination of factors offers sufficient ground to distinguish the mercenary from, say, a South African rifleman on AU peacekeeping duties in the Sudan, who might easily display exactly these characteristics. And finally, it is evident once more that there is nothing about this bundle of characteristics that make them a necessary feature of being a mercenary – as we have seen above, a private warrior could quite easily lack all of these characteristics and still fit the definition of a mercenary that I set out earlier in this chapter.

It seems, therefore, that an investigation into the reasons that Machiavelli gives for counting the mercenary to be morally lacking offers little support for the traditional vilification of the class of all private warriors. This is clear enough in Lynch and Walsh's paper, and were this all there is to be said, this chapter would offer nothing particularly new to the discussion. But there is at least one more angle of attack that is levelled at the private warrior that neither Lynch and Walsh nor Coady analyse closely, albeit a vague and unclear one, and that is that mercenaries are the 'whores of war'. What remains for this chapter is to take a closer look at this analogy that is often supposed to hold between prostitutes and mercenaries.

## Whores of war?

As I have said, an intriguing and yet under-analysed analogy is often held to apply between those who contractually provide sexual services and those who contractually provide military services. Both forms of employment vie for the title of the oldest profession, and both are generally considered to be ethically problematic. But just what is it about mercenaries that supposedly makes them the 'whores of war'? A necessary starting point in assessing this is to consider what is it that is taken to be ethically troublesome about prostitution.

It's worth noting from the start that prostitution is no longer as universally vilified as it once was. In an interesting parallel with the rise of private military companies, prostitutes are increasingly re-labelling themselves as 'sex workers' and demanding recognition as legitimate members of an economic society. Arguments in favour of this sort of view tend to be of the liberal contractarian brand advocated by Lars Ericsson, who argues that 'If two adults voluntarily consent to an economic arrangement concerning sexual activity and this activity takes place in private, it seems plainly absurd to maintain that there is something intrinsically wrong with it.'[17] Such arguments are of little interest to us here, of course, for we are in search of reasons why prostitution might be considered to be bad.

The response to Ericsson's paper by Carol Pateman sets up nicely one of the dominant lines of the argument against prostitution, which emerges from some quarters of feminism. As Pateman puts it, 'The central feminist argument is that prostitution remains morally undesirable, no matter what reforms are made, because it is one of the most graphic examples of men's domination of women.'[18] Related to this are objections to prostitution on the grounds that it oppresses, endangers or harms the prostitute,[19] or that prostitution results in a violation of one's autonomy.[20] Again, however, this does not help us very much. For those fond of comparing mercenarism with prostitution are quite obviously not trying to argue that the mercenary is at risk of exploitation or some other abusive harm,[21] and that *this* is what is wrong with mercenarism!

What we are looking for here is some sort of objection to prostitution that would justify the sort of moral censure that lies behind such Biblical injunctions as the command to burn to death a priest's daughter if she turns to prostitution (Leviticus 21:9). What is obvious is that this objection lies within the bounds of the claim that it is not appropriate to offer sex for money. But why is it not appropriate? We have already indirectly dismissed the idea that the problem here is an overriding desire for money (lucrepathology), for though this might well be considered to be morally problematic it is not specific enough to enable us to point the moral finger at the prostitute.[22] So if it is not simply an overriding lust for money that is the problem, it must be that there is something about the nature of sexual relations that makes offering sex on a commercial basis immoral. Here, perhaps surprisingly, the Bible is of some help to us, for in it the nation of Israel is often compared with a prostitute when 'she' turns away from the God who has created, chosen and rescued her (see for example Ezekiel: 16). What seems to be at stake here is a particular relationship – prostitution is problematic because it involves a violation or breach of what is deemed to be the appropriate relationship.

Whether this is a legitimate reason for the negative moral judgement on prostitution is not relevant here. The question for us is whether there is a successful analogy between mercenaries and prostitutes, where success is measured by the justification of apportioning moral censure on mercenaries. Asking this question requires us to heuristically take as given the most conservative view of prostitution, regardless of what we actually believe to be true of the morality of prostitution. The first thing we note here is that there is at first glance an apparent disanalogy between offering sex commercially on the one hand, and offering military services commercially on the other. In the case of prostitution, the act in question takes place between the two parties involved in the contractual relationship, presumably for mutual benefit. Mercenarism, on the other hand, involves one party contracting with another, for mutual benefit, to fight against some third party (presumably not for said third party's benefit!). This disanalogy does not, however, seem to be morally significant, and can be dissolved by replacing the term 'fighting' with something like 'defending' – then in both cases there is a contract for mutual benefit in which the first party pays the second to perform a desired service on his (or its) behalf.

So then, what is it about commercial soldiering that is like offering sexual services for pecuniary reward? More specifically, what appropriate relationship is violated or disrupted by mercenarism? The main candidate in view here is that of the relationship between the citizen and the state. Just as it might be argued that the only morally appropriate relationship for the exercise of sexual relations is that between a husband and wife,[23] so the implied argument here is that the only morally appropriate relationship for the exercise of martial skills is that between the citizen and the nation of his citizenship. Thus, just as prostitution and other forms of adultery or fornication are violations or disruptions of the morally appropriate sexual relationship, so mercenarism is a disruption of the morally appropriate martial relationship.

If this is, indeed, the crux of the analogy between the prostitute and the mercenary, then, to state the obvious, the question we must here ponder is whether the relationship between citizen and state is indeed the only appropriate one in service of which the warfighter can legitimately apply his deadly skills? It is generally accepted that killing is a morally serious matter, and it is this seriousness that, within civil society, seems to make it ethically appropriate for the state to hold the monopoly on violence, for this shifting of violence from the individual to the state is supposed to reduce the overall level and destructiveness of violence in society. For similar reasons, it is generally accepted that it is the organs of the state which bear responsibility for defending the state's citizens from outside attack.[24] Does this, therefore, mean that because states ought to defend their citizenry, citizens ought only to fight in the service of their states? The most coherent version of this thesis is based on the idea that, for individuals, the employment of violence is only ethically legitimate in cases of self-defence, and that the state's right to defend itself from attack derives in turn from the individual's right to self-defence. If this is true, the argument continues, then clearly the right to employ violence in defence of a state or other relevant group cannot extend to persons who are not members of that state or relevant group.

The view that a state can derive its right to defend itself from the individual's right to self-defence is subjected to close scrutiny in a recent book by David Rodin.[25] Rodin's rigorous analysis leads him to the following conclusion:

> The argument which draws a connection between personal self-defense and national-defense is at once beguilingly simple and intuitively appealing. It has informed moral and philosophical thinking on warfare since at least the time of the Christian Fathers and has had a powerful influence on the development of modern international law. But I have argued that the analogy cannot be philosophically sustained. National-defense cannot be reduced to a collective application of personal rights of self-defense, and it cannot be explained as a state-held right analogous to personal self-defense.[26]

Not surprisingly, Rodin's book has drawn a range of responses, but very few of these seem to undermine his conclusions. The one response to Rodin that seems to offer some hope of redeeming the state's right to defend itself from attack, one I explore elsewhere,[27] rests on the notion of human development as the central concept justifying the proportionate employment of armed force, both in defence of a state and for the purposes of humanitarian intervention. But if this is true, there is nothing particular about the state that gives it the authority to intervene using force in the interests of human development.

Even if it were granted that the state's right to defend itself from attack derives from the individual's right to self-defence, it does not necessarily follow that this makes the private warrior a violator of the relationship between the citizen and the state. For it is questionable why the right to intervene in order to protect a citizen or group thereof should extend only to the state. Surely, what matters is that said citizen or group of citizens is protected. In matters of life or death, it seems self-evident that the promiscuity of defenders is desirable. If we take the analogy with individual self-defence seriously, then it must not be forgotten that there is a right for individuals to intervene to defend others as well as themselves, and there is nothing about this being a contractual arrangement that would undermine that right. Consider the case of Jane, who finds that she has to walk through a bad neighbourhood at night. Jane is a taxpayer, and is therefore rightfully under the protection of the local police. However, the local police are not sufficiently effective to ensure her safety. Believing (rightly) that her chances of being attacked are high, Jane enters into a contractual arrangement with a bouncer at a nightclub she happens to pass, who agrees to protect her on her walk through the bad neighbourhood for an agreed fee. As it happens, Jane is attacked, and her companion does intervene to save her. Do we think that Jane's companion is in some sense unethical? No. True, we might have valued his actions more highly if he had offered his protection for free. But we do not somehow consider his actions to be *unethical*. This example reflects the dynamic that exists between state police and private security forces. It has not, to my knowledge, been argued that rent-a-cops are somehow deeply immoral because their occupation violates the citizen–state relationship with respect to the employment of force. Why then, should this suddenly become an issue when military force is involved?

Even if the preceding argument is not accepted, this still doesn't necessarily leave the private warrior out in the cold. For why could a state not contractually employ private warriors who are its own citizens, as, for example, the US government does when it employs the services of Blackwater USA?[28] Furthermore, it is not at all clear how the state–citizen relationship justifies the use of force in cases of humanitarian intervention and other 'peace operations', and yet it is increasingly recognized that in some cases such interventions are ethically required. Why then could private warriors not be employed for armed interventions of this kind?[29]

The flip side of this issue (and it must be admitted that this is a consequentialist consideration, not one directly relevant to the virtue of the private warrior himself) is that it seems that a good argument could be made for the view that states ought always to prefer foreign mercenaries to citizen soldiers, for if the state has a duty to protect its citizens then that duty must surely extend also to those citizens who happen to make up the nation's armed forces. As Coady points out, Thomas More makes exactly this point in articulating the strategies of his wise Utopians.[30]

## Conclusion

While one short paper cannot hope to settle this issue, my analysis leads me to be inclined to concur with Lynch and Walsh when they write that

> many writers…base their hostility to mercenarism on a moral analogy with prostitution. But if the strategy is a common one, nonetheless it is inadequate, depending on an extraordinary idealization of appropriate sexual and military relationships, and on a mistaken equation of the morality of intimacy with that of organized violence.[31]

Furthermore, as we saw, Machiavelli's arguments regarding the moral character of the mercenary are generally unconvincing. Of course this does not mean that some mercenaries have not done or will not do bad things – this is obviously not true. But the point is that there is nothing particular about their being mercenaries that makes them intrinsically bad. Our investigation also does not show that, even if soldiers-for-hire are not necessarily bad in themselves, the exercise of this trade might not result in bad consequences for the world. But if it turns out that there are ways of regulating the private military profession such that these private warriors may be employed in ways that are generally beneficial, then it seems to me there is then no further reason for African policymakers to deny them a role in the management of armed conflict. In conclusion, it is my claim that we should agree with Lynch and Walsh when they write that 'The Good Mercenary is neither logically impossible nor psychologically implausible.'[32]

## Notes

1 I use the male pronoun here because, with a few exceptions, warriors-for-hire are male. The exceptions to which I refer are almost entirely limited to the private military industry, where some former female soldiers and police officers have lucrative contracts interrogating and guarding women suspected of involvement in the Iraqi and Afghan insurgencies.

2 C.A.J. Coady, 'Mercenary Morality' in A.G.D. Bradney (ed.), *International Law and Armed Conflict (Archiv für Rechts- und Sozialphilosophie, Beiheft* 46), Stuttgart: Franz Steiner Verlag, 1992, pp. 55–69.

3 T. Lynch and A.J. Walsh, 'The Good Mercenary?', *The Journal of Political Philosophy*, 2000, Vol. 8(2), pp. 133–53.

4 Uwe Steinhoff, 'What are Mercenaries?', Ch. 1, p. 28.

5 Uwe Steinhoff, 'What are Mercenaries?', Ch. 1, p. 21.

6 Uwe Steinhoff, 'What are Mercenaries?', this volume, Ch. 1, p. 22.

7 Steinhoff refers, by way of example, to 'mercenaries like the famous Count von Rosen who are so selective about the wars they fight in that they can hardly be distinguished from ideologically motivated volunteers.' Another relevant example would be the American pilots of the 'Flying Tigers', or the American Volunteer Airgroup, under the command of the legendary Captain Claire L. Chennault, who fought for China against Japan prior to US entry into World War II. Flying Tigers airmen were US Army and Navy pilots who resigned their commissions in order to sign one-year contracts with the Central Aircraft Manufacturing Company, to 'manufacture, repair and operate aircraft'.

8 Niccolo Machiavelli, *The Prince*, Trans. Harvey C. Mansfield, 2nd edn, Chicago: University of Chicago Press, 1998.

9 Lynch and Walsh, 'The Good Mercenary?', p. 136.

10 Again one raised by Lynch and Walsh.

11 This presumes that the idea of just cause or right intention applies to the individual soldier in a conflict is itself a contentious claim.

12 Lynch and Walsh, 'The Good Mercenary?', p. 138.

13 See, for example, the website of Blackwater USA, which declares that the company offers its services 'in support of security and peace, and freedom and democracy everywhere', www.blackwaterusa.com/about/, accessed 9 October 2007. Historically, we can again think of the case of the Flying Tigers. Chennault himself seems to fall quite neatly into this category.

14 Interestingly, Tobias Masterton and others have put forward the idea of a non-profit PMC that works exclusively for the United Nations. See www.corpwatch.org/article.php?id = 8989, accessed 9 October 2007.

15 Lynch and Walsh, 'The Good Mercenary?', p. 140.

16 Ibid., p. 140.

17 Lars Ericsson, 'Charges against Prostitution: An Attempt at a Philosophical Assessment', *Ethics*, 1980, Vol. 90(3), pp. 33–9.

18 Carole Pateman, 'Defending Prostitution: Charges against Ericsson', *Ethics*, 1983, Vol. 93(3), p. 561.
19 See, for example, the arguments put forward at www. prostitutionresearch.com/, accessed 9 October 2007.
20 Scott A. Anderson, 'Prostitution and Sexual Autonomy: Making Sense of the Prohibition of Prostitution', *Ethics*, 2002, Vol. 112(4), pp. 748–80.
21 This may in fact be a very real risk. However, this possible objection to merce-narism has not, to my knowledge, been explored in scholarly literature.
22 That this is one version of the 'mercenaries are prostitutes' objection is made clear by Lynch and Walsh when they write that 'It is a commonplace that mercenaries are evil because they receive "blood money". Sometimes there is talk of "the whores of war". Such epithets point to a common moral criticism of mercenarism; namely, that mercenaries kill for money. The mercenary's killing motives are morally inappropriate because they are in a determining sense financial.' Lunch and Walsh, 'The Good Mercenary?', p. 135.
23 Or (less conservatively) between two parties in a committed love relationship.
24 This generally accepted view is not, however, without its difficulties. David Rodin's book *War and Self-Defense*, Oxford: Oxford University Press, 2002, provides an excellent account of these difficulties. See also Deane-Peter Baker, 'Defending the Common Life: National Defence after Rodin', *Journal of Applied Philosophy*, August 2006, Vol. 23(3), pp. 259–75.
25 Rodin, *War and Self-Defense*.
26 Ibid., p. 162.
27 Baker, 'Defending the Common Life'.
28 While the security clearances required for almost all Blackwater positions makes it virtually inevitable that its employees are US citizens, it's worth noting that citizenship is not a requirement for employment by the US military.
29 As it happens, this is precisely the market that the private military industry is working hardest to make its own. See for example the articles available on the website of the International Peace Operations Association, www.ipoaonline.org/home, accessed 9 October 2007.
30 Coady makes reference to Thomas More, *Utopia*, Harmondsworth: Penguin, 1974, p.112.
31 Lynch and Walsh, 'The Good Mercenary?', p. 134. They seem poised at this point in their paper to go on to offer a detailed analysis of just why this analogy is inadequate. Oddly, however, they continue instead with this point:

> The latter mistake is of particular importance, for too often the case against mercenarism rests on a failure to appreciate an insight contained in the liberal tradition. For it does not at all follow that encouraging virtuous motives in individuals ('righteousness') will contribute to the end of social justice, indeed on occasions the opposite may well be true. The attempt to maximize the virtue of the individual's participation in organized violence may have as a result more – and more bloody – violence than under a moral regime in which the virtue of such actions lies more generally in the merely pecuniary.

32 Ibid., p. 141.

# 3 Regulating anarchy

## The ethics of PMCs in global civil society

*Mervyn Frost*

There is a widespread belief that private military companies, when evaluated from an ethical point of view, are problematic. Such companies perform a range of different functions from 'sharp end' action to 'backup support'. Their activities include providing logistical support to states, non-governmental organizations and international organizations; providing security to these organizations; providing training to security and military forces of states undergoing reconstruction and so on. For the moment direct combat operations have not been privatized.

A whole range of different problems have been mentioned with regard to such private military companies (PMCs). These include their lack of accountability and transparency, a suspicion that they pose a threat to human rights, a suspicion that they will be able to circumvent international humanitarian law, and many others. A good example of a general evaluation of PMCs is to be found in P.W. Singer's *Corporate Warriors*.[1] Here, he lists a whole number of different problems associated with this type of companies:

- PMCs might have different interests to the agent employing them.
- PMCs might act in ways that are difficult for employers and the public to monitor.
- PMCs may be tempted to cut corners, overcharge or to 'cut and run'.
- PMCs might become more powerful than those employing them and thus become a threat.
- In order to pay the PMC the employer (often a state) might pawn its most valuable assets (access to natural resources).
- Those actors (states) with more cash to hire PMCs will become more powerful than others.
- Weak states with cash can become interventionists with the aid of PMCs.
- The executive branch of governments, by using PMCs, can bypass the controls of legislatures.
- The ability of weak states to provide internal security becomes dependent on their relationship to rich states who are prepared to pay for the services of PMCs.

Many of the problems mentioned in this list are standard ones applicable to any private company in any field of operation. One can see this by replacing the phrase 'private military company' with 'mining company', 'oil company' or simply 'corporation' in the paragraphs above. Any private corporation may end up posing similar problems for any buyer making use of its services; these are not problems specific to PMCs. What I am concerned about in this chapter is: do PMCs pose particularly difficult ethical problems for us other than the practical problems mentioned above? What are the problems and how ought we to think about them? This chapter offers a framework which I believe will contribute to our thinking about ethical issues arising out of using PMCs towards specific ends.

## Practice theory

What we need to understand at the outset are the ethical constraints operating on actors who set up PMCs. The people who set up PMCs are not isolated individuals acting in a social vacuum. To the contrary, they are constituted as actors of a certain kind within specific social practices. The practices in which they are constituted as such have embedded in them fundamental ethical norms. Were the actors to disobey these norms, they would cease to be actors in good standing within these social practices and would not be regarded by the other members of the practices as being the kind of actors entitled to set up a PMC. What are the relevant practices which constitute the actors who set up PMCs?[2]

In order to set up a PMC one has to be both a civilian and a citizen. These two actor statuses can only be held within two very specific global social practices. To be a civilian is to be a rights holder in global civil society. To be a citizen, is to be a participant in the society of sovereign states. Let us examine each of these rather bald assertions in turn.

## Global civil society

The actors who create companies (including PMCs) must be understood in the first place as rights holders within the practice of global civil society.[3] To illustrate the point here let us consider a single civilian, Tim Spicer, the founder of Aegis Defence Services. The first actor status Spicer needed in order to form the company is that of a rights holder. This is a status which one holds when one is recognized as an actor in good standing in civil society. Let us call such a rights holder a civilian. Spicer is a rights holder in civil society. As such, he is recognized by other members of global civil society, such as you and me, as the one who has the right to own property, the right to make contracts, the right to freedom of speech (how could one make contracts if one were not free to speak to other rights holders?), the right to freedom of movement that entitles him to move amongst his fellow civilians seeking to make contracts for his firm, the right to freedom of association with other rights holders, a right to redress in those cases where contractees default on their contracts and so on. We, his fellow participants in civil society, do not consider that he has these rights because he is a member of a specific state or because he is located in some specific territory. He has these rights because he knows how to claim them and because he recognizes them in others wherever they happen to be. Even in areas where the state has broken down (or does not function well) we still recognize his civilian rights.[4] These civil society rights are embodied (more or less successfully) in the common law of Britain and in the domestic law of the rest of the 193 sovereign states worldwide that participate in the global market which, itself, is a major component of global civil society. Spicer, like the rest of us, knows how to be a rights holder and he knows how to interact with other rights holders. Knowing this is a precondition for his being able to function within civil society. I do not need to spell out any more detail here. Suffice it to say that Spicer, like you and me, is constructed as a certain kind of actor, a rights holder, in that elaborate system of mutual recognition which is global civil society. Global civil society is a social construct within which we who have constructed it have accepted rules which constrain us not to behave in certain ways. In particular, we have accepted rules which require us not to infringe the basic human rights of our co-participants in this society.

Clearly within civil society we as civilians are free to set up companies that offer different kinds of services to our fellow civilians. We may set up construction companies, private universities, motor-car manufacturing companies and so on. If we think there is a demand, we may set up private military companies. The normal constraints operative upon rights holders pertain in all these cases. We are entitled to use our rights to set up companies provided that the companies do not threaten the very rights we make use of in order to establish them. So, just as rights holders are not entitled to set up companies expressly designed to steal other people's property, so too, rights holders are not entitled to set up private military companies, which have as their express purpose the infringement of other people's rights. The point is a very general one that applies equally to companies providing services to individuals or to states.[5]

Just as civilians are entitled to set up private military companies provided they do not infringe the rights of other civilians, so too, do civilians have the right to make use of the services of such companies. In our private capacity we are entitled to employ such companies to protect, amongst other things, our persons and our property. As part of a public authority such as the state, we are entitled to make use of such companies to provide protection in specified areas (e.g. protecting key installations), provided, of course, that in doing so the company does not infringe the rights of other civilians wherever they happen to be (at home or abroad). The ethical constraints on the members of such companies, and on those who make use of their services, are precisely the same as the ethical constraints operative on any other company in civil society. According to this logic there is nothing about such companies which makes them more difficult to understand from an ethical point of view than any other company. All such companies have to uphold the ethical norms embedded in civil society.

It is important to note that although such companies are *private* they are not *secret*. They are still subject to scrutiny in the public domain in the same way that all companies are. Just as Microsoft has to submit its annual accounts to scrutiny by authorized auditors and just as Microsoft's activities have to be seen to be above board and within the law, so too, must Aegis Defence Services subject itself to public audit. In like manner, Aegis, like all private firms, is eligible to be the subject of inquiries launched by the press. Similarly, just as more and more firms are voluntarily subjecting themselves to public scrutiny to determine their adherence to codes of corporate social responsibility, so, too, are the PMCs, as a glance at their websites will prove. Such firms are not clandestine organizations. If they are to flourish they have to be seen to be successful in the market place (which is a public space). They have to be seen to be acting in terms of the laws which we have established to protect our rights. They have to be seen to be acting in terms of the commonly accepted standards of corporate social responsibility. For it is only in this way that they will gain further business. So, although there might be incentives for them to attempt to cut costs, if they do so by performing their jobs poorly, they will be penalized. The market has built-in checks to make sure that companies do what their employers have employed them to do.[6]

## The society of sovereign states

The second practice within which those who set up PMCs are constituted as actors is the society of sovereign states. Everyone in the world is a participant in this practice. In this practice the participants, through an elaborate system of mutual recognition, constitute one another as *citizens*. It is worth noting that the practice in its current form is one in which the participating states either are democracies or declare themselves to be *en route* to that status. In order to elucidate what is involved in being a citizen, let us once again consider Tim Spicer as an example. He is a *citizen* of Britain. As such he has a whole set of political rights. These include the right to stand for political office, the right to vote in elections, the right to form political parties and to participate in them, the right to information about the activities of the elected government, the right to criticize the elected government, the right to certain services from his elected member of Parliament and so on. In order to continue to enjoy these rights, he is required to recognize the rights of his fellow citizens. Furthermore, for him to enjoy his citizenship rights, it is crucial that the sovereign state within which he enjoys them is recognized as sovereign by other such sovereign states. Were his sovereign state to be colonized by another, his citizenship rights in the colony would not hold the value they currently do in a fully sovereign state.

Underpinning the complex set of rules which comprise the practice of sovereign democratic and democratizing states is a set of ethical values. Once again, in a short-hand way, we might say that the values entrenched in the system are those linked to the notion of individual human freedom. In this sense the ethic is similar to that which underpins civil society. However, the freedom one enjoys as a citizen in a sovereign state, especially a democratic one, is an improvement on that which one enjoys as a civilian. It is a supplement to civilian freedom. The improvement is to be found in the following feature of the society of sovereign states. As a citizen one is recognized as one who is entitled to participate as an equal with one's fellow citizens in the business of self-government. One becomes a co-determiner of the rules of the polity within which one is constituted as citizen. As a citizen one is the source (or ground) of the authority of the government of the state within which one lives.

It is crucial to notice that the practice within which citizenship in its modern form is established is not simply the individual state within which a given person is established as a citizen, but the whole practice of sovereign states. To be a free person as we understand it today involves one being recognized as such in his/her state and having his/her state recognized as a free state by the other 193 states in the community of states.

For citizens who are setting up a PMC, it is crucial that they do not flout the rules of the practice within which they are constituted as citizens. It is crucial for Tim Spicer to be recognized as a British citizen in good standing. That he has an OBE (Officer of the Order of the British Empire) status no doubt helps in this regard. For if he were to be seen as an enemy of the state, as an international terrorist, as a person guilty of treason and so on, this would undermine the standing of his PMC in the public domain.[7] It is a condition of the success of his company that he be seen, in general, as behaving in an unimpeachable way, as one who upholds the ethic embedded in the society of sovereign states.[8]

Looked at in the round we can now see that there are very severe constraints on Tim Spicer and all others like him. If their private military companies are to prosper then they must ensure that they, together with all the employees of their companies behave in ways that do not undermine their civilian and citizenship rights. This requires of them that they not undermine the civilian and citizenship rights of others.

Of course, in practice there will always be some people in PMCs who break the ethical norms pertinent to them as rights holders in these practices. Just as in the domestic sphere there are always criminals who breach domestic law.

On the face of the matter then, it would seem that within the two dominant global practices (global civil society, and, the society of democratic and democratizing states) the creation of private military companies is ethically legitimate and that those setting up such companies are constrained by the ethical criteria of good behaviour contained in both practices. It is easy to understand that any PMC falling foul of these constraints would be dealt with harshly by market forces (in the context of civil society) and also by the society of sovereign states. A 'corporation' that set out to undermine the latter global practice would soon be branded an 'international terrorist group'. There is no need to suppose that this kind of security corporation is any more (or any less) ethical than any other kind of private corporation.

## Are there some functions which ought not to be privatized?

In light of the above it is worth asking why the misgivings about the ethicality of PMCs persist. A different way of considering the ethics of PMCs is to ask the question: Are there some functions of the state which ought never to be privatized?

Let us first of all consider the case of the state. In the history of the modern state the relationship between the citizens and the military has been a particularly close one. Indeed, some theorists, like Charles Tilly, have argued that the formation of the modern state has everything to do with developments which were brought about by the requirements of modern military establishments.[9] It has been argued that the modern state developed in the way that it did in response to the imperatives of modern warfare. This may or may not be true, and I shall not go into this argument here. However, what is clear is that at the level of meaning, the relationship between states, citizens and war fighting is a close one. In many states, if not in most, the citizens regularly pay homage to those who died for the state in previous wars. In the rhetoric on these occasions it is said that the soldiers who fell 'gave their lives for their country'. Courageous deeds are honoured. Dying for one's country is understood as a self-sacrifice for a greater good. The fighting of war is seen as a collective deed, it is something for which all citizens are responsible. Where the military is successful, all citizens, it is supposed, do (or ought to), feel pride. Where the military is unsuccessful, all citizens are thought to feel shame. This is the domain of collective responsibility. To refuse military service is to demonstrate one's lack of moral fibre.

The contrast between the understanding of military service outlined above, with the understanding of the military service provided by PMCs and those working in them, is stark. There would be no dishonour in a PMC leaving the service of one state to serve a different state. There would be no dishonour in an employee of a PMC walking away from his/her PMC to find employment with an alternative (rival) PMC that offered better pay and employment conditions. The whole notion of honour seems not to be relevant here. In terms of the traditional model of soldiering a soldier serves his/her country, which is quite different to what the 'soldiers' who work for PMCs do. Instead they see themselves as serving the global practices that I have outlined.[10] As indicated above, organizations such as Blackwater see themselves as standing for the values embedded in global civil society and the society of democratic states.[11]

Is there something ethically suspect about the idea that a state and the citizens in them should regard the defence of its legitimate interests as a job to be done for the upholding of global standards, rather than a duty owed by citizens to the defence of some particular nation/state? It would only matter if the people in them were constituted as members of a community within which their constitution as worthy people depended on their willingness to fight in wars in defence of a particular country. There is little doubt that throughout history there have existed communities in which people were constituted in this way. What is clear, though, is that the global practices within which we operate nowadays are not such practices. Neither global civil society nor the community of democratic and democratizing states have built into their structures the notion that wars are only just (or right) when fought by citizens who fight voluntarily for a single specific state and whose very idea of selfhood depends on their being prepared to fight in defence of that state.

Consider the matter from the point of view of a single citizen – you. Would it (and should it) matter to you that your state is being defended by a private military corporation rather than by soldiers serving the sovereign? Would it matter to you that border security in your state (at airports, for example) is being provided by a private security firm rather than the law enforcement agency of the state (the police)? I think not. What matters to us is that the wrongdoers are kept at bay. Who does the keeping at bay should be irrelevant, provided that the task is done with due consideration for the rights of all affected parties. In a democracy, from the citizens' point of view, what matters is that the policies and laws guiding the establishment of the contract with the private firms are made by the elected government. What matters is that the private company being used must be understood by me, the citizen, as being subject to the laws and regulations laid down by my legitimate (because properly elected) government, and must be seen as carrying out the tasks set by it.

## Privatization, regulation and ethics

The act of privatizing functions that were once run by a public body is an interesting institutional manoeuvre when seen from an ethical point of view. When one then takes into account the task of regulating the privatized units, it becomes fascinating, particularly when the function in question is military action abroad. Let us examine the ethics of privatization in more detail.

As outlined earlier, we are constituted as civilians in global civil society and also as citizens in the practice of sovereign democratic states. Both are of fundamental importance to us from an ethical point of view. In the second of these practices, as citizens we accord to one another the status of co-participants in the business of self-rule. One of the things we, the citizens of democratic states, may do through our elected governments is privatize certain functions of the state. Those who gain control of the privatized functions are, through the act of privatization, authorized to use their property rights to advance their self-interests. They are entitled to seek profits for themselves. What we see in this privatizing manoeuvre by the state is the reverse of the sequence outlined in Hegel's account of the progress achieved in the movement from civil society to the state. In that account we were asked to see civil society as a set of private relations between the owners of property rights. Civil society, it was said, produced certain ethical problems such as competition, unequal power relations, conflict and alienation. These were then remedied, according to Hegel, when rights holders formed states within which the tensions experienced in civil society are resolved through the creation of a 'general will' which is deployed to solve public problems.[12] The privatization manoeuvre that we are currently discussing does precisely the reverse. Here we see the public authority, authorized by the citizens, deciding to re-create a set of civil society property rights. What was once an exclusively public function, the military one, is now made (wholly or partly) a private one.

Why do governments, with the support of their electorates, do this? Why do we do this? From an ethical perspective is this not a movement backwards? Why do we seek to reverse the Hegelian ethical progression? Why do we seek to backtrack on the belief common to so many social democrats, socialists and communists, who, taking their cue from Karl Marx, actively pursued a belief that progress would consist in taking into public control, many social functions that had been private before? The answer is the self-evident one that in these cases the body politic is of the opinion that privatizing these functions will benefit the public, without doing damage to our ethical infrastructure. The outcome of these newly created private interests, each pursuing its own profit, will, it is argued, benefit the citizens of the polity in general. Why? The answer is well known. Having public goods supplied by private, profit-seeking actors in open competition with one another, will result in these goods being delivered more efficiently. Where public provision often results in slow and inefficient provision, private provision results in vigour and efficiency. So the story goes.

Where a good previously supplied by a public body, like a military establishment or estate, is privatized, what is being deliberately created is an *anarchy*. I use the term in its technical sense, to refer to a social arrangement which is not centrally controlled by a government. In an anarchy actors, with specific freedoms, pursue their own plans, whatever they happen to be, within a framework of commonly recognized constraints. There is a sense in which an anarchy, as I am defining it, is similar to a practical association as described by Michael Oakeshott.[13] We who participate in anarchies justify them on the grounds that they constitute us as actors in a domain of freedom. In this domain we are property holders in that we have the final say about the deployment of certain assets. Within anarchical systems, we are free to use the rights we have within them, as we see fit, subject only to the constraint that we allow the other rights holders to do the same.

Let me make this set of abstract assertions more concrete. Where there was once a public body, the US military, who in a monopolistic way supplied all the military services required by the US government, the government has privatized some of these military functions. In this privatized domain there is now an anarchy of PMCs competing with one another to supply certain services to the US government. Each actor in this anarchy seeks out the contracts it wants, organizes itself in the way it deems best, supplies the service in the way that it thinks most efficient, makes its own decisions about the best use of its resources and so on. This autonomy is guaranteed to PMCs, they have not merely been given notional discretion on some matters. The CEOs of such PMCs are specifically not officers of the state.

It is important to remember that the people who work in the privatized companies are not people who have given up their citizenship status in their respective states and their civilian status in global civil society. They still hold these roles and still value the ethical standing they confer on them. They are still constrained not to do anything that undermines their statuses as such. Their new roles in privatized companies are constituted within the macro structure of global civil society and the society of democratic states.

We have seen then, that we citizens justify the privatization of some public functions by referring to the long-term consequences of the operation of the new anarchical order. The benefits, we believe, come from the granting of autonomy to the actors in the anarchical order. The argument in favour of the creation of such anarchies is a consequentialist one. The consequences of the private provision of public services, it is believed, will be beneficial to the public. Because the whole process is justified in consequentialist terms, it will come as no surprise that in societies that have completed this manoeuvre, the measurement of outcomes, the setting of goals, targets and so on will increasingly become a central activity of the government that buys the services of such companies. As private military provision becomes ever more common, we must expect that the setting of goals, the measurement of outcomes and the creating of the tables pertaining to such companies, will become commonplace. Governments will progressively seek to regulate these anarchical practices. Crucially, though, to regulate is not to govern directly. It is a different kind of activity.

When we, the citizens of democratic states, privatize certain functions (like the military), how can we ensure that our creation, the anarchy within which we have created a set of rights holders (the PMCs) in anarchic competition with one another, will provide the public goods we seek? The answer is that we seek to do this by means of regulation. Let us look more closely at what regulation involves. It is the tricky activity of trying to maintain an anarchy in a given field of autonomous competition, of actively not destroying the freedom enjoyed by the participants in it, while, at the same time, directing it to achieve the ends we desire. It is the problem of directing without central planning. This is the definition of regulation. How does one direct an anarchy? One might say that regulation involves *indirect rule*. The regulator does not command what the participants in the anarchical order must do, but achieves the outcome desired by setting targets and specifying what constraints are to operate on how these might be achieved.

In order to regulate, one must have accurate measures of the consequences of the privatized activity over time. One must have good data to get the measurement right. This is relatively simple in an open and stable society. It is easy to privatize some commodity, such as the supply of clean water and to monitor the outcome. For here we have a clear measure, litres per household, and easy ways of gaining data revealing whether targets have been met, and so on. Train services are similarly easy to measure and monitor. Activities abroad are much more difficult. What is especially difficult to monitor is the supply of war-making functions and security functions in other sovereign states, particularly in the areas that are extremely unstable and dangerous. The following are particularly difficult:

1   Specifying what is to count as the successful delivery of security in the unstable conditions that by definition apply in these circumstances. What kind of outcomes will be judged to be successful security outcomes? Complete peace? Partial peace? How are these to be specified and measured?
2   Putting in independent monitors to measure the specified outcomes. Such monitors who operate in the crisis-ridden

environments will find it difficult to determine who is doing what, and to whom.

3   Monitoring (which is crucial to the regulation of the private supply of these services) is made especially difficult by the following consideration. In almost every case a PMC would be able, plausibly, to claim that it would be detrimental to its achieving its goals to have monitors present at the point of provision.

4   Once it becomes clear how difficult it is to monitor PMCs in unstable environments, then it becomes easy for the governments of democracies to stop worrying about monitoring the performance of such companies, because the governments themselves will be able to avoid adverse judgements about the outcomes of the activities of the PMCs they have set up. They can do so by claiming that the outcomes are more or less impossible to measure. Citizens themselves will have little or no measure of the success or failure of the PMCs in these circumstances, so they will have little reason to hold their government to account for a set of adverse outcomes.

5   On ethical matters it will be difficult to monitor whether those who work for the PMCs are upholding the basic ethical standards that they ought to be upholding as civilians and citizens. This follows, once again, from the difficulty of monitoring what the PMCs are doing in the unstable and dangerous conditions under which they operate.

6   All of this becomes even more difficult when the PMCs start subcontracting out parts of what they have contracted to provide to local contractors.

Within modern democratic states we have highly developed systems for regulating private companies that sell services to the public. The branch of law known as regulatory law is one of the fastest growing and most interesting aspects of contemporary jurisprudence. Regulation is achieved through a number of different mechanisms which include framework laws provided by ordinary legislation, executively enacted regulations, the press itself which can keep an eye on the activity of such companies, and private non-governmental watchdogs which monitor the activities of private companies. In the United Kingdom a prominent group of these watchdogs monitors the privatized rail companies. Finally, governments themselves are subject to ongoing public scrutiny and periodic competitive elections. My main contention is that there is nothing intrinsically ethically problematic about PMCs (or private companies that provide other kinds of services), but like other actors in anarchical practices they may attempt to flout well-established ethical norms. The challenge is to devise regulatory regimes which prevent this, but which do not destroy the fundamental anarchical structure of the practice from producing the desired outcomes.

## Conclusions

In this chapter I have argued that the creation of private military companies does not offend or contradict the ethical values built into the most fundamental global institutions of our time, global civil society and the society of democratic states. We who hold civilian and citizenship rights are entitled to use our rights to create private companies offering services to other rights holders, provided that in doing so, we do not abuse the rights of our fellow rights holders. I have provided a brief account of why citizens in democracies might, with good reason, seek to privatize some functions normally carried out by public bodies. Furthermore, I have indicated how doing this need not offend our fundamental ethical commitments. Privatization is a public act, by a public authority, for the achievement of a public good. It involves the creation of an anarchical institution, for the achievement of public goods. In the last part of the chapter I have discussed how the public in a democracy might seek to prevent ethically noxious outcomes coming about as a result of the process of privatization, without at the same time destroying the anarchical structure within which privatized companies must, by definition, operate. The key to preventing such outcomes is regulation by public bodies. Within stable democratic states, this kind of regulation is relatively easy. However, within some unstable and dangerous territories beyond the borders of one's own state, greater problems are encountered in attempting to monitor and regulate the activities of PMCs. Solving these is a major task awaiting us in contemporary international relations.

## Notes

1  Peter W. Singer, *Corporate Warriors: The Rise of the Privatized Military Industry*, Ithaca, NY and London: Cornell University Press, 2003.
2  On practice theory in general, see Theodore R. Schatzki, *Social Practices: A Wittgensteinian Approach to Human Activity and the Social*, Cambridge: Cambridge University Press, 1996.
3  For the purposes of this chapter I simply stipulate that global civil society is the society made up of all those people who claim first-generation rights (i.e. political and civil rights) for themselves and recognize them in others.
4  Whether he is able to enforce them is a different question. We often claim these rights, and have our claims recognized as legitimate, in those circumstances where we do not have the power to enforce them. The Kurds in Iraq under Saddam Hussein's rule provide a good example.
5  The point applies both to organizations such as Aegis Defence Services and to private security firms within the suburbs of sub-Saharan cities.
6  In some cases, the markets fail to constrain the participants in them in the ways outlined as a result of what economists call 'market imperfections'.
7  Consider the current standing of Mark Thatcher as a demonstration of this point.

8 This is incorporated into the mission statements of the larger and better-known PMCs.
9 Charles Tilly, *The Formation of National States in Western Europe*, Princeton, NJ: Princeton University Press, 1975.
10 For related account of the changing military cultures in the contemporary world, see Christopher Coker, *Humane Warfare*, London and New York: Routledge, 2001.
11 See Blackwater's website where it articulates its vision as seeking to 'support freedom and democracy everywhere', www.blackwaterusa.com/, accessed 9 October 2007.
12 See the discussion of Hegel's understanding of the state provided in Dudley Knowles, *Hegel and the Philosophy of Right*, London: Routledge, 2002, ch. 13.
13 Michael Oakeshott, *Hobbes on Civil Association*, Berkeley: University of California Press, 1975, pp. 109–110.

# 4   Benevolence, honourable soldiers and private military companies
## Reformulating Just War theory

*Joseph Runzo*

The ethics of warfare continuously evolves from an intersection of legal, moral, religious and political ideas contextualized by the facts of military history and a reasoned appraisal of future military conditions and parameters. The rise of private military companies (PMCs) raises a number of ethical issues which must be addressed within the wider context of a universal ethics of warfare. Any viable ethics of warfare today must address the exigencies of the fight against international terrorism. One military response to terrorism can be humanitarian intervention. And one military means of supporting humanitarian intervention can be the employment of PMCs. So how do these three factors – terrorism, humanitarian intervention and PMCs – affect the evolving ethics of warfare? We shall see that a key to this question is understanding what it means to be an honourable soldier, and this, in turn will lead to a suggested reformulation of Just War theory.

## Just War theory

In the Western theory of Just War developed by theologians and then by the proponents of international law, an attempt is made to limit the evils of war, an attempt which is divided into two levels. At the first level are *jus ad bellum* considerations, which are an attempt to limit the number and possibility of wars. Thus, war is to be

1   seen as a last resort;
2   carried out with right intention;
3   carried out for a just cause;
4   a proportional response to the injustice being addressed and
5   there must be a formal declaration of war by a proper authority.

Once a people engages in a war, the second level of *jus in bello* considerations come into effect

1   *discrimination*, including the treatment of prisoners as non-combatants, and

2   *proportionality*, including considerations of both quantity (the amount of death and destruction) and quality (the use of weapons of mass destruction, weapons with unusually cruel effects, and weapons with long-term effects).

That is to say, to be just, warfare must be directed towards the appropriate targets and coupled with the attempt to avoid direct intentional harm to non-combatants, and to be just, warfare must be carried out with an intensity which is appropriate to the kind and degree of injustice putatively requiring rectification. Broadly speaking, what underlies Just War theory is the assumption that one is taking the moral point of view.

I have argued elsewhere that the three characteristics of taking the moral point of view are

1   one taking others into account in his/her actions because he/she sees and respects them as persons with equal rights (benevolence);
2   the willingness to take into account how one's actions affect others by taking into account the good of everyone equally (justice or impartiality);
3   abiding by the principle of universalizability – for example, the willingness to treat one's own actions as morally permissible only if similar acts of others in comparable circumstances would be equally permissible.[1]

## The problem of verminification

Responding to the stupefying and senseless slaughter of World War I, Thomas Hardy wrote these lines in his poem 'The Man He Killed':[2]

> Staring face to face,
> I shot at him as he at me
> And killed him in his place.
> I shot him dead because –
> Because he was my foe,
> Just so: my foe of course he was;
> That's clear enough; although ...
> Yes, quaint and curious war is!
> You shoot a fellow down
> You'd treat if met where any bar is,
> Or help to half-a-crown.

So how could one kill an 'enemy' who would be friend at another time and place? Or how is it that 800,000 Tutsi could be slaughtered in Rwanda between April and May 1994 – ironically leaving heaps of corpses in churches – while the Western world watched this 'black on black' violence?[3] At the start of World War I, the Carnegie Endowment for International Peace stated regarding war between Greece and Bulgaria, that

> Day after day the Bulgarians were represented in the Greek press as a race of monsters, and public feeling was roused to a pitch of chauvinism which made it inevitable that war, when it should come, should be ruthless.... Deny that your enemies are men and you will treat them as vermin.[4]

It is easier to violate the rights of – and even wantonly kill – those whom we do not see as persons, those whom we do not treat, under universalizability, with benevolence and justice. Thus, the Imperial Japanese military intentionally brutalized its soldiers and inculcated in them the belief that the Chinese were inferior beings well before the invasion of China in 1937 and the subsequent horrors like the slaughter of 350,000 civilians in the Rape of Nanking. And on the other side, the Australian General Blamey said of his Japanese opponents:

> Our enemy is a curious race cross between the human being and the ape...Fighting the Japs is not like fighting normal human beings.... We are not dealing with humans as we know them. We are dealing with something primitive. Our troops have the right view of the Japs. They regard them as vermin.[5]

## Terrorism

In general, terrorists are unable to achieve their political goals using conventional means, so they turn to terrorizing members of the public, often the very people they are ostensibly 'liberating', to promulgate their political and sometimes religious message, attempting to coerce the public and/or political authorities into accepting their demands. Guerrilla fighters can become terrorists if their initial attempt to produce a popular uprising fails.

The 1999 US Government report *The Sociology and Psychology of Terrorism: Who Becomes a Terrorist and Why* identifies various strategies which terrorists use to rationalize their violence toward other humans, one of which is to dehumanize victims, that is, the use of the designation 'infidel' by radical Islamic Fundamentalists, or the Italian and German terrorist references to victims as 'tools of the system'.[6] This shows the extraordinary and formidable nature of terrorism, for while verminification is a problem in all warfare, verminification is also part of the necessary life-blood of the terrorist. Once the moral point of view is abrogated, once we stop treating others as persons, atrocities and terrorism are inevitable.

Dealing with terrorism tests the limits of the *in bello* principle of discrimination. However, the history of brutal reprisals against civilian populations in regions of terrorism is a history of ever-escalating counter reprisals. But more important than the utilitarian failure of counter reprisals is the ethical failure: we must always adhere to the principles of benevolence and universalizability.

## Humanitarian intervention

One of the strongest cases for offensive military action is humanitarian intervention in cases like ethnic cleansing or genocide or rampant terrorism. Dr James Orbinski, who was the international president of MSF (Doctors without Borders) when they received the Nobel Peace Prize in 1999, and had been in charge of Rwanda for MSF during the massacre, said in his Nobel acceptance speech that 'The founding principles of humanitarian action [are] the refusal of all forms of problem solving through the sacrifice of the weak and vulnerable. No victim can be intentionally discriminated against, or neglected to the advantage of another.' Even though MSF had asked for military intervention in Rwanda, he went on to say that 'We must criticize those interventions called military-humanitarian.' For on the one hand, he said 'Humanitarianism occurs where the political has failed or is in crisis.... It must be free of political influence, and the political must recognize its responsibility to ensure that the humanitarian can exist'; yet on the other hand, 'Humanitarian action exists only to preserve life, not to eliminate it.' I count Orbinski as a friend, and have an unqualified admiration for his humanitarian work, but I am not so sure whether a clear distinction can be made between humanitarianism and military intervention necessitated by humanitarian concerns.

Orbinski is right about the danger that self-interested military action will hide under the protective mantle of a spurious 'humanitarianism'. But as even MSF's experience in Rwanda shows, the impulse to humanitarianism may be subverted by the lack of secure conditions to carry out any aid. Even more acute is the problem of proper authority (clause 6 of the *jus ad bellum* criteria) when international authorities – for example, the UN – fail to act to protect humanitarians. Addressing this issue in 1999, the Dutch Institute of International Affairs identified five criteria which might form the basis of future international consensus on 'unauthorized' humanitarian intervention which does not have a legal basis in current international law:

1  there are 'serious violations of human rights or international humanitarian law';
2  the Security Council 'fails to act';
3  the intervention is taken multilaterally, if possible;
4  any uses of force are necessary and proportionate and
5  the intervening state or states are relatively disinterested.

I think this set of criteria is a good starting point for discussion and I will return to them at the end.

## Private military companies

Throughout military history, mercenaries have been attached to regular armies not only because they expand the numbers of fighting forces, but also because they have often been the experts in specialist weapons which armies have turned to each time warfare 'modernized'. The modern corporate entity which the PMC is potentially provides both these services and ostensibly provides an ideal organized force to aid in military humanitarian intervention when national means or will fails.

To deal with the proliferation of mercenaries, Additional Protocol I has been added to the Geneva Conventions.

Additional Protocol I of the Geneva Convention states:

A mercenary is any person who

1   is specially recruited locally or abroad in order to fight in an armed conflict;
2   does, in fact, take a direct part in the hostilities;
3   is motivated to take part in the hostilities essentially by the desire for private gain and, in fact, is promised, by or on behalf of a Party to the conflict, material compensation substantially in excess of that promised or paid to combatants of similar ranks and functions in the armed forces of that Party;
4   is neither a national of a Party to the conflict nor a resident of territory controlled by a Party to the conflict;
5   is not a member of the armed forces of a Party to the conflict; and
6   has not been sent by a State which is not a Party to the conflict on official duty as a member of its armed forces.

And given the enormous rise of both mercenaries and PMCs in Africa, the Organization of African Unity has adopted Additional Protocol I and added the strong probation that 'A mercenary shall not have the right to be a combatant or a prisoner of war.' I shall argue in support of the first half of this prohibition, though I think the situation at Guantanamo Bay casts doubt on the advisability of the latter half of the prohibition.

## Outsourcing war

In the United States, the move towards increased privatization of former military functions is seen as having the double benefit of (1) competition-based savings and (2) higher-quality weapons and services, since the US military will not need to maintain expensive experts and weapons systems which are more cost-effectively maintained by a private firm. Moreover, employing PMCs addresses several overriding features of the current US (and largely Western) way of waging war, what Martin Shaw calls 'risk-transfer warfare': war must minimize casualties to Western troops, the enemy must be killed not only quickly and efficiently but also discretely, and wars must minimize the electoral risks for politicians.[7]

There are many issues to discuss here, but two problems with employing PMCs in conflict zones are (1) unlike military professionals, the personnel of a PMC neither systematically study military law and Just War theory nor operate under the purview of military law, and (2) while being efficient at the techniques of short-term warfare, PMCs are not constituted to address the long-term process of peace.

Regarding the first point, outsourcing war has many of the same negative moral and practical consequences as the sort of outsourcing of torture we find in the CIA's policy of 'extraordinary rendition', in which terrorist suspects captured abroad are sent to countries like Egypt, Jordan, Morocco, Pakistan and Uzbekistan that are known for torturing prisoners. Since 11 September 2001 more than a hundred terrorist suspects have been subjected to 'extraordinary rendition'. The problem with participating in torture, whether directly or indirectly, is that torture inherently subverts morality. To be moral, a nation, like an individual, must do more than generally act rightly. To be a moral individual or nation, dispositions of character and rational perspectives must be built by repeated execution of processes of careful, self-reflective adherence to the right and the good. To be moral, at the least, is to take the moral point of view: to act benevolently towards others, to act in a just and fair manner and to understand one's own actions as universalizable. Or as Immanuel Kant put the latter point in religious terms, original sin is thinking that you are the exception to the rule. Thus, if torture is wrong, it is wrong for everyone: to be moral, one should never treat the torture of others as a just means to one's own ends; and torture treats the other merely as a means to one's own ends. Similarly, offensive military action carried out by mercenaries treats the 'enemy' as a means to material aggrandizement. And just as torture occurs outside the bounds of morality, so too, mercenary warfare is conducted outside the moral bounds of peacemaking.

Regarding the second point, to defeat terrorism we must understand why people become terrorists. The frustration–aggression hypothesis suggests that 'every frustration leads to some sort of aggression and all aggressive acts result from some prior frustration.' This hypothesis has been applied to violent movements by Ted Robert Gurr as follows: 'The necessary precondition for violent civil conflict is relative deprivation, defined as actors' perception of discrepancy between their value expectations and their environment's apparent value capabilities.'[8]

But this means that success depends on attacking terrorism with a comprehensive plan to deal with the problems underlying the acts of terrorism. There is a clear parallel in attempts to combat the international drug trade which often finances terrorist groups. For example, the act of aerial spraying over the opium fields in Afghanistan, which produces 87 per cent of the world's illegal opium, goes to show that such an act is inadequate, for it simply moves the problem only to resurface in another region, while ignoring the underlying need to encourage the finding of alternative ways to help the poverty-stricken farmers of Afghanistan make a living. Similarly, there are no merely military solutions to international terrorism, for in the long term we must reduce the 'frustration–aggression' syndrome by reducing the sense of relative deprivation behind violent civil conflict, and it places an intolerable burden on the military which would do well not to ignore this fact.

Reconstruction alone is not enough – for to reconstruct after a war may simply mean putting back in place the very structures that led to war in the first place. Perpetual peace entails the construction of new structures and the cultivation of new relationships which centre on reconciliation and not vengeance, and which bring not retributive justice but justice that is fair. So the real shortcoming of employing PMCs for warfare is both moral and practical: they are not in the business of reconciliation – which is the ultimate goal of a Just War – and, indeed, reconciliation may be inimical to their commercial goals. As Sun Tzu observed, some 2500 years ago, the most successful army is the one which does not need to fight, but PMCs need conflict zones and perpetual peace puts PMCs out of business.

## A global ethic for the honourable soldier

As Sun Tzu notes:

> War is a grave matter; one is apprehensive lest men embark upon it without due reflection.... Therefore, appraise it in terms of the five fundamental factors.... The first of these factors is moral influence [Tao]; the second, weather; the third, terrain; the fourth, command; and the fifth, doctrine.[9]

So for Sun Tzu moral considerations are more paramount than any other considerations about warfare. He elucidates this notion of the 'Tao' further as follows:

> Those skilled in war cultivate the *Tao* and preserve the laws and are therefore able to formulate victorious policies.... The *Tao* is the way of humanity and justice; 'laws' are regulations and institutions. Those who excel in war first cultivate their own humanity and justice and maintain their laws and institutions. By these means they make their governments invincible.[10]

One element of cultivating humanity and justice in ourselves is to undertake war only with full knowledge and wisdom.

Religious ethical systems hold that there are underlying moral structures – whether the *Tao* or the Mind of God or Allah or *Dharma* – which supersede the mere tactical, strategic and political rules of warfare. To see this, consider the other two, non-Western, paradigms of the honourable soldier: the *bushido* tradition of Buddhist samurai Japan and the notion of *dharma* in the Hindu *Bhadgavad Gita*.

The first military government of Japan was established in 1186 CE in Kamakura. This eventually led to the establishment in 1603 in the new city of Edo (modern Tokyo), north of Kamakura, what became 250 unbroken years of Tokogawa samurai rule until 1867. Paralleling the Western notion of an 'officer and a gentleman', the samurai of the Tokogawa regime were both imbued with the morality of religion – in this case Zen Buddhism – and also expected to develop both knowledge and wisdom. Samurai frequently became scholars and physicians. The author of the *Bushido Shohinhu*, or 'Bushido for Beginners', a Confucian scholar and military scientist, sets down the essence of the Tokogawa bushido code in which he proclaims that, 'In the way of the warrior, it is essential to do it right from root to branch. If you do not understand the root and the branch, there is no way for you to know your duty.'[11] This is reminiscent of Sun Tzu's injunction that one must cultivate the Tao of humanity and justice if one is to be skilled in war.

Now, in February 2005 *The New York Times* reported that Lt Gen. James N. Mattis, the commanding officer of the Marine Corps Combat Development Command in Quantico, Virginia, said that

> Actually, it's a lot of fun to fight. You know, it's a hell of a hoot. It's fun to shoot some people. I'll be right upfront with you, I like brawling.... You go into Afghanistan, you got guys who slap women around for five years because they didn't wear a veil.... You know, guys like that ain't got no manhood left anyway. So it's a hell of a lot of fun to shoot them.

This failure to take the moral point of view and the verminification of the Afghans reflected badly on the American military, as Secretary Rumsfeld noted at the time. But on 3 April 2005 *The Observer* reported that Gary Jackson, the president of the PMC Blackwater, quoted in *Tactical Weekly*, the firm's electronic newsletter, endorsed Mattis' un-bushido-like attitude, saying that terrorists

> need to get creamed, and it's fun, meaning satisfying, to do the shooting of such folk.... All of us who have ever waited through an hour and a half movie, or read some 300 pages of a thriller, to the point when the bad guys finally get their comeuppance know this perfectly well.

Not only does Jackson compound the initial problem, but his comments also introduce a second problem: PMC personnel are not subject to the same strictures and legal constraints as members of the American military who ultimately answer to military justice, the Secretary of Defence and the President, the legal representatives of the bushido notion of 'humanity and justice'.

The rules of engagement can be morally problematic even in a highly professionalized national army. When I spoke at West Point in 2003, I came in from the airport with a colonel who had just come off the National Security Council. He was saying even then that the British forces in Iraq were trained to wait longer than American troops were trained to wait before firing at vehicles apparently breaching security check points. His own sense was that the British response – which he regarded as wiser – resulted from experiences like Northern Ireland where one misplaced bullet at a checkpoint killing an innocent civilian can produce incredibly negative – and justified – criticism, undermining the larger objective of peace.

However, at a University of Cambridge conference for Senior Officers of the British military this spring when I related this American colonel's analysis of why American soldiers shoot more quickly at check points it was rejected. In particular a group of captains in the Royal Marines, who had worked extensively with the Pentagon in preparation for the current war in Iraq, said that the deciding factor was the American 'gun culture'. As one captain put it (and I quote) 'We do not use guns the way you do. We do not use guns to kill people.' These sorts of problems are only likely to be compounded among the personnel of PMCs.[12]

Another aspect of *bushido* is the emphasis placed on facing death wisely. Again in the *Bushido Shoshinhu*, it says:

One who is supposed to be a warrior considers it his foremost concern to keep death in mind at all times.... When you assume that your stay in this world will last, various wishes occur to you, and you become very desirous. You want what others have, and cling to your own possessions, developing a mercantile mentality....When you always keep death in mind, covetousness naturally weakens, and to that degree a grabby, greedy attitude logically does not occur. That is why I say your character improves.[13]

This anti-mercenary Buddhist samurai notion that humans should not, and warriors especially should not, cling to the things of this world is actually derived from Hinduism, the basis of Buddhism. The great Hindu text the *Bhagavad Gita* is set in the midst of the great epic battle between the Kaurava family and their cousins the Pandavas. Though the Pandavas eventually win, many of their relatives and friends are slaughtered. In the *Gita*, one of the Pandava brothers, Arjuna, discusses with his chariot driver – who turns out to be the God Krishna – whether it is his duty to fight against his relatives and friends or his duty *not* to fight against his relatives and friends: that is, Arjuna wants to know what is his *dharma*, what is the underlying moral structure of the universe which he ought to follow. As Arjuna says

> I do not want to kill these men
> though I myself am slain,
> not even for the three-world rule,
> much less an earthly gain.[14]

The moral underpinnings, the *dharma*, of Arjuna's duty is expressed in chapter 12, verse 13:

> Be friendly and compassionate
> released from ego selfishness,
> patient, hate not any being,
> the same [as you] in pain and happiness.[15]

Thus, in the midst of battle, the advice of the *Gita* is to be benevolent in all actions. Of the benevolent person, the *Gita* declares,

> A man like that is not destroyed
> in this world or the next, my friend,
> for nobody who acts aright
> can have an evil end.[16]

To become a knower of one's own soul one must acquire wisdom. As Robert Nozick says, wisdom is 'itself a way of being deeply connected to reality'.[17] In Confucian terms, wisdom connects one to the *Tao*, in Hindu and Buddhist terms wisdom aligns one with *Dharma*, and on the perspective of Western monotheism, wisdom offers a glimpse of the Mind of God. Whether or not it is understood in religious terms, a universal truth which must be part of any universal ethic of warfare is that the honourable soldier pursues wisdom for humanity and justice. There is no honour without wisdom, and the wise soldier is honourable.

I would suggest that the honourable soldier is one:

1   who has systematically studied both warmaking and Just War theory;
2   who is honest about the possibility of the utilitarian failure of warfare;
3   who is not materialistic and so faces death with resolution, not regret;
4   who sees enemies as persons and humanity as one community;
5   whose guiding goal is peace;

6    who sees weapons not as a means to kill people but as a means to effect and defend peace and
7    who, if religious, both sees the spiritual value of all persons and assiduously guards against substituting the state for the transcendent.

There is no guarantee that the mercenary accords with criteria 1 and professional military personnel are more likely than mercenaries to fit criteria 3, 4 and 6. Hence, professional soldiers are more likely than mercenaries to be honourable soldiers. The last point 7 is also important because most of the world's population is religious and consequently most soldiers are, to some extent, religious. This can lead to two related problems: soldiers substituting the state for the transcendent and religious egoism. Regarding the first problem, the Christian, Islamic and especially Jewish traditions have often theologized violence. Thus, in Islamic wars gone wrong, the greater *jihad* of Islam – the struggle with the self – becomes subjugated to the lesser *jihad* of struggle with the *dar al-harb*, the 'house' or territory outside the Islamic state 'transforming the meaning of *jihad* from a religious concept of striving on the path of God into a rationale for warfare on behalf of the ends of [the Muslim state as a] political community'.[18] As an example of the second problem, the supposed superiority of Spanish Christianity – what I call religious egoism–lent support to the Conquistadors' slaughter of Native Americans, against which Francisco de Vitoria felt compelled to develop the notion of 'innocents' *vis-à-vis* the *in bello* consideration of proportionality and discrimination.

## Future Just Warfare criteria

Drawing the foregoing observations together, a preliminary sketch for a future Just War theory which takes terrorism, humanitarian intervention, the phenomenon of PMCs and what it is to be an honourable soldier into account might look like this.

*The Moral Point of View* (benevolence, justice and universalizability) governs the following *jus ad bellum* and *jus in bello* considerations:

*Jus ad bellum* considerations:

War must be

1    a last resort;
2    against an imminent threat to peace and justice;
3    carried out with right intent for a just cause;
4    with both a reasonable hope of success and a reasonable plan to achieve success;
5    as a proportional response to the injustice or threat to international peace being addressed and

6    initiated with a formal declaration of war by a proper authority. This includes the Rwandan Principle: If there is a military humanitarian intervention, the proper authority may be a single state or collection of states not directly threatened if

   a    the intervening state or states are relatively disinterested and motivated primarily by humanitarian considerations,
   b    there are publicly documented and extremely serious violations of human rights or international humanitarian law, such as genocide, ethnic cleansing, the systematic killing of civilians as a tactic of terror, the systematic use of rape as a military weapon, sanctioned slavery or widespread forced starvation,
   c    the Security Council fails to intervene, or fails to act sufficiently expeditiously, in order to avert further crimes against humanity and
   d    the intervention is multilateral and, if not, only unilateral as a last resort.

*Jus in bello* considerations:

*The Principle of Discrimination*    places limits on what constitutes legitimate targets of violence and includes, for example, the treatment of prisoners as non-combatants.

   *The Principle of Proportionality*    places limits on the degree of force employed – which should not inflict more damage than the just cause for the war merits – and includes considerations of both quantity (the amount of death and destruction) and quality (the use of weapons of mass destruction, weapons with unusually cruel effects, and weapons with long-term effects) of the force employed.

   *The Principle of Military Professionalism*    restricts offensive combat operations to professional military personnel specifically trained in Just War theory and restricts any private militarized forces (mercenary), if publicly and properly contracted, to ancillary roles such as security, logistics and technical/material support.

A Military Professional is honourable if he/she

1    has systematically studied both warmaking and Just War theory;
2    is honest about the possibility of the utilitarian failure of warfare;
3    is not materialistic and so faces death with resolution, not regret;
4    sees enemies as persons and humanity as one community;
5    whose guiding goal is peace;
6    and so sees weapons not as a means to kill people but as a means to effect and defend peace;
7    and who, if religious, both sees the spiritual value of all persons and assiduously guards against substituting the state for the transcendent.

The current pressures of international terrorism, and the current unrestrained nature of PMCs as an alternative to using professional soldiers entail our drawing at least one practical conclusion here: democracies must increase the size of their professional armies to meet the security demands of nations and the moral necessity of humanitarian intervention. An ethical conclusion we can draw is this: we need a global citizenry and citizen soldiers who understand justice as something which transcends politics and which embraces the commonality of humankind and treats each individual as a person. And while the absence of war (negative peace) is desirable, the establishment of peace (positive peace) is the greater good. Negative peace as *status quo* is peace as a means to justice; the positive peace of the transformation of conflict-riven societies is a just end in itself. To this end we need national professional soldiers who are both peacemakers and peacebuilders – peacemakers to give us a liveable present and peacebuilders to give us a liveable future. In this context of a Just War theory for the future, since the personnel of PMCs are unsuited to peacebuilding and are, at best, poor at peacemaking, they should not serve in offensive combat roles.

## Notes

1 Joseph Runzo, 'Ethics and the Challenge of Theological Non-Realism' in Joseph Runzo (ed.), *Ethics, Religion and the Good Society*, Lousville, KY: Westminster Press, 1992, p. 90. n. 45.
2 Thomas Hardy 'The Man He Killed' in John Hollander (ed.), *War Poems*, New York: Knopff, 1999, p. 237.
3 Geoffrey Robertson, *Crimes against Humanity: The Struggle for Global Justice*, London: Penguin, 1999, p. 72.
4 Tim Allen and Jean Seaton (eds), *The Media of Conflict: War Reporting and Representations of Ethnic Conflict*, London: Zed Books, 1999, p. 46.
5 Quoted from John Dower, *War without Mercy: Race and Power in the Pacific War*, London: Faber and Faber, 1986, p. 71, in Yuki Tanaka, *Hidden Horrors: Japanese War Crimes in World War II*, Boulder, CO: Westview Press, 1998, p. 132.
6 US Library of Congress, *The Sociology and Psychology of Terrorism: Who Becomes a Terrorist and Why?* Washington, DC: Library of Congress, September 1999, p. 39 www.loc.gov/rr/frd/pdf-files/Soc_Psych_of_Terrorism.pdf, accessed 9 October 2007.
7 Martin Shaw, *The New Western Way of War*, London: Polity, 2005, 71f.
8 Ted Robert Gurr, *Why Men Rebel*, Princeton: Princeton University Press, 1970, p. 224.
9 Sun Tzu, *The Art of War*, Samuel B. Griffith (trans.), Oxford: Oxford University Press, 1963.
10 Ibid.
11 Thomas Cleary (trans.), *The Code of the Samurai: A Modern Translation of the Bushido Shoshinsu*, Boston, MA: Tuttle Publishing, 2000, p. 7. The Buddhist underpinnings of the perspective can be seen in the death poem of Ouchi Yoshitaka, a sixteenth-century samurai general, the last lines of which are taken from the Diamond Sutra of Mahayana Buddhism: Both the victor and the vanquished are but drops of dew, but bolts of lightening – thus should we view the world.

12 Instructively, even in the American West, where guns *were* used 'to kill people', Colt's 1873 revolver the Peacemaker was not named ironically. This gun was particularly popular among lawmen in the extra-long barrel version known as the Buntline Special because it was often used, to not kill, but to subdue miscreants by hitting them alongside the head with the barrel.

13 Cleary, *The Code of the Samurai*, pp. 3 and 5.

14 Geoffrey Parinder (trans.), *The Bhagavad Gita, a Verse Translation*, Oxford: Oneworld, 1998, ch. 1, verse 35, p. 8.

15 Ibid., ch. 12, verse 13, p. 83.

16 Ibid., ch. 6, verse 40, p. 47.

17 Robert Nozick, *The Examined Life: Philosophical Meditations*, New York: Simon and Schuster, 1990, p. 276.

18 James Turner Johnson, *Morality and Contemporary Warfare*, New Haven, CT: Yale University Press, 1999, p. 173.

# 5 Private security companies and corporate social responsibility

*Christopher Kinsey*

It is reasonable to argue that the international community's attitude towards the privatization of security is polarized. While some of us see private security companies (PSCs) as a force for good, for example, able to facilitate elections in Iraq, others are not so generous and point to the actions of DynCorp contractors in Bosnia who participated in the country's sex trade.[1] Those opposed to the use of PSCs frequently quote such behaviour, while they also point to the lack of control over and accountability of such companies. At the same time, demand for private security services has surged since the attacks of 11 September 2001 (9/11), with no indication of demand slowing down in the immediate future. For that reason, their role and conduct is under far greater scrutiny today than ever before.

While so many questions about their utility, accountability and legal status remain problematic – see Emanuela-Chiara Gillard's chapter on the legal status of PSC/PMC staff in this volume[2] – many individuals are uneasy about endorsing a business activity that raises serious ethical questions without first evaluating the behaviour of PSCs and where necessary subjecting them to pressure to bring about change. Many critics argue that it is not enough for PSCs to simply enforce a minimum standard of behaviour on their employees. In the absence of any ban, there is a need for a set of minimum regulatory requirements.[3] If PSCs want to be considered socially responsible, they must achieve suitably high standards in their working practices. Only by going beyond the minimum standards will they be seen as socially responsible and start to enjoy the level of public confidence and legitimacy associated with the defence industry in general. Unfortunately, the working practices of some PSCs suggest there is still some way to go before reaching this point. As one contractor argued 'for some companies, Iraq represents the wild west, while their contractors behave as if they are a 21st century cowboy.'[4] So far, not a single foreign contractor in Iraq has been held accountable for any criminal misconduct, while the same is not true for American and British soldiers.[5]

Security companies need to evaluate, or even re-evaluate in some cases, their objectives in line with a thorough assessment of corporate social responsibility (CSR). Moreover, there is growing public demand for security companies to do more to improve the social consequences of commercial decisions, even though there is little agreement on how to achieve this. At the same time, the nature and extent of the changes needed are still unknown, though no one doubts the need for change. This is very much the case since 9/11. Without a clear understanding of the extent and nature of these new demands for change, private security in general, and in Iraq in particular, will continue to face difficulties in convincing a naturally sceptical civil society of its legitimacy and the advantages of that legitimacy to the wider community.

The chapter explores the extent to which PSCs have engaged in socially responsible behaviour; what is frequently referred to as 'corporate social responsibility' (CSR). The chapter is intended to identify the extent to which PSCs go beyond their social obligations when fulfilling their contractual requirements to ensure the well-being of other individuals and organizations affected by their activities. Following on from this, the chapter goes on to identify the constituent elements of a CSR that underpin the private security industry. It then examines the extent to which PSCs undertake to fulfil their social responsibilities towards these constituent elements and the problems they face in the process of doing so. Finally, the focus of the chapter is on the industry in general though it does, in places, draw heavily on the behaviour of PSCs in Iraq.

## Understanding corporate social responsibility (CSR)

CSR is not new. Indeed, as a movement it has been evolving over the last three decades and now fully embraces the principle of human rights. More importantly, 'some companies have always acknowledged a wider responsibility towards the community.'[6] According to Johnson and Scholes, 'corporate social responsibility is the detailed issues on which an organization exceeds its minimum required obligation to stakeholders.'[7] Mondy, Sharplin and Flippo, on the other hand, argue that 'social responsibility is the implied, enforced, or felt obligation of managers, acting in their official capacities, to serve and protect the interests of groups other than themselves.'[8] Both definitions point to the voluntary acts that move beyond legal compliance and include investing more in human capital, the environment and stakeholders. To simplify matters further, 'when a corporation behaves as if it had a conscience, it is said to be socially responsible.'[9]

As will be made clear later, social responsibility is not just about discrete issues suggested by Johnson and Scholes, but affects every aspect of a company's business and is tied to concerns for moral issues. To behave socially responsibly in one area of business is not enough;

corporations must act in a socially responsible manner in all areas of business. How is this achieved? Mainly through policy statements, adapting practices over time, training and strong moral leadership by managers. This last claim can be considered culturally specific and may create problems for managers who fail to realize the impact of their own cultural values on the decisions they make concerning the local community.

CSR is concerned with both internal and external actors. These concerns will either manifest themselves as legal requirements or social obligations. In the latter case, corporations and society enter into a contract, what Mondy, Shaplin and Flippo refer to as a social contract; 'the set of rules and assumptions about behaviour patterns among the various elements in society'.[10] Continuing, they explain that 'much of the social contract is embedded in the customs of society.'[11] Furthermore, CSR supposedly makes no moral distinction between internal and external groups, though in practice this is not always the case, especially when resources are limited. From the perspective of the actors, their concerns carry the same weight as each other and may even impact equally on the well-being of the corporation. Neither is it a top-down task driven solely by managers. It is as much a concern of the workforce and is a concept that is driven from the bottom-up as much as it is driven from the top-down in many respects. Nor does the idea always sit comfortably within companies, since embracing CSR may involve changing the mindset of the company for it to work without any guarantee of success. However, time and effort is necessary to force CSR into becoming an integral instead of remaining a marginal component of the company's culture.

## The constituent elements underpinning CSR within PSCs[12]

The organizational structure of PSCs, as with all businesses, is designed to utilize corporate resources to maximize profit for shareholders. In the past, the rules and methods used to conduct business were externally set, while it was the responsibility of corporate officers to abide by such rules and methods to the advantage of the shareholders. The authority of the corporate officer did not extend beyond the need to maximize profits and certainly did not include the use of corporate resources to undertake social engineering or other non-profit-making functions unless they could be seen to have a direct impact on the well-being of the corporation. More importantly, the impact on private security of changing social values has meant that corporate officers are being given responsibility for functions in the areas they have little experience of, let alone being accountable for, through a mandate from the shareholders. Lack of understanding of the concept of CSR may also be behind the industry's wish to know more about it, a point made by the Director General of the British Association of Private Security Companies.[13] According to Beese, confusion over its meaning may also be 'the result of the broad definition given the term and interpreted differently by every business and businessman'.[14] While the urgency to understand the concept points to a turning point for the industry, albeit a small one, it demonstrates an increased awareness of the social environments it operates in and the social responsibilities that go with operating in those environments.

Nevertheless, changing social values has meant changes to corporate strategy for PSCs. The actions of PSCs are increasingly being influenced by ethical considerations to the extent that some companies have their own ethical policy and standard operating procedures (SOPs) to ensure their staff behave properly in all situations.[15] Even so, company policy and SOP are sometimes marginalized, or even forgotten, in the heat of business, as the company staff cave in to such demands fearing the risk of being punished. Neither should we underestimate the degree to which PSCs take their social responsibilities seriously. As Enzer explains:

> corporate responsibility is defined by those restraints imposed on a commercial organization by specific standards [s]et by government legislation... and client and the responsibility expected by the shareholders... in this context, corporate responsibility extends beyond the social and employment aspects normally understood. It also extends to corporations not actively pursuing business that is knowingly involved in an attempt to interfere in a democratic political process whether that is undertaking work to remove a regime or indeed support an unacceptable regime to survive against a defined democratic process.[16]

For the companies, it is not just about their individual reputation, but the reputation of the industry in general. They believe the extent to which they take their social responsibility seriously is reflected to a degree in their determination to sanction members of staff and contractors who break the rules.[17] According to Beese, for example, it is 'a top priority for ArmorGroup, its management, employees and shareholders'.[18] More interestingly, over the last few years more PSCs have come to realize that their future success will be determined more and more by how socially responsible they behave and not solely by their ability to find new markets for their services.

Ethical considerations are also determined by the ethical stance a PSC may choose to adopt as an integral element of its corporate strategy, while also influencing its ethical agenda. As with any business, PSCs may choose between four possible ethical stances: short-term shareholder interests; long-term shareholder interests; multiple shareholder interests and the role as a shaper of society.[19] Again, the decision as to which stance to take is the responsibility of the senior management. Nevertheless, it is very unlikely that PSCs would fall into the last two categories since it is only the companies in these two categories who would be prepared to bear any reduction in profitability for the social good.[20] Instead, their actions tend to suggest they belong to the second category; shareholder interests are tempered with recognition that a well-managed relationship with other stakeholders can benefit the company in the long term.[21] This position is also reflected in a PSC's ethical agenda and, according to Johnson and Scholes, 'is concerned with corporate social responsibility to the various stakeholders, particularly those with little formal power'.[22] Four fundamental issues underpin the ethical agenda of PSCs. They include: concern over the impact of the industry on stakeholders, especially those with little formal power to influence their actions, but who could be directly affected by them, concern over the lack of transparency in the industry; concern over the lack of regulation, including self-regulation; and finally, concern over the lack of oversight and accountability. These are the issues that a socially responsible security industry should be addressing.

## PSCs and the extent of their social responsibility

### Stakeholders

As mentioned earlier, stakeholders are actors who can either be external or internal to a business and affected by its behaviour. For private security the external group includes, but is not exclusive to, the PSC's home government and its agencies, the local government of the country where the operation is taking place, the company's clients, and the local community. The workforce normally represents the internal group. For the purpose of this chapter it will focus on only two stakeholders, security contractors and the local community. The former represents internal interests while the latter represents external interests.

Those who study the industry meet the idea that PSCs take corporate responsibility towards stakeholders seriously with mixed reaction. The fact that CSR is a relatively new concept for private security to understand is partly due to the fact that it only started to make itself felt in the last decade. Nevertheless, some companies appear better able to act beyond their immediate obligations towards their stakeholders than other companies. Why this is so is not clear. Certainly, the more established companies will have a vast array of experience that they can use to enhance their operational and management procedures to ensure they can meet, or move beyond, the expectations of their stakeholders. They may also try to exploit CSR, seeing it as an opportunity to gain a commercial advantage over their rivals. On the other hand, new companies to the industry are unlikely to have the same level of resources to direct at CSR and consequently may decide to adhere to minimum requirements instead. To suggest, however, that the degree to which a company is prepared to accept CSR is somehow linked to the length of time it has been in business is to oversimplify a much more complex issue. Other concerns also influence how companies behave socially, most notably the attitude of senior managers. Their willingness, or lack of, to engage in CSR is an important factor here. For this group, while there may be immediate advantages to cutting the cost of an operation by disregarding certain interests of stakeholders, the more astute managers understand that in the long term competitiveness is as much to do with the quality of the service offered as it is with profit.

From a CSR perspective, the case of Blackwater's operation in Falluja is interesting. In March 2004, four US security contractors working for Blackwater got lost driving through Falluja, which at the time was a stronghold of Sunni resistance to the US occupation. Shortly after entering the city the two vehicles became stuck in traffic that enabled armed men to open fire on the convoy from behind. The men were repeatedly shot at point-blank range before their bodies were dragged from the vehicles, desecrated, burnt and then the remains of two bodies left hanging from a bridge over the Euphrates River. The gruesome image was immediately broadcast around the world.[23] The actions of the company on that day are now a matter for a US Court after the families of the men killed decided to sue Blackwater for wrongful death. As the family's attorney, Marc Miles explains, 'this is a precedent-setting case... once they lose the first case, they'd be fearful there would be other lawsuits to follow.' Legal arguments aside, the incident is also very interesting from a CSR perspective. The company's attitude towards security operations in dangerous environments also contributed to the success of the ambush. Without going into the event too deeply, the company had joined forces with a Kuwait company, Regency Hotel and Hospital Company, and won a security contract with Eurest Support Services (ESS) to guard convoys transporting kitchen equipment to the US military.[24] According to one newspaper report, 'the original contract between Blackwater/Regency and ESS... recognized that the current threat in the Iraqi theatre of operations would remain consistent and dangerous and called for a minimum of three men in each vehicle on security missions with two armoured vehicles to support ESS movements'.[25] However, in a later contract signed between Blackwater and Regency, which specified security provisions identical to the original one, the word 'armoured' was deleted, saving Blackwater an estimated $1.5 million from not having to purchase armoured vehicles.[26] Neither was the security team adequately staffed or armed or allowed enough time to conduct a pre-route assessment. It also appears that the company failed to supply the contractors with maps of the area.[27] Indeed, the pending lawsuit states '[t]he team was sent out without the required equipment and personnel by those in charge of Blackwater... adding that the four would be alive if Blackwater [had] provided them with certain safeguards it promised in contracts they signed.'[28]

The company, itself, argues that 'the contractors in question knew the perils they could face during the course of their duties.'[29] Even so, the company could have extended its social responsibilities to the contractors beyond that which was in the contract. For example, Blackwater could have chosen to adopt operating procedures that would have prevented the men from travelling without the necessary arms and training and to hold managers responsible for any breach of such policies. Instead, either operational procedures were ignored or were simply not there. Most companies have strict operating procedures that contractors must follow for their own safety and that of their clients. Ignoring such procedures can even be a dismissible offence. In the case of Blackwater it appears the drive for profit took precedence over the safety and well-being of their contractors.

As with all organizations, a key strategic issue is the ethical stance that is taken regarding the organization's obligation to its stakeholders. For managers, it is a key issue and they must know its extent and application as far as their organization is concerned.[30] In the case of Blackwater, to ensure such an incident does not happen again they may have to reposition certain stakeholders to alter the influence of some key players in favour of other key players. For example, contractors could be given greater responsibility to determine operating procedures, or at least share such responsibility with managers. In the end, a poor relationship between a Blackwater manager and a contractor appears to be partly to blame for the horrific incident and was further compounded by the ethical stance the managers took, reflecting what appears to be a short-term shareholder interest.

Another stakeholder directly affected by the ethical stance of PSCs is the local community. This is particularly so in Iraq, where local citizens have paid with their lives for the poor standards of some PSCs.[31] Unlike contractors, this group represents external interests. Other stakeholders, but who can also be clients of PSCs, include government agencies,[32] international organizations and business corporations. While the reasons for their reliance on private security may differ, they all have a common interest in ensuring their reputation is not damaged in any way because of the behaviour of PSCs they employ.

In the majority of cases PSCs take stakeholder/client responsibility seriously. They know that not to impose the highest-possible standards on their workforce can have a detrimental impact on their business. Government contracts demand high standards of any company including PSCs. As Goring explains:

> government contracts are much more specific on rules for the use of force[33] and training, standards of operators, clearance and audit. On a commercial contract the emphasis is on doing everything cheaply to maximize the client profit, but government contracts have to take into consideration political sensitivity.[34]

This is, in part, because government officials have a responsibility that extends beyond monetary value to take account of the welfare of government officials, the reputation of the government and the interests of the electorate; no civil society wants to be associated with ethically questionable government contractors and may show their displeasure of such contracts through the ballot box. When tendering for government contracts the government must decide between cost and services. It is not always the case that a government department will accept the cheapest tender. They normally accept the bid that reflects the greatest under-standing of the security environment and how the company will ensure the government achieves its aims within that environment safely. Moreover, the cheapest bid may not always take account of contingency planning, while those PSCs that adhere to a normative approach to business – it ought to be done this way because it is the right way to do it and not just about maximizing profit – frequently include such planning in their bids. As Andrew Dunnet, Director of the CSR Academy explains, 'the drivers for good business vary according to sector.... Some businesses adhere to the normative case that it's the right thing to do, while others have identified tangible bottom benefits through CSR.'[35] The point of the discussion is that PSCs act no differently from other types of business. Some companies will attempt to cut their costs so as to submit a very competitive bid, while other PSCs will want their bids to reflect their normative approach to business and thus include contingency planning.

In the case of the Matrix contract, for example, it soon became apparent that AEGIS security details required flame-resistant overalls after a contractor was burnt as a result of an attack on the convoy he was protecting. Demand for the overalls came from the contractors, with the support of managers, and the client agreed there was a need for them, while the contract allowed for such a contingency.[36] Socially responsible attitudes towards working conditions are of course necessary, especially when working in dangerous environments wherever those environments may be. But, being socially responsible is only possible if contracts allow it. Certainly, government contracts are looked on more favourably by PSCs than a private contract probably because they enable managers to take account of the welfare of their employees more easily as the conditions on the ground change. Fixed-price contracts between security and commercial companies, particularly in Iraq, may not have the same degree of financial flexibility in the case of contingency planning, leaving the PSC to renegotiate its contract if the situation on the ground suddenly deteriorates beyond redemption.

At the strategic level the majority of PSCs have implemented company ethical/social policy that determines the behaviour of the company generally and in specific situations.[37] They risk, however, such exercise being seen as nothing more than a marketing gimmick for the sake of promoting CSR but without any real enforcement powers. For the client, ensuring PSCs comply with their own Code of Conduct is problematic.

For example, the client may not have the resources necessary to monitor their behaviour. Whatever the problem, it leaves in place their moral, if not legal, responsibility, to ensure the contracted PSC acts in accordance with the law and its own ethical and social policy. After all, such policies may have been a deciding factor in the client's choice of PSC. The client's only workable option is to write clauses into the contract prohibiting the PSC from certain actions and enforcing standards, while threatening legal action if the company ignores those clauses.[38] This may be why government contracts are prescriptive in relation to accounting and the adherence to procedures.[39] At least this way, the PSC can be held to account. For the PSC, on the other hand, client integrity is taken very seriously. In the case of ArmorGroup, for example, the company refused to deploy their security team to Iraq to look after UK government officials without protective vests. The vests were held up because the Department of Trade and Industry (DTI) was slow in issuing ArmorGroup with the necessary licence to export the vests into Iraq. The company took the view that it was far too dangerous for its staff and clients to move around the country without the correct protective equipment even though the client was also responsible for the delay in the contract.[40]

Finally, armed protection, the very nature of their work, makes them a potential threat to the community. In Iraq, for example, there have been, and continue to be, incidents of contractors shooting dead local civilians. Moreover, the attitude of some contractors towards the local population could be described as arrogant.[41] Other contractors realize they have a social responsibility to the community and will shape their behaviour to reflect the concerns of the local community. They understand the threat they pose to the community by carrying arms. As one ArmorGroup contractor commented, 'to do this job properly you have to continually train, refining or adopting new drills to reduce the threat you pose to the local community and stay alive.'[42] The death toll among contractors is not insignificant.[43] Thus, training has become a central issue with contractors, who spend the majority of their time rehearsing drills when not actually working.[44]

### Transparency

To reduce some of the criticism that has been levelled at the industry in the past there is a realization that more may need to be done to make the industry more transparent, especially if it is to gain the confidence of the wider community. As with other commercial organizations, PSCs have at least a moral obligation to inform us of their activities, who their customers are, and where they operate. The international community is also entitled to know about the nature of the companies themselves and the individuals responsible for them. At the same time, the industry is entitled to the same confidentiality arrangements other commercial organizations receive. Just because the industry lends itself to conspiracy theories does not give the international community any extra rights over confidentiality than with less-controversial industries. For example, the international community should not expect PSCs, which are after all simply commercial organizations, to release commercially sensitive material, or operational details to public scrutiny. It does not happen with other business organizations, so why should we expect it of this particular industry? It is not as if they can escape scrutiny. The companies are subject to domestic law and as Sandline International found out to their detriment in 1998, the police and Customs and Excise can seize company documents if they believe a crime has been committed. Again, there is the question of obligation here. Do PSCs have a greater obligation towards their staff or to the international community? Releasing operational material may please their critics, but may place the lives of contractors and their clients at risk. Prioritizing the interests of different stakeholders is a part of any business. But, in the case of private security, there is an additional concern that people's lives may be put at risk just to satisfy journalistic curiosity.

In the case of Iraq, the international community mainly relies on the media for information concerning the activities of PSCs. The companies themselves have discussed their role in the reconstruction of the country, but little else. The problem is not necessarily the fault of the companies, but is, as implied from the statement above, a consequence of their operational environment. No company wants to give its operational procedures away to the insurgency by having journalists write about them in the press. The operational environment aside, part of the problem may lie with the lack of political will shown by the US and UK governments to encourage greater transparency in the industry. Both governments could start by being more explicit about their own use of private security. They may also want to consider the use of government monitors to ensure PSCs comply with national and international laws.

*Self-regulation*

In the absence of appropriate national and international legal frameworks that can adequately regulate the activities of PSCs, leading British companies have established the British Association of Private Security Companies (BAPSC) to promote standards in the industry. The Association was launched in February 2006.[45] The industry recognizes that in the absence of government support for regulation there is a need for self-regulation. At present, only two countries have introduced a regulation to control the sale of PSC services. They are the United States and South Africa.[46] PSCs can also join the International Peace Operations Association (IPOA) in the United States, which again promotes better standards within the industry.[47] It is intended that membership of these

Associations will encourage and promote professional standards and expertise in an environment that lacks an adequate legal framework.

Whether one agrees with this or not, the companies that elect to join will almost certainly argue that membership demonstrates how seriously they take social responsibility in the absence of any formal regulations. At the same time, we should not forget that such a demonstration has economic advantages, especially if it removes the less-savoury element of the industry. As Bearpark explains, 'the ultimate incentive for self-regulation lies... in the increase of competitiveness in the race for lucrative contracts with major clients, such as Western governments.'[48]

The introduction of voluntary regulation in the United Kingdom is designed to go some way to addressing the growing accountability gap that has arisen out of a collective failure to assign responsibility for human rights functions vacated by governments.[49] It should not, however, be seen as a replacement for well thought-out legislation to control the conduct of PSCs. The idea behind self-regulation is simple; by becoming a member of a trade association the government would regard such companies as providing an assurance of respectability.[50] More importantly, the primary function of the association, in consultation with the government and human rights organizations, is to draw up a Code of Conduct for overseas work covering respect for human rights, respect for international law and respect for sovereignty.[51] Any company that fails to abide by the Code faces the prospect of being expelled.[52]

In reality, members are governed by a set of general principles that include

> Disclosure of their corporate structures and relations with offshore bases, partners and subcontractors, committing themselves to follow all the rules of international humanitarian and human-rights law as well as international protocol and conventions' and enshrined in the Association's Charter.[53]

According to Bearpark:

> [The companies] sign a charter embodying these principles, as well as additional agreements on standards and detailed membership criteria. Companies undergo a thorough vetting process to ensure their transparency and integrity before being admitted as members, allowing for the sanctioning of companies that do not comply with the legal and ethical standards of the majority.[54]
>
> Furthermore, imposing strict standards on [the companies] is intended to become the kitemark of the industry.[55]

The problem is that while self-regulation may promote socially responsible behaviour, control of the industry is only feasible within a wider framework that includes setting an international code for standards and national regulation. While the leading companies may act responsibly, not everyone will view self-regulation in the same light. Without the threat of sanctions, the less socially responsible companies may pursue a course of action that is plainly contrary to the public interest.

## Accountability and oversight

The final element underpinning CSR in the industry is accountability and oversight. Mondy, Sharplin and Flippo define accountability as 'any means of ensuring that the person who is supposed to do the task actually performs it and does so correctly'.[56] While their definition applies to individuals, it can also apply to organizations. Accountability in the context of private security is both an issue between organizations and within organizations. In the first instance, it is about PSCs being held accountable to a higher authority for their actions, in the second instance it is about individual contractors being held accountable to managers for their behaviour. The two levels are related in that while contractors must account for their behaviour to managers, the managers may then have to account for their contractor's behaviour to a legal authority outside of the organization. Scanlan and Keys describe the flow of accountability in this situation as upwards.[57] In the case of responsibility, however, the situation is reversed. Governments have a responsibility to prosecute managers and contractors who act unlawfully, while managers have a responsibility to ensure contractors are aware of their position and their relationship to other organizations including the courts.[58]

Clearly, governments are failing in their responsibility by ignoring the legal issues that surround the industry. There is an urgent need for governments to establish official bodies to monitor the activities of PSCs, and to hold them to account if they act unlawfully. As Iraq has shown, where the institutions of law and order are failing, there are no external legal mechanisms that can hold companies to account. Coalition Provisional Authority Order 17 gives contractors immunity from Iraqi legal process, making them instead subject to the exclusive jurisdiction of their sending states.[59] Even though there is a provision within Order 17 that allows the sending state to waiver the immunity of the contractor (Section 5[3]), this is unlikely to happen at present until the Iraqi criminal justice system is able to achieve a standard that can guarantee its integrity. Consequently, all the Multinational Force can do is to hold contractors who they believe have acted unlawfully and then hand them over to the contractor's own government who is then responsible for prosecuting the contractor. Such an approach is not ideal, mainly because of the difficulty in collecting evidence by the sending state for a successful prosecution, and thus raising fears that contractors who act unlawfully will likely escape prosecution. The reported actions of some contractors in Iraq certainly point to the indiscriminate use of force that has resulted in the deaths of innocent civilians and yet no contractor has been prosecuted.[60]

The lack of accountability and oversight is a problem for the industry, but one it cannot tackle by itself. Holding PSCs and their contractors legally accountable for their actions is a matter for the courts. Ultimately only they can impose sanctions on the contractors who have been found to act unlawfully. Nevertheless, the companies that hire PSCs also have a legal and moral responsibility to ensure security contractors abide by the law. Moreover, it is quite possible they may also find themselves facing legal action if they fail to ensure this happens. Nor does this remove any of the PSC responsibility to its stakeholders. Again, they are also legally bound to making sure their employees or contractors behave themselves according to the law and, where necessary, to hold them to account for any breach of company rules they may have committed. At the same time, human rights organizations have a moral obligation to monitor the activities of PSCs and where such activity is legally questionable to bring it to the notice of the international community. In the case of Iraq, they may even try to bring to bear political pressure on the government of the sending state to waiver immunity so a prosecution can take place, though, as noted above, this is unlikely to happen in the immediate future given the poor state of the Iraqi judicial system. On the other hand, if a human rights violation involves a US PSC then a human rights organization, such as Human Rights Watch, may seek to bring legal redress through the Alien Tort Claims Act.[61]

While some progress has been made in this area, there is still some way to go. In the United Kingdom, for example, there is a need to set industry-wide minimum standards that the behaviour of companies can then be judged against and if necessary be held accountable to an independent auditor or, as suggested by Bearpark, an independent Ombudsman,[62] if they fail to meet those standards. Setting standards is the responsibility of the BAPSC and its members. Appointing an auditor is another matter. The association could take on the role, but may find a conflict of interests arising if they do. Members may even go so far as to threaten to withhold registration fees if not given a clear bill of health from the association. A far better approach may be to appoint an external auditor instead. The companies, on the other hand, would need to be able to account for their standards through an internal audit trail to the external auditor. For example, they may need to prove that their contractors are firearms proficient by keeping records of each time contractors receive firearms training on the ranges. Companies may also need to keep records in relation to first-aid and human rights training to mention only two areas of concern. Moreover, the degree to which companies comply with standards, but are also able to show how compliance occurs will, in part, reflect how serious they are about CSR.

# Conclusion

The chapter identifies four constituent elements that underpin corporate social responsibility within the private security industry. They include safeguarding the interests of stakeholdes, ensuring transparency, promoting self-regulation and encouraging accountability and oversight. PSCs need to engage in these areas beyond the minimum requirement if they want to be considered as socially responsible actors. At the moment, it seems the industry is conscious of the concept and that it applies to them, as it does to every industry. Beyond that, there appears to be a lack of understanding about exactly what it represents. And yet, as Iraq demonstrates, companies, though not all of them, generally act in a socially responsible way. Why is this so? The main explanation is probably to do with competition and future markets. Enlightened customers, in particular, are more likely to engage with socially responsible PSCs and thus increase their profits. As a socially responsible industry they may find it easier to penetrate new markets than if they were to simply ignore the subject.

   Nor is the drive for socially responsible behaviour a top-down process, but as the chapter explains, demand for change can also be driven from the bottom-up. Finally, as we know, CSR is a relatively new idea to PSCs. As mentioned above, the industry is still struggling to understand the concept and the arguments that surround it. More importantly, they are still learning how to turn the principles associated with it into practice. Ultimately, the industry needs to fully embrace the concept if it is to draw benefits from it. Specifically, companies need to take a holistic approach to the concept. Social responsibility of a PSC cannot be exclusive to one area of operations while in another area its behaviour is ethically questionable. In this respect, CSR is an inclusive concept. It affects every aspect of a PSC's business.

# Notes

Much of the data for this chapter is drawn from discussions held with managers and contractors during a trip to Baghdad, 29 April to 3 May 2006.

1 Stewart Payne, 'Teenagers Used for Sex by UN in Bosnia', *Daily Telegraph*, 25 April 2002.
2 Emanuela-Chiara Gillard, 'Private Military/Security Companies: the Status of Their Staff and Their Obligations under International Humanitarian Law and the Responsibilities of States in Relation to Their Operations', in Andrew Alexandra, Deane-Peter Baker and Marina Caparini (eds), *Private Military Companies: Ethics, Policies and Civil–Military Relations*, London: Routledge, 2008, pp. 264–284.
3 Campaign against the Arms Trade, 'Comments on the Green Paper on PMCs', www.caat.org.uk/publications/government/mercenary-0802.php, accessed 22 May 2006.
4 Interview with private security contractor, Baghdad, 2 May 2006.
5 United States Government Accountability Office, *Rebuilding Iraq: Actions Needed to Improve Use of Private Security Providers*, GAO-05-737, 2005, p. 21, fn. 18.

6 Company owners have often felt a responsibility to look after their employees. This was particularly the case in Victorian Britain. Two Victorian businessmen Richard and George Cadbury who were both great industrialists and social visionaries, for example, established the Bournville Village. The story of the village is one of industrial organization and social planning that sought to build a factory in a pleasant environment in complete contrast to the normal oppressive working conditions Victorian workers had to endure. See Cadbury Chocolate website at: www.cadbury.co.uk/EN/CTB2003/ accessed 2 February 2006.

7 Gerry Johnson and Kevan Scholes, *Exploring Corporate Strategy*, London: Prentice Hall Europe, 1999, p. 230.

8 Wayne Mondy R., Arthur Shaplin and Edwin Flippo, *Management Concepts and Practices*, London: Allyn and Bacon, Inc., 1988, p. 632.

9 Ibid.

10 Ibid., p. 634.

11 Ibid.

12 I would like to thank Lt Col Jason Wright for helping to identify the four constituent components of CSR that underpin its relationship to the private security sector.

13 Andy Bearpark, Director General, British Association of Private Security Companies, Interview, 27 April 2006.

14 Christopher Beese, Chief Administration Officer, ArmorGroup, reply to questionnaire, 22 December 2005.

15 Interview with AEGIS staff, Iraq, 1 May 2006

16 Peter Enzer, Operations Director, Group 4 Securicor, reply to questionnaire, 11 January 2006.

17 A number of PSCs, for example, have made the negligent discharge of a round from a weapon a dismissible offence. Eric Gough, Operations Manager, ArmorGroup, Interview, 10 March 2006.

18 Christopher Beese, reply to questionnaire, 22 December 2005.

19 Johnson and Scholes, *Exploring Corporate Strategy*, p. 227

20 The Quaker companies of the nineteenth century are a good example of companies that would fall into category three. Category four represents the ideological end of the spectrum. The aims of the companies/organizations in this group are to shape society, while financial rewards are regarded as secondary in importance.

21 Johnson and Scholes, *Exploring Corporate Strategy*, p. 226

22 Ibid., p. 203

23 Jeremy Scahill, 'Blood is Thicker than Blackwater', www.thenation.com/doc/20060508/scahill, accessed 21 April 2006.

24 Ibid.

25 Ibid.

26 Ibid.

27 Joe Sterling, 'Family's Lawsuit over Slain Contractors Stalls', http://edition.cnn.com/2005/LAW/04/11/blackwater.lawsuit/index.html, accessed 21 April 2006.

28 Ibid.

29 Ibid.

30 Johnson and Scholes, *Exploring Corporate Strategy*, p. 225.

31 Nick Butterly, 'Inquiry into Shooting of Academic', *Advertiser*, 31 March 2006.

32 Details released under the Freedom of Information (FOI) show that armed protection in Baghdad and Basra for UK government officials is supplied by ArmorGroup and Control Risks Group. FOI Request from Dr Christopher Kinsey to the Foreign and Commonwealth Office, 27 April 2005. Published on

the FCO website at, www.fco.gov.uk/Files/kfile/FCO%20&%20Security %20contractors.doc, accessed 26 April 2006.

33 The US military does not allow security contractors to use the term 'rules of engagement', which is understood to be a military term. Security contractors must use the term 'rules for the use of force' when engaged in an act of hostility. Interview with ArmorGroup staff, Iraq, 1 May 2006.

34 John Goring, Country Manager, ArmorGroup International, Iraq, E-mail communication, 12 May 2006.

35 Andrew Dunnett, Director, CSR Academy, 'Is it Good Business to Be a Good Business', *Corporate Social Responsibility: Your Guide to Business with a Conscience*, London: Distributed in *The Times*, 24 April 2006.

36 Interview with AEGIS staff, Iraq, 1 May 2006.

37 An examination of the websites of the following companies: Control Risks Group; ArmorGroup; Erinys International; Military Professional Resources Incorporated (MPRI); AEGIS Defence Services and DynCorp International show they all have corporate governance/Code of Ethics polices in place. The International Peace Operations Association (IPOA) has its own Code of Conduct that all its members must adhere to as part of their membership agreement.

38 In the case of the Foreign and Commonwealth Office (FCO), to make sure contractors follow agreed standards, the provisions of [the Iraq] contracts have been very carefully drafted by FCO Contract Advisers. Overseas security managers and other FCO staff meet regularly with representatives from the above companies to review the contracts to ensure that they are able to meet FCO changing needs. Another of the FCO requirements is that all security contractors working for the FCO must receive FCO security clearance before they start working on FCO projects. Freedom of Information request, Dr Christopher Kinsey, FCO, 27 April 2005, www.fco.gov.uk/Files/kfile/FCO %20&%20Security%20contractors.doc, accessed 26 April 2006.

39 John Goring, E-mail communication, 12 May 2006.

40 'The DTI has now put more effort into the licensing mechanism with the result that we do not experience the delays the companies used to.' Christopher Beese, Chief Administrative Officer, ArmorGroup International, E-mail communication, 26 April 2006.

41 Christian Miller, 'Private Security Guards in Iraq Operate with Little Supervision', *Los Angeles Times*, 4 December 2005.

42 Richard Platt, Security Contractor, ArmorGroup International, Interview, 7 February 2006.

43 David Isenberg, 'A Government in Search of Cover: PMCs in Iraq', London: British American Security Information Council, 2006, p. 7.

44 Interview with ArmorGroup and AEGIS staff, Iraq, 1 May 2006.

45 The British Association Private Security Companies, www.bapsc.org.uk, accessed 16 May 2006.

46 In the United States, any article and service that is deemed to be a defence article and defence service must be licensed before it can be exported abroad. See International Traffic in Arms Regulations (ITAR), www.pmdtc.org/reference. htm, accessed 16 May 2006. In the case of South Africa, the government introduced the Regulation of Foreign Military Assistance Act 1998. The Act seeks to control all forms of foreign military and security services, including advice and training. The Act may soon be superseded by 'The Prohibition of Mercenary Activity and Prohibition and Regulation of Certain Activities in An Area of Armed Conflict Bill, 2005', which is intended to be even tougher on those individuals who sell military and security services abroad without first gaining permission from the government.

47 IPOA Code of Conduct, www.ipoaonline.org/conduct/ accessed 14 April 2006.
48 Andy Bearpark, 'Self-regulation is Key for Private Security Industry', *Jane's Defence Weekly*, London, 22 March 2006.
49 Christopher Kinsey, 'Regulating Private Military Companies: The Legislative Dimension', *Contemporary Security Policy*, Vol. 26(1), 2005, p. 96.
50 The Foreign and Commonwealth Office, *Private Military Companies: Options for Regulation*, London: Stationery Office, 2002, p. 26.
51 Ibid.
52 Ibid.
53 Bearpark, 2006.
54 Ibid.
55 Ibid.
56 Wayne Mondy R., Arthur Shaplin and Edwin Flippo, *Management Concepts and Practices*, p. 249.
57 Burt Scanlan and J. Bernard Keys, *Management and Organizational Behaviour*, New York: John Wiley & Sons, Inc., 1979, p. 92.
58 Ibid.
59 Coalition Provisional Authority Order 17, 27 June 2004, p. 4.
60 Jonathan Finer, 'State Department Contractors Kill Two Civilians in Northern Iraq', *The Washington Post*, 9 February 2006.
61 The oil companies Total and Unical and their operation in Burma is frequently cited by human rights organizations as an example of injustice, leading to the displacement of people and government repression. The Alien Tort Claims Act (ATCA) in the United States offers a means to bring legal redress in US courts. Victims who are not US citizens can use the US judicial system to sue corporations for injustices committed abroad.
62 The idea of an independent Ombudsman was first suggested by Andy Bearpark at BAPSC's First Annual Conference, 30–31 October 2006.

# Part II
# Policies and law

# 6   Mars meets Mammon

*Andrew Alexandra*

One of the fundamental tasks of a state is to provide physical security for its members – to create conditions for peaceful intercourse between its citizens and to prevent the violent usurpation of political authority, from within or without. Typically, states have constructed institutional providers of coercive force, such as police forces and armies, as one of the means to the achievement of that task. Private military firms (PMFs) have emerged over the past twenty years as non-state organizations which have the capacity to provide significant coercive force, alongside, in place of, or in opposition to, state institutions. My focus in this chapter is on the increasingly important role that PMFs are playing in the provision of national defence. In particular, I want to consider the possibility of PMFs becoming the dominant providers of such services, and explore some of the implications of such a state of affairs.

## Background: PMFs as providers of military services

Two sets of factors have intersected to stimulate the emergence of private military firms as important players in the international security sector. The first were geo-political changes consequent on the end of the Cold War. During the Cold War many states aligned themselves with one of the two competing superpowers, which provided them with the means – including military support – they needed to protect themselves against internal subversion or external invasion. The demise of the Soviet Union left those states which had relied on its support without a backer, while the United States no longer had the same generalized incentive to stand behind any state which might otherwise align itself with the USSR. In a number of fragile states, particularly in Africa, where the government possessed only tenuous legitimacy and limited coercive power, government and non-government actors alike were forced to look for other sources of security services. One of the other immediate effects of the end of the Cold War, a rapid drop in expenditure on arms and armies (the 'peace dividend'), helped ensure that those services were available. It is estimated that in the 1990s 10 million soldiers were discharged from national armies, into a world awash with military equipment. A number of elite units, especially from the USSR and South Africa, in effect moved holus-bolus from working for the state into employment in PMFs.

The simultaneous need for, and availability of, non-state military forces explains the growth of private provision of such force. It does not explain the distinctive form that those providers have taken on. PMFs are, in a straightforward sense, mercenary organizations – they provide services, including the provision of coercive force, for a fee. But if they are mercenaries, they differ in important, perhaps fundamental ways from military mercenaries as they have traditionally been understood and operated. As Peter W. Singer puts it, the 'critical factor is their modern corporate business form'.[1] To understand why they have taken on this form, we need to look at the second set of factors that have shaped the emergence of PMFs, developments within developed liberal democracies consequent on the adoption of neo-liberal ideas by the policy elite.

One effect of the adoption of those ideas has been a change in the understanding of the role of the state in delivery of services to its citizens – from 'government' to 'governance'. While the state still takes responsibility for the availability of a range of services, it oversees the provision of such services, rather than delivering them directly through its own agencies. As part of this change many state agencies have been privatized. There appear to be two main motivations for such privatization. First, it is held that private agencies, subject to the discipline of the market, will provide the needed service more efficiently than public sector organizations. But, second, it is often thought that there is a fund of available resources, skills and so on, locked up in public sector organizations that can generate greater economic returns, first for the state itself, and then for the community more generally, if their economic potential is exploited in the market.

Neo-liberal ideology thus renders the provision of military services by private, rather than public, providers at least *prima facie* desirable. At the same time, neo-liberalism has also contributed to the need for private provision, by changing the relationship between citizens, mediated through state institutions. Fraternity has long been one of the animating values of Western states, expressed, for example, in welfare programmes such as age pensions and health care systems. Norms of loyalty, mutuality and exclusivity, and preparedness to sacrifice individual interests for the greater good, all of which can be seen as specifications of the value of fraternity, have also been embodied in institutional arrangements for national defence, as well as in attitudes to those arrangements (and in turn hostility to mercenaries and mercenary forces reflect their incompatibility with the value of fraternity). In recent decades, with the ascendancy of neo-liberalism as the guiding political ideology fraternal social values have been eroded. In effect, risk has been re-privatized. But, of course, norms of sacrifice and the like, on which the citizen army has been founded, inevitably are undermined in such circumstances. Perhaps military service is on the way to becoming another good that only can be provided through commercial means.[2]

Corporatized private military providers, then, have both the expertise that is in demand by wealthy governments, and the organizational form that makes it possible for governments to turn to them, as they do to other corporate service providers, as they increasingly 'outsource' the provision of services that were formerly delivered by public sector organizations. Probably the most well-publicized exploits of PMFs have involved companies such as Sandline International and Executive Outcomes in providing combat service for governments in Sierra Leone and Angola.[3] However, most PMFs are based in Europe and North America, with the US government being the biggest client of PMFs.[4]

In understanding the role of PMFs in the provision of military services it is important to distinguish the different functions which can be undertaken by PMFs: combat service; military training and strategic advice; logistics and technical support. Following Peter Singer the relationship between these different functions can be represented by the image of a spear, with engagement in battle representing the tip of the spear.[5] In first-world countries the place at the tip of the spear has of course been, and largely continues to be, occupied by national armies, with PMFs increasingly providing non-combat functions such as training for national armed forces that tended in the past to be provided 'in-house'. However, the line between PMFs and national forces is becoming increasingly blurred, both functionally and organizationally. Functionally, the increasingly mechanized nature of modern war makes it more difficult to draw clear lines between those who are at the tip of the spear, and those who provide them with technical assistance. In the US invasion of Iraq in 1991, for example, when unmanned Predator drones and B-2 stealth bombers went into action their weapon systems were operated and maintained by non-military personnel working for private companies. Furthermore, PMF personnel who are not part of the military chain of command nevertheless now do many things that traditionally would have been done by soldiers on active duty, and that would lead to their being classified as combatants during war-time. Many of the estimated 25,000 plus private military contractors currently operating in Iraq, for example, are occupied guarding installations and personnel – Paul Bremer, the US head of the Coalition Provisional Authority in Iraq in 2003–04, was guarded by members of a PMF, not US soldiers – and it is predicted that the United States is likely to turn much of the role currently played by its armed forces in Iraq over to private providers.

The increasing structural integration of PMFs into national armies is exemplified in developments promoted by the Blair government in the United Kingdom. Under so-called Private Finance Initiatives private companies tender for contracts of between ten to forty years duration for the construction, servicing and maintenance of military facilities. In 1996, the United Kingdom introduced the Sponsored Reserve concept, whereby PMFs provide services in conflict zones by enrolling some of their workers as voluntary Sponsored Reserves, who become reservist members of the armed forces, becoming part of the military chain of command when on active service. So far these Reserves have been used only for non-combat functions (such as working in the meteorological unit, and providing in-flight refuelling services). Nevertheless, again, in virtue of their organizational status and role, they would clearly be classified as combatants in war-time.[6] Other European countries are following, somewhat more cautiously, in Britain's footsteps.

In short, then, PMFs have rapidly become massive corporate structures, capable of providing the full range of functions traditionally undertaken by national armed forces. Increasingly their personnel are in fact displacing enlisted members of the armed forces in carrying out those functions, either within the organizational structure of national armies, or alongside that structure, or even instead of it. If current trends continue, all or much of the capacity to deliver armed force in developed nations could eventually be in the hands of private providers.

The prospect of PMFs becoming the dominant or sole providers of those military functions that for at least the past couple of centuries have been provided by national armies throws into doubt the viability of the particular political paradigm which we have come to accept as the *status quo*. In the rest of this chapter I want first to outline some of the features of that paradigm, and then to speculate about dangers and opportunities that may arise as a result of the displacement of public national armies by PMFs.

## The current paradigm

On the current paradigm, the world is divided into a number of sovereign states, each of which claims sovereignty over a discrete territory. One of the implications of that claim is that each state has a right to defend its sovereignty from attack by other states, and to possess the means to do so – typically through the institution of a standing citizen army. The post-World War II settlement had it that these armies could only rightfully be used in response to an unjustified attack on their own, or some other, state.[7]

Implicit in this paradigm is a certain normative view about violence, and hence of institutions dedicated to the provision of violent force. On this view agents are not justified in using violence either as an end in itself, or as a means to their ends. Nonetheless, violence or the threat of violence, can become justified in as much as it is necessary as a means to deter or prevent the violation of rights, or to rectify such violations if they nevertheless occur, and consequently so can institutions dedicated to the provision of such violence. Institutions dedicated to the provision of legitimate violence, then, are by their nature guardians. The ideal world is one in which there is no violation of rights and hence no need for violence. The best possible world is the one in which as much as possible of what would happen in the ideal world still happens: it is to the realization of this world that institutions of state violence are dedicated.

There are thus two overriding desiderata for such institutions: the first, obviously, is effectiveness in preventing and limiting violence and other rights violations; the second, perhaps less obviously, is what might be called neutrality. The thought here is that these institutions should, as much as possible, operate without impinging in any way on the legitimate activities of the public they protect. Of course, in practice they will always have some impact, if merely because they are costly, so a system of taxation or the like will have to be put in place to fund them. Though these two desiderata – effectiveness and neutrality – are not logically incompatible there is a kind of pragmatic tension between them. Many of the most obvious ways of increasing the effectiveness of institutions of violence, such as giving them greater powers to monitor and restrict suspect actions or people, clearly reduce neutrality. In any case, since these institutions have no independent intrinsic value, the desideratum of neutrality tells us that they should be as small and non-intrusive as is compatible with effectiveness.

Broadly, institutions of state violence have two orientations: first, to what happens within the state – the domain of police forces – and second, to what happens between states – the domain of military forces. In both cases these institutions are supposed to provide a public good – that is, a good that is available to all members of a group. In the case of the police, the public good they provide is the opportunity to go about one's business free from the fear of having one's personal rights violated. The group to which they provide this good is all those who inhabit the relevant jurisdiction. In the case of armies, the public good they provide is the freedom from the fear of having one's political institutions usurped by violent force, and from the disruption and danger that follows from the attempt to so. In the first instance, the public to which they provide this good is the citizens of the state to which the army belongs. But more broadly, given the interdependence of nations, the large and unpredictable effects of serious international conflict, and the benefits that flow from peace, the relevant public is the human race.

Although both police and armies have often fallen spectacularly short of meeting the demands of the guardianship model of institutions of state violence outlined above, at least in some cases police have, in my view, come somewhere near to doing so. In places such as Australia and England high levels of civility are now taken for granted in the day-to-day dealings most people have with each other.[8] This is an achievement, standing in stark contrast to the situation in earlier times and in other places, and it is clearly due at least in part to the operation of police forces. That is, police have achieved a high degree of effectiveness. Furthermore, to a large extent the social life of these societies is not fundamentally affected by the presence of police forces in their midst, so police have also come somewhere near satisfying the desideratum of neutrality.

The situation is quite different in respect of armies. Far from the world becoming more pacific, it appears to have become steadily more and more war-like over a long period of time. The financial costs of armies has grown steadily over the past couple of centuries (even allowing for the dip in the 1990s alluded to above),[9] and is currently estimated at over $US1 trillion – 2.6 per cent of global gross domestic product.[10] Unsurprisingly, in the light of this spending, and of technological advances, armies' capacity to wreak destruction on each other – and on the civilian population – is also greater than it has ever been. And armies consistently use that capacity, with the number of deaths in wars over the past couple of centuries continuing to grow, in both relative and absolute terms.[11]

There is a structural problem here. In the case of police in well-functioning societies, the state possesses an overwhelming superiority in the capacity to deploy coercive force. Once that superiority has been achieved, police can prevent the emergence of any potential challengers that might threaten to subvert its effectiveness. But no state, not even the most powerful, possesses anything like that superiority in relation to other states. In the face of the potential threats to its security posed by other states, a state generally increases its capacity to deploy violent force, through the development and purchase of more powerful weapons systems and the like. Since most weapons systems possess offensive as well as defensive capacities, such action in turn makes that state a greater potential threat to other states, which respond in kind, which causes the first state to increase its preparations – thus the paradoxical but apparently remorseless logic of the arms race, where the attempt by the armies of each state to act effectively, means that all progressively become less effective. Armies thus have become increasingly less effective in protecting both the population of their own states, and more broadly the global population. States therefore face a collective action problem: while it is reasonable for each state to increase its preparation for war as the international environment becomes more threatening, the effect of each doing so is to make all of them less secure.

Furthermore, even as armies have become *actually* less effective, their *attempts* to retain or increase their effectiveness have undermined their neutrality. Far from armies functioning as invisible guardians for societies, the need to prepare for and fight wars has had a profound effect on political and social life in modern states. Many of the characteristic formal arrangements and institutions of the state, from taxation to passports, have developed as means to support armies and their activities. Armies and associated institutions such as the armaments industry possess great political and economic power. The political culture of modern states generates the material and political support which is the condition for the effectiveness of armies. Even in a country as geographically untouched by international conflict as Australia, for example, stories of military glory and sacrifice are at the heart of the narratives by which national – and hence personal – identity is constructed.

The relationship between armies and the societies they are supposed to protect is a complex one. As I have just been claiming, as the size of those armies has grown in an attempt to retain relative effectiveness, so has their effect on the functioning of societies. But it is also the case that social forces can impact on armies to undermine their effectiveness. There is a standing temptation for politicians to use the offensive capacities of armies to promote their national interests, or even their own partisan agenda. Politicians can, and often do, exploit the xenophobic and bellicist strains in popular thought for short-term political gain, creating and exploiting tension with other states in order to bolster their own political standing. So armies can be pushed towards, or even into wrongful wars by social forces – and that push contributes to the ratcheting up of global military activity, and its consequent impact on society.

On the other hand, social forces can adversely affect the effectiveness of armies by unduly retarding their operations. Gil Merom's recent book *How Democracies Lose Small Wars*[12] is instructive in this regard. Merom points outs that in a number of small(ish) wars, such as the Vietnam War and the Israeli occupation of Lebanon, the side which clearly possessed overwhelming and continuing military and material superiority never-theless lost the war. They did so, Merom plausibly maintains, because popular opposition to the wars within the more powerful states grew to a point where the domestic political costs were too great for the powers-that-be to bear. That opposition was fuelled both by moral outrage, but also by popular unwillingness to pay the ongoing costs in soldiers' lives and military spending. While arguably the small wars that Merom dis-cusses were all unjustified wars in the first place, this obviously does not mean that small wars have to be unjustified. Merom identifies three inter-twined factors relevant to democracies' tendency to fail in pursuing small wars, which he calls:[13]

*Instrumental dependence* – the state's degree of reliance on the society to provide the resources, mostly manpower, needed to carry on military activity;

*Normative difference* – the distance between the state and the popular opinion about the legitimacy of *sacrifice* (of the democratic state's soldiers and resources) and *brutal conduct* (towards the enemy) and

*Political relevance* – the amount of influence societal forces have over policy-choice or their outcomes.

Prudent political leaders would seem well advised to refrain from military involvement that would bring all the three factors into play to a high degree, whatever the overall merits of the case for such involvement. The difficulty of 'selling' small wars to domestic populations in democracies does, in fact, seem to have conditioned the behaviour and policies of politicians over the past couple of decades. Consider the response of Western powers to the breakdown of order in former Yugoslavia. Western leaders were reluctant to make the relatively small commitment to the use of force that could have at least ameliorated the worst excesses that followed from that breakdown; when the United States did finally get involved in Kosovo, it relied on air power, as a method of delivering force with relatively low risk of (US) military casualties.

But of course none of the factors Merom points to is immutable. Normative difference, for example, disappears when the populace believes that their nation is facing an existential threat. Indeed, in such a case military force – and the political leaders who direct it – gain overwhelming support. The lesson to be learned by political leaders, obviously, is to present military action as a response to such a threat – an attack on 'our way of life' – and to have sufficient control over the organs of popular opinion to be able to do so persuasively. But it is also possible to reduce instrumental dependence by, for example, developing mechanized and automated weapons systems (which has been one of the consequences of the so-called Revolution in Military Affairs), or by drawing personnel from outside one's own society. In turn, one of the effects of reducing instrumental dependence is to diminish what Merom calls political relevance. To the extent to which policy makers do not rely on the ongoing popularity of the commitment of military forces to make such a commitment viable, they are largely insulated from political forces. As I have implied above, in the light of the normative views about the proper role of armies such insulation is not necessarily a bad thing, since there are occasions when popular opinion can deter political leaders from committing to or continuing military options where it would be desirable for them to do so. On the other hand it is not necessarily a good thing either, since where political leaders do not have to reckon with the reluctance of their people to become involved in non-essential wars, they may be tempted to use the army as simply another tool available to further their aims.

## Where to from here?

So much for the situation we find ourselves in – what about where we might be heading? I assume, though without anything like absolute conviction that at least for the foreseeable future something like the current system of states will remain in place. The scenario I want to focus on is one in which PMFs displace public national armies as the providers of the violent force capacity that is supposed to prevent and resolve conflict between states.

One possibility is that the only thing that changes is that national armies continue in pretty much their current form, with the state simply 'contracting out' for the provision of services that are currently provided by public armies. English-speaking countries, at least, are familiar enough with this kind of development across a range of services that were previously provided directly by state instrumentalities, from public transport to water and power.

In my view, this would be a bad outcome, for at least a couple of reasons. The first is that, as I have argued above, the current system, of which this would be a close continuant, is itself seriously and increasingly flawed in terms of both of the desiderata of effectiveness and neutrality. Retention of the structure of national armies, each of which is charged with being prepared to meet the threat that may be posed by other such armies, means the perpetuation of the collective rationality problem pointed to above, where the attempt by each to discharge their responsibilities means that all become less able to do so.

But, second, it may be that such a system would actually exacerbate these problems, given the structure of incentives that would face PMFs in such a system. As standard 'invisible hand' explanations of the workings of markets point out, the competitive structure of markets means providers of goods have an incentive to find ever more effective and efficient methods of production. In general, this is desirable, when the commodities being produced are things that are in themselves good or even just harmless. But when what is being produced is the capacity to inflict violence, then given the collective action problem pointed to above, greater productive efficiency is actually undesirable. Furthermore, we know that corporations do not simply meet existing demand, but take measures to generate more demand. This could be done in a variety of ways in the sort of scenario under consideration, but one obvious way is through political influence. Money speaks, and as the financial size of PMFs increases, so does their likely political influence. As their voice becomes louder it is likely that the voice of the populace will be muted: it would seem that the privatization of armies will decrease what Merom calls political relevance – the amount of influence that societal forces have over policy choice – as their workings become of less-direct public concern and less sensitive to public opinion. As I have claimed, this *need* not be a bad thing. The worry, however, is that it *will* be a bad thing, as political leaders of rich countries give in to the temptation to use the capacity for the deployment of force that their wealth gives them to further their ambitions, a temptation that will be encouraged and exploited by PMFs for their own purposes. Finally, the peculiar nature of coercive force as a market good should be noted. With standard market goods (such as cars or frozen chickens), demand drives supply.

With coercive force, on the other hand, demand is a function of supply – the greater the amount of such good in the hands of others, the greater the demand for it by those who do not have matching resources.

This all sounds alarming. The question is, is there a viable alternative? At least in very broad terms I think that there is. First, we need to reduce or even remove the opportunity that political leaders have to misuse military force. There are a number of state agencies that are at 'arms length' from direct political control, for just these sorts of reasons, including central banks and public broadcasting corporations, who are relevant models for the relationship between the state and the agency that controls its purchase of defence services.

Second, PMFs should not be seen as simply privatized analogues of current national defence forces. The point is that armies are supposed to provide security – the build-up of coercive force is justified only in as much as it is a means to that end. National defence forces must calculate the level of coercive force that they should have at their disposal relative to that possessed by potential opponents. From the point of view of each force that context is, to a large extent, a given. Hence, it is rational for each to increase its own capacities to deliver violent force as and when that context becomes more threatening, even though the long-term consequence of such behaviour is to make all less secure. We need to find a way to change the context, so that what is rational from the point of view of all states (and in the long term) is also rational from the point of view of each individual state (and in the short term).

Here the workings of existing insurance markets provide an instructive model. When Benjamin Franklin set up the first fire insurance mutual company in Philadelphia he saw it originally as a scheme of risk-sharing, so that losses caused by fires would not have a catastrophic effect on their victims. It was soon realized, however, that it was also possible to use the company as a means to reduce both the likelihood of fires occurring in the first place, and to reduce their severity if they nevertheless did occur. The likelihood of fires occurring could be reduced in two ways: first by giving members of the scheme incentives to behave in safer ways, by making adoption of safety measures such as proper fire-places and the like a condition for membership, and rewarding those who avoided fires through lower premiums; and second by using premiums to support research into technologies that would allow members to behave more safely. The severity of the fires which nevertheless occurred was reduced through the action of fire brigades, again funded from premiums.

Similarly, I would suggest, we should be able to institute a market in international security insurance, in which states pay premiums for protection against invasion, and the evils consequent on such invasion, and receive compensation where this protection fails. On this approach, PMFs should be conceived as providers, not of coercive force *per se*, but rather of security. The current paradigm of national defence in fact already shares a number of characteristics with fire insurance schemes. First, war, like fire, is seen as a bad, something to be avoided if possible. Second, defence forces, like fire brigades, are supposed to act to limit the damage if that bad nevertheless occurs. The problem with the current paradigm, as claimed above, is that the methods which are used to ensure the ability to deal with war if it occurs, also make it more likely that it will occur.

This kind of problem could be overcome if PMFs as insurance providers become the dominant, or even sole, providers of security for states. Qua commercial entities PMFs have an incentive to engage in the (expensive) use of coercive force only when they are obliged to do so. At the same time they have both an incentive and the capacity to change the international context in which they operate to make it less threatening, including pressuring national leaders to avoid provocative behaviour, to institute effective arms limitation and reduction treaties, and the like. In turn, national leaders would have an incentive to comply with such pressure in order to reduce the premiums they pay. Finally, it would seem essential to remove conflicts of interests that PMFs might face in this sort of situation by ensuring that they do not have interests in armaments companies and the like that benefit from conflict and instability.

## Conclusion

The idea of a market in international security insurance is presented in the previous section in the sketchiest of outlines. It faces a range of obvious objections and difficulties. There is, for example, the question of how a state – or its citizens – could be compensated if a PMF fails in its protective role and an invader succeeds. Moreover, how could we prevent a single PMF coming to dominate the market in international security insurance, and thereby obtain a monopoly of coercive force, putting it in a position where it could effectively do as it pleased?[14] Space precludes me from addressing these problems in any detail. There are, however, two broad points bearing on them and related objections which can be made here.

First, in trying to assess the desirability of alternative institutional arrangements for the protection of the political realm from violent usurpation, we are engaged in a comparative exercise. The question is not whether some suggested alternative is flawless: it is whether it is superior to the status quo. No doubt an insurance scheme cannot provide a watertight guarantee against (successful) invasion, or promise adequate compensation if it occurs. But we already lack any such guarantee, and our current system (as I have argued above) is structured in such a way as to generate (growing) insecurity rather than security. PMFs qua insurers, on the other hand, could have both the incentive and capacity not only to protect states against existing threats, but also to reduce such threats.

In respect of the worry that PMFs might usurp the political authority of their employers, again we currently have no guarantee that national armies will not do just this, as of course many have. In any case, the corporate nature of PMFs provides at least some reassurance. PMFs qua corporation should ultimately be motivated by profit. A properly structured market in private national security provision should align the interest of PMFs with the preservation of a properly functioning political and legal framework, within which the PMF can operate, and whose stability they regard as a necessary condition for the achievement of their own goals.

## Notes

1 Peter W. Singer, 'Corporate Warriors: The Rise and Ramifications of the Privatized Military Industry', *International Security*, 2001–02, Vol. 26(3), pp. 186–220.
2 For a more elaborated discussion of this issue see Elke Krahmann 'The New Model Soldier and Civil–Military Relations', this volume, Ch. 17.
3 HC 577 *Private Military Companies: Options for Regulation*, Foreign and Commonwealth Office, London: The Stationery Office, 2002, pp. 11–12.
4 Elke Krahmann, 'Controlling Private Military Companies in the UK and Germany: Between Partnership and Regulation', *European Security*, 2005, Vol. 13(2), pp. 277–95, also as presented to the International Studies Association Annual Convention, 2003, www.isanet.org/portlandarchive.html#, accessed 12 October 2006, p. 2. PMFs also work for private clients, of course, including NGOs.
5 Peter W. Singer, 'Corporate Warriors: The Rise and Ramifications of the Privatized Military Industry', pp. 202–5; cf. Peter W. Singer, *Corporate Warriors: The Rise of the Privatized Military Industry*, Ithaca, NY: Cornell University Press, 2003.
6 Ibid., p. 9.
7 See, for example, the Charter of the United Nations at www.un.org/aboutun/charter, accessed 12 October 2006. Recent attempts to claim rights to pre-emptive strikes and to humanitarian military intervention in defence of groups whose human rights are being egregiously violated by, or with the complicity of, their own state, can be understood (perhaps with some strain) as fitting within this paradigm. Pre-emptive attacks are claimed to be a kind of 'forward defence', while it is held that sovereignty does not give a right to systematically violate – or ignore the violation – of human rights, so intervention in defence of such rights cannot be seen as a violation of sovereignty.
8 See Norbert Elias, *The Civilizing Process, Vol. 1. The History of Manners*, Oxford: Blackwell, 1969.
9 The years immediately after the end of the Cold War saw a substantial drop in global military spending. Military expenditure resumed its upward trend in 1998–99, and accelerated further after 11 September 2001. It is now at least at the level it was at the end of the Cold War. See *SIPRI Yearbook 2002: Armaments, Disarmament and International Security*, Oxford: OUP, 2002, pp. 323–70; 'Summing up Disarmament and Conversion Events: Change and Continuity after September 11', *Conversion Survey 2002: Global Disarmament, Demilitarization and Demobilization*, Baden-Baden, Germany: Nomos Verlaggeschellschaft, 2002, pp. 13–20.
10 'Global Arms Spending up to $US1 Trillion', *The Age*, 6 August 2005, reporting on findings of the Stockholm International Peace Research Institute.

11 But see the claim by the Human Security Centre (HSC) that despite the resumed upward trend of military spending, both the incidence and severity of state military conflicts (and indeed of all kinds of armed conflicts) have trended substantially downward since the end of the Cold War. See Human Security Centre, *Human Security Centre Report 2005*, Oxford: Oxford University Press, 2006, esp. Part V. While data concerning the number of inter-state armed conflicts is broadly uncontroversial, this is not true in the cases of deaths (and more broadly casualties) that have been caused by such conflicts. First, there is a difference between counting (or trying to count) deaths *in* war, and deaths *consequent on* war. In the latter case, we should include not only, for example, those who die prematurely after the cessation of hostilities because of their wounds, ill-health produced by war conditions and so on, but also those who die in non-state conflicts, civil disorder and so on, which have come about as a result of wars. Second, there are obvious and notorious methodological problems in counting war-related deaths. The HSC, for example, uses a (mainly press) report-based methodology for calculating its figures. As they acknowledge, there can be large discrepancies between the figures generated in this way and those produced by, for example, epidemiological surveys or historical investigations. The magnitude of such discrepancies was vividly illustrated by the recent publication of an epidemiologically based calculation of deaths consequent on the US invasion of Iraq. See G. Burnham, R. Lafta, S. Doacy and L. Roberts, 'Mortality after the 2003 Invasion of Iraq: A Cross-Sectional Cluster Sample Survey' at www.thelancet.com/webfiles/images/journals/lancet/s0140673606694919.pdf, ast (accessed 12 October 2006), which produced estimates of deaths more than ten times greater than those generated by report-based methods. Notwithstanding the large variations in estimates of numbers of deaths caused by wars over time, there appears to be a broad consensus that these numbers have increased through time, and that that increase tracked growth in military spending. Of course, the (intuitively plausible) link between military spending and armed conflict is merely contingent, and the authors of the HSC Report point to a number of political, social and economic factors which currently militate against resort to arms.
12 Gil Merom, *How Democracies Lose Small Wars*, Cambridge: Cambridge University Press, 2003.
13 The terms are Merom's (Merom, ibid., pp. 19–21), the explanations of what they mean are my paraphrases of Merom.
14 This is, of course, a variant of one of the standard concerns about mercenaries.

# 7 Private military companies

## Markets, ethics and economics

*Jurgen Brauer*

> Our ultimate purpose then is not so much to provide a defence of
> mercenarism, but to attack a certain kind of anti-mercenarism, under-
> pinned by that Machiavellian *virtu*, which extols *inter alia* the virtues of
> a citizen's willing subordination of his or her personal interest to the
> communal good.[1]

The perennial quarrel between and among legislators, commentators and
practitioners regarding private military companies (PMCs) and private
security companies (PSCs) has intensified since the end of the Cold War,
and especially since private sector companies contracted to perform
military services for states such as Sierra Leone in Africa and Papua
New Guinea in southeast Asia.[2] The recent discussion has revolved
around (1) the creation of a useful taxonomy of modern non-state forces,
(2) a complex of issues regarding legality, legitimacy, accountability,
transparency and issues of state sovereignty and economic exploitation
and, with all that, the motives of key players such as states, factions in
failed states, international organizations, PMCs and business and humanitarian communities, (3) practical aspects and the peacemaking and
peacekeeping 'efficiency' of PMCs and (4) the prospects for adequate legislative regulation, executive branch supervision of industry participants
and international law.[3] Many of these topics overlap.

Inasmuch as dollars, cents and vested interests are involved, economics
plays a role in the debate but it tends to be the sort of economics that
non-economists do, an economics inappropriately amalgamated with
other fields and topics such as business, finance, budgets, efficiency and
cost-effectiveness – as if all of these were synonymous – a pop-economics
that has as little to do with economic analysis as a scientific discipline that
generates theory, falsifiable hypotheses and empirical tests.[4] To reduce
economic analysis to efficiency is like reducing Mona Lisa to her eyes:
an incomplete and usually partisan view results. If this only ruffled
economists, which might be alright, but when the debate on PMCs
swerves to make economic concepts such as efficiency the arbiter of

whether PMCs 'should' or 'should not' be permitted, then the discussion becomes normative and leaves the realm in which economics can claim sole jurisdiction. By analogy, as science can inform about the veracity of certain religious claims but not decide whether one is to believe in supernatural forces, so economics can inform the PMC debate but not decide it. As medicine can explain contributive causes of respiratory disease but not by itself make society switch to the use of non-polluting fuels, so economics can explain the waxing and waning of PMCs but not by itself make interested parties raise or dissolve them.

To be sure, economics – like medicine – can carry normative implications. For instance, there is no question that the way certain totalitarian governments run their economies is severely injurious to those living within their jurisdiction (e.g. North Korea, Zimbabwe), and most people would regard it as unethical to conduct a state's affairs in a way that is harmful to its citizens. But, although it may explain and influence their formation, economics is not primarily about norms.[5] Instead, economics is about how individuals make choices and about the collective outcome these choices generate.[6] One of these outcomes regards the formation and operation of markets.

The purpose of this chapter is to present a set of selected economic concepts and apply them to show just why PMCs are controversial. The first section develops the concepts, the second applies them and the final section concludes. The thesis of this chapter is that what is at issue is not *how* force is organized (i.e. public or private) but how force is *organized* (regulated). One implication is that there is considerable scope to reconcile divergent positions among legislators, commentators and practitioners to work toward a regulatory framework that takes full account of what markets and governments can and cannot do.[7]

## Economics

A decision, or *choice* from among alternatives, requires an *objective* the achieving of which is subject to *constraints*. Objectives, be they formulated by individuals or by collectives across the spectrum from families to armies, are the starting points of economic study.[8] In practice, economists leave the explaining of how people come by certain objectives to psychologists, sociologists, anthropologists and other social scientists and instead devote themselves to elucidating the constraints under which choices are made and to recording how changes in constraints lead to changes in the choices made.

The objectives are referred to as preferences. Wholly subjective in nature, examples range from inconsequential personal likes and dislikes – such as the texture, firmness, colour, size and taste of a favourite fruit – to fundamental issues such as how armed force is to be organized. People explain, debate and argue about how and why they arrive at a particular preference and try to convince each other that one objective is preferable to another. As individuals, economists have preferences as well, but as professionals they generally abstain from addressing the issue of preference formation. Preferences constitute a 'black box', only recently being peeked into by a branch of social/economics study – a twig, really – known as behavioural economics. The constraints are grouped into two broad classes, prices and resources. If preferences denote what one wishes to 'get', then prices mark what one must 'give' in exchange, and resources signify the pot of gold from which one can do the giving.

The interaction of preferences with the various possible prices one faces and the resources one can draw on defines one's *demand* for goods and services, an agent's willingness and ability to pay for the benefit the good or service is expected to yield. In an exchange, as one good is received, another good (often, but not necessarily, money) is given up.[9] The benefit received is greater than the value of what is given up, or else the agent would not wish to buy. To purchase, the ratio of benefit to cost has to be greater than one. On occasion, demanders make mistakes and buy goods with a benefit/cost ratio of less than one. But unless the purchaser uses another agent's resources to make the purchase, we do not expect such mistakes to be repeated over time, at least not for the repeat purchase of the same item. People learn. One may buy milk once, but if one does not like it (benefit/cost $< 1$), one will not buy it again.[10]

Most people enjoy experimenting and like to sample different foods and fashions, for example. What is purchased is not only the expected benefit of the item itself, but also a life-style of searching and sampling. If sampling across items yields ratios below 1, we expect the person to reduce sampling and settle into a routine. Variety can lose its appeal. The expectation of benefits is massively influenced by one's economic, political, cultural and natural environment (e.g. peer pressure, commercial advertisement, trade law, climatic conditions), as are the costs (e.g. peer disapproval, limited income to expend, fear of imprisonment for wishing to 'purchase' political dissent). No one is sovereign.

Likewise, *supply* arises from an agent's willingness and ability to furnish goods. What is given up is the good produced, or rather the resources used in its production, in exchange for which another (usually, but not necessarily, the purchase price in terms of money) is received. The supplier, too, ordinarily will count on a benefit/cost ratio greater than one, or else it would not make sense to supply. On occasion, suppliers make mistakes and they lose money, that is, the benefit received is smaller than the cost. Unless the supplier uses another agent's resources to supply the good, we do not expect the supplier to continue to trade.

*Trade*, the exchange of goods, refers to two agents' *differential valuation* of two goods being exchanged, one for the other. For example, in the academic labour market, I supply my ability to provide scholarly labour services in exchange for a monetary income (and, perhaps, health, pension and other benefits), and I do this because I ultimately value the money I receive more than the hours I agree to give up in exchange. In contrast, the demander (the university) values my labour services more than the money it has to give up. Although it is common practice to regard me as the supplier and the university as the demander of labour, agents simultaneously are both suppliers and demanders: I supply labour and demand money; the university supplies money and demands labour. My benefit/cost ratio (money/labour) must be greater than one or else I would not wish to trade. Likewise, the university's benefit/cost ratio (labour/money) must be greater than one or else it would not wish to trade.

The ratios of money/labour as compared to labour/money would appear to cancel out. That they do not stems from the fact that I value the dollar I receive more than the university values the same dollar it gives up, and that I value the hour I give up less than the university values the hour it receives. The same dollar has two valuations, as does the same hour. Even more stylized, if I have an orange and you have an apple, we both might find that I'd like your apple and you'd like my orange. Naturally, we exchange and both of us will be the happier for it. Different valuations of two items by two agents drives trade that is perceived as mutually beneficial (benefit/cost ratios > 1).

Mutually beneficial trade by one pair of demander and supplier can bestow benefits or impose costs upon others who are not party to the trade. If my mining company hires a private security company, there may result spill-over effects (*externalities*) to those living in the neighbourhood around the mining area. Whether these effects are positive or negative is an empirical matter. If overall neighbourhood security improves, the effect would be positive: people receive a benefit for which they did not pay. If overall neighbourhood security declines, the effect would be negative: people bear a cost for which they are not compensated. The external effects can be mixed in that some in the neighbourhood receive a benefit while others suffer a cost. Even the prospect of differential externalities can lead to unsettling community dynamics, with those who expect to gain being opposed by those who foresee uncompensated losses. But even if a local community were only to gain or only to lose, larger communities' interests may be differentially affected. If we suppose, for the sake of the argument, that everyone within a local community agreed that the hiring of PMCs in Sierra Leone in the 1990s had resulted only in benefits, then we would still be arguing the pros and cons of the employment of PMCs elsewhere, or of employing them in Sierra Leone at another time.

Trade implies *property*. One cannot trade away resources one does not own. But since resource endowments are unequally distributed, the sum total of trade necessarily benefits the rich more than the poor, even as each trade the poor undertake does benefit them as well or else they would not trade out of their smaller endowments. The poor are equally smart traders, only more constrained in their means. By force of confiscation (*taxation*), some societies compel the redistribution of earned current income and accumulated assets so that the poor have more resources to trade with. Since this discourages the accumulation of assets available for redistribution in the first place, other societies prefer to stress voluntary transfers (grants) and equal opportunity for skill development to enhance trading potentials in current and future generations. In truth, societies mix approaches to redistribution, differing only in the balance chosen. In addition, even the poor can trade against expected *future* property and endowments. For example, banks loan money to students against repayment in the future.

Trade implies *contract*. I agree to give you my orange, and you agree to give me your apple. Contracts can be *honoured* or not, and if the latter then they must be *enforced* (or not) and *punishment* must be meted out (or not). If I give you my orange, and you give me your apple, everything is fine. If I give you my orange, and you do not give me your apple, I will seek to enforce the contract. I can run after you myself and take back the apple (self-policing), or I can run to an arbiter (external policing) to secure the apple in my stead. If I run after you, I can fail to catch you, but so can the arbiter. If I catch you I must beat you up – just as I would expect to be beaten up had I broken the contract – or else running away with the orange (or the apple) would on average be profitable.[11] When a contract is not honoured, one side to the trade loses (benefit/cost < 1). In a society where contracts routinely fail to be honoured, trade will decline and otherwise mutually beneficial exchange will not take place. Society becomes impoverished as each agent is compelled to make due with his or her own resources, unable to trade some or all of them for higher-valued resources another agent might offer.

Agents realize that in the long run when trade fails they all arrive at the socially destructive end of what is privately profitable in the short run – reneging on contracts (cheating). For their own private long-run good, they will seek collective *remedies*. In addition to *law* and *culture* at the societal level – both costly – they develop *trust* and *trustworthiness* (i.e. *reputation*), or *discipline*, at the individual level.[12] One foregoes the opportunity to cheat today in order to be able to trade for gain tomorrow. One engages in intertemporal trade with oneself: the long-run benefit of honesty is greater than the short-run cost of giving up benefits to be had from cheating. This is why settled communities have always viewed itinerant traders with suspicion. He who has *mobility* need not come back and has greater incentive to cheat. Therefore, the stationary agent will want to place a burden of proof on the mobile agent who may be asked to leave behind deposits or securities such as a person who is part of the trader's entourage, that is, a *hostage* to be released when the trade is completed. But itinerant traders needed to be wary as well: he who is settled is likely to have more friends ready at hand to compel an unwilling exchange. Dangers of *shirking* or of *appropriation* (partial or no contract fulfilment) lurk in every trade. Trade entails *risk*.

Like law and culture (law, for short), the development of trust and reputation (trust, for short) are costly. They require time (repeat transactions) and the development of risk management tools. Well-off societies are societies that have managed to evolve high levels of trust or law relative to the cost of providing them. *Competition* arises only under relative equality of trust or law. If I have an orange to offer and one kid offers one apple but a second offers two, then I will trade with the second kid only under comparable conditions of trust or law. If I am not sure of the trade with the second kid's two apples, I may opt for the safer choice of the trade with the first kid's single apple. The degree of *certainty* is an important determinant of trade volume. If trade relies on degrees of certainty, *signals* must be developed that reliably *inform* about qualities of trust or law (hence brand-name marketing, or tradesmen advertising their services as bonded and insured), but information can be manipulated, just as culture can be flouted and law corrupted which is why all these three – information, culture and law – are juicy targets for abuse.[13]

The danger of abuse ties into the all-too-common confusion of *free markets* with *unfettered markets*. To ensure the securing of mutual benefit, societies see to it that free markets are appropriately *regulated*. Unfettered markets are unregulated or ill-regulated, and the risk of abuse and failure to deliver maximum mutual benefits is high. Numerous conditions that make for 'market failure' have been identified.[14] Many market failures can be mitigated by appropriate intervention (i.e. regulation) but the converse danger – 'government failure' – also arises. Economists passionately argue in favour of the virtue of well-regulated free markets; none argue for unfettered markets. In contrast, market participants constantly try to gain advantage by *lobbying* for the presence or absence of regulations, whichever happens to favour one side of the market over the other. If successful, this results in *market power*, the power to skew the benefit/cost ratio in one's favour. Problems stem not – as many mistakenly believe – from the presence of well-regulated free markets but from their very absence.

Not all markets can be equally well-regulated. One reason for this is that regulation requires (cultural or legal) jurisdiction, within and cross-jurisdictional agreement on what is to be regulated, and agreed powers of enforcement. Since even spouses have difficulty agreeing on how to regulate (and enforce) their children's behaviour, it does not surprise that scaled up to communal, even global, dimensions, the problems to be tackled would multiply. Consequently, markets tend to be either over or under regulated. Market conditions change, and vested interests – each vying for influence – have to be reconciled. The resulting compromises are not necessarily ideal. Good law sets market participants free to trade for mutual benefit, but the law can also imprison either by inhibiting otherwise beneficial exchange when undue market power is permitted or created or by compelling otherwise non-beneficial exchange. The economists' prototype of the 'free market' refers to an ideal middle ground that permits society at large to allocate its resources in such a way as to maximize mutual benefits from trade. Such markets, and only such markets, are referred to as *efficient*.

Efficiency, then, is a technical concept within economics, and its achievement is predicated upon a set of conditions that must be met. Some of these have been outlined in the foregoing pages, such as the requirement for the presence of reliable information available in equal measure and quality to both sides of the trade, the presence of enforceable contracts, the presence of regulation and conflict management tools to resolve conflicts over resources and their (re)distribution, pricing, market power, agenda setting for private and collective preference formation, and variegated other issues. Dispute resolution mechanisms need to be formulated, funded and maintained, both within and across societies. Thus, far beyond mere law, markets are very much based upon *ethics* and *morals* – the code of values that individuals and the groups they form establish, and behaviour in accordance with the code.

## Private and public force – a false dichotomy

If it needs to be spelled out, the foregoing pages illustrate how the ample differences among commentators on the issue of PMCs can arise. Those who would reduce the debate to whether or not free markets for PMCs 'work' betray a measure of ignorance of the economics of markets. Everything is conditional. As Shearer and others have pointed out, in practical terms, some PMCs have in fact stopped violence and slaughter. The conditions for the market to deliver mutual benefits had been attained. Detractors of PMCs will have to explain how to justify the continuing slaughter in many African and other states. Waiting for state-approved or UN-sanctioned intervention has cost millions of people their very lives. By the same token, there is no question whether PMCs' abuses have taken place or not. The conditions for markets to deliver mutual benefits have not been attained. The same of course is true for *public* forces which also deliver net benefits to society only when certain conditions hold, frequently identical to those applied to private forces such as transparency and accountability.

Some in the PMC industry call for market regulation. This does not surprise, as regulation comes with a complement of licensing or similar devices that limit market entry. Keeping the competition out of course increases profits of those who are inside. We have seen this in other industries, even mundane ones such as dieticians or hairdressers. But as this chapter has explained, the call for regulation should not be scoffed at and dismissed as some commentators have done. Instead, the call for regulation should be welcomed as it permits civil society to specify the rules of engagement. Once proper regulation is in place, new competitors will arise because the vast majority of business investors prefer a stable, certain regulatory environment over an uncertain one. Had global civil society established such rules by the late 1990s, instead of being tied up in a tiff over the morality or immorality of 'mercenary' services, the subsequent slaughter in western Sudan and elsewhere might have been more limited.

There are additional complications. For example, in the United States, prostitution (sale of in-person sexual services)[15] is illegal in most states, but not in Nevada. Underage sex is outlawed, unless an underage bride (rarely a groom) is married off 'legally'. Gambling is illegal in most states, but not when it involves 'Indian reservations' or state-sanctioned gambling (lotteries that amount to self-taxation by the poor). Many non-medicinal drugs are classified as illicit, but not alcohol and tobacco, both of which are powerfully addictive. It is illegal to acquire some categories of firearms, but plenty of other categories are legally and easily purchased at local retail outlets. Armed security guards for private housing compounds, office buildings or shopping malls are easily and legally hired, but the 'security' offered by criminal protection rackets cannot be legally hired. International trade in endangered species or pathogens is generally outlawed, and yet there are exceptions involving zoological associations and medical researchers. In a word, many markets for functionally identical goods or services exist, yet a part of these markets is deemed legal, another is not. Which is which depends on social mores – the ethics of the group or groups in question. It is these social mores that determine which items are considered 'goods' or 'services' and which are 'bads' or 'disservices'. The function of regulation of markets for goods and services is to procure maximum mutual benefits among traders (demanders and suppliers); likewise, the function of regulation of markets for bads and disservices is to procure minimum mutual benefits (to regulate these markets out of business altogether).

Just which is a good or a bad, a service or a disservice, depends on one's views. Social mores change. What once was regarded as immoral has become commonplace, and vice versa. Taking photographs of people once was, and in some societies still is, considered immoral behaviour ('stealing a person's soul') but is now routine. The habitual use of foul language, rude behaviour and violence once were considered marks of a depraved person but is now standard fare in popular culture. Tarring, feathering and flogging once were considered acceptable punishments for miscreants but – thankfully – not anymore.[16] Along with social mores, market conditions change. Social mores influence market demand and supply. Ancient Rome had a standing army. Empires ranging from the Inca and Aztecs to those of Egypt, India and China also managed to accumulate a public monopoly of force, the better to obtain monopoly rents (taxes) for rulers by offering peace to their subjects.[17] With Rome, its standing army fell as well. By the time of the Italian Renaissance, the use of PMCs– the *condottieri* – was commonplace throughout Europe. Machiavelli's famous rallying cry against the employment of mercenaries came after the high-point of their use had already passed. Apart from political factors and changes in military technology, a key turning point was that the contracts after whom the *condottieri* – the contractors – are named proved too onerous to enforce.[18] Mutual benefits were scant.

Standing armies revived, even well before 1648, but with hefty mixtures of 'nationals' and 'foreigners' – in the American Civil War as in the European colonial wars in the mid-1800s for instance – and saw their more purely nationalistic heyday only in the twentieth century. The aberration is not the use of private forces in warfare, but the almost exclusive use of 'nationals' in state forces during the twentieth century. It is puzzling that in a world in which young, educated, mobile people are straining to burst nation-state borders, serious scholars would wish to make so much hay out of one's 'nationality'. Are Kurds in Iraq Iraqis? Are nationalized Turks Germans? Are South Africans with a British passport British? Just who is Indian or Indonesian? By whose design and natural right are people to submit and identify themselves with their putative 'nation'?[19]

With Lynch and Walsh (2000), I am so not much arguing in favour of PMCs as to challenge a certain type of anti-PMC cogitation that divulges more fear than reasoning. For an economist the key is not *how* force is organized (private or public provision) but how force is *organized* (regulated). The differentiation between private and public force is an empty differentiation. A false dichotomy, it distracts from the real issue, the proper regulation of the market for force. We are not at any rate dealing with a binary variable – public or private forces – but with a continuous variable, one with many gradations from private security guards at Australian shopping malls, to privately guarded neighbourhoods in South Africa, to community policing in Brazil, to university police at American campuses, to private detectives hired by suspicious spouses or for industrial counter-espionage, to private intelligence services hired by public agencies, to private security companies hired by mining corporations in Asia or humanitarian relief agencies in Africa, to those hired by international organizations such as the United Nations in support of peacekeeping operations. Further more, the United States, to take a prominent example, operates military-nuclear installations and research laboratories under private management, it hires its public armed force on the private labour market, and it builds its considerable arsenal of weaponry in factories run by privately owned, stock-market traded firms. The key in all cases is effective regulation by the public sector (society's government). The emergence of an expanded field of military-related activities served by private-sector actors thus cannot be the reason *per se* for the discomfort many feel with PMCs. In principle, these 'new' activities could be regulated, just as the 'old' ones have been regulated.

Contrary to much scholarly, political and public opinion the debate surrounding the privatization of force is not about economic efficiency – that is a canard – but about regulation, that is, accountability and legitimacy,[20] and an assessment of contracts and transaction costs within the regulatory framework.[21] Sometime a case can be made for PMCs, sometimes (maybe many times) not. Just as there are ample cases of *PMCs* that operate unaccountably and illegitimately, there are equally ample cases of *public* military forces that operate in like fashion. Similarly, just as private *military* companies are sometimes caught doing awful things, so private *non-military* companies are sometimes caught doing awful things as well: the US accounting scandals of the 2000s serve as an example. Further, many of the commentators that express fear of private *military* companies running amok would, one hopes, also express shock at *civilian* leadership if, in the name of democracy, it pressed armed forces into service. The notion that civilian leaders can be as dangerous as (private or public) military leaders should not be new to observers of political history.

The history of organizing human warfare shows cyclical movement: sometimes more private, sometimes more public, always a mixture, rarely the exclusive provenance of one or the other. What changes are the conditions under which this or that organizing principle is better suited to the purpose of war-making, or peacekeeping. Like ethics, the organization of warfare continuously evolves in response to changes in the environment. That environment can be influenced, and in my view it would behoove commentators to lay aside the 'good' or 'bad' mentality with regard to PMCs that since the late 1990s has effectively condemned victims by the thousands to the absence of any humanity at all.

## Conclusion

Most people would agree that world society's ultimate objective, the ultimate benefit sought, is peace and security. If that is the demand, it will be provided in some fashion, 'privately' or 'publicly', even if imperfectly. Even tyrants need to purchase the labour services of their henchmen, and modern nation-states purchase the services of 'privates' on the labour market as well.[22] Neither implies efficiency, but both imply trade. As this chapter has illustrated, trade depends on a very large complex of factors and conditions that must be met for markets to function as intended, to yield the net benefits its participants expect. Ann Markusen (2003) specifies three minimum conditions for economically successful privatization of force: (1) 'the service to be contracted by the public sector must be open to true and sustained competition,' (2) 'the client himself must have a clear understanding of what kind of services are expected,' and (3) 'the client must be in a position to control and verify the services delivered.'[23] This chapter has identified many more. At issue is not *how* force is organized (public or private provision) but how *organized* the force is (regulated)? The use of 'public' force can be just as efficient or inefficient as the use of 'private' force. To achieve proper regulation of force, not its mixture, is the task at hand. This is not a new realization or conclusion,[24] but it is arrived at from a more thoroughly economic perspective than has hitherto been the case.

## Notes

1 T. Lynch and A.J. Walsh, 'The Good Mercenary?', *The Journal of Political Philosophy*, 2000, Vol. 8(2), p. 134.

2 Unless otherwise noted, the remainder of this chapters use 'PMCs' as a convenient shorthand to denote all non-state armed forces and associated services.

3 A sampling of the literature: On taxonomy see, for example, Herbert Wulf, *Internationalization and Privatizing War and Peace*, New York: Palgrave Macmillan, 2005, esp. pp. 43–7, and Robert Mandel, *Armies without States: The Privatization of Security*, Boulder, CO: Rienner, 2002. On mercenary history, see, for example, Janice E. Thomson, *Mercenaries, Pirates, and Sovereigns: State Building and Extraterritorial Violence in Early Modern Europe*, Princeton, NJ: Princeton University Press, 1996; Deborah Avant, 'From Mercenary to Citizen Armies: Explaining Change in the Practice of War', *International Organization*, 2000, Vol. 54(1), pp. 41–72; and J. Brauer and H. van Tuyll, *How Much Does This Castle Cost? Economics and Military History*, Chicago, IL: The University of Chicago Press, forthcoming in Spring 2008. On contemporary relations between and among security providers, private corporate interests, state interests and 'end-user' citizen interests, see, for example, Peter W. Singer, *Corporate Warriors: The Rise of the Privatized Military Industry*, Ithaca, NY: Cornell University Press, 2003, and K.R. Nossal, 'Roland Goes Corporate: Mercenaries and Transnational Security Corporations in the Post-Cold War Era', *Civil Wars*, 1998, Vol. 1(1), pp. 16–35. On discussions about the security gap that failed states and failed UN actions create for PMCs to enter, see, for example, David Shearer, *Private Armies and Military Intervention*, Adelphi Paper 316, International Institute for Strategic Studies, Oxford: Oxford University Press, 1998; K. O'Brien, 'Military-Advisory Groups and African Security: Privatized Peacekeeping?', *International Peacekeeping*, 1998, Vol. 5(3), pp. 78–105, and Doug Brooks, 'Messiahs or Mercenaries: The Future of International Private Military Services', *International Peacekeeping*, 2000, Vol. 7, pp. 129–44 on one side, and N. Cooper, 'Peaceful Warriors and Warring Peacemakers', *The Economics of Peace and Security Journal*, 2006, Vol. 1(1), pp. 20–4, D.J. Francis, 'Mercenary Intervention in Sierra Leone: Providing National Security or International Exploitation?', *Third World Quarterly*, 1999, Vol. 20(2), pp. 319–38, Abdel-Fatau Musah and J.K. Fayemi (eds), *Mercenaries: An African Security Dilemma*, London: Pluto, 2000; William Reno, 'Internal Wars, Private Enterprise, and the Shift in Strong State–Weak State Relations', *International Politics*, 2003, Vol. 37, pp. 57–74; and X. Renou, 'Private Military Companies against Development', *Oxford Development Studies*, 2005, vol. 33(1), pp. 107–15. On international law of mercenaries, see, for example, J.C. Zarate, 'The Emergence of a New Dog of War: Private International Security Companies, International Law, and the New World Disorder', *Stanford Journal of International Law*, 1998, Vol. 34. Among many others, Abdel-Fatau Musah,

'Privatization of Security, Arms Proliferation and the Process of State Collapse in Africa', *Development and Change*, 2002, Vol. 33(5), pp. 911–33 argues that PMCs undermine government accountability, at least in the African context. S.J. Zamparelli, 'Competitive Sourcing and Privatization. Contractors on the Battlefield: What Have We Signed up for?', *Air Force Journal of Logistics*, 1999, Vol. 23(3), pp. 8–17 provides a view on private contractors from within the US Air Force. On regulation, see, for example, *UK Green* Paper, Private Military Companies: Options for Regulation, February 2002; Anna Leander, 'The Market for Force and Public Security: The Destabilizing Consequences of Private Military Companies', *Journal of Peace Research*, 2005, Vol. 42(5), pp. 605–22. Much of the literature addresses these and other themes simultaneously.

4 Few *bona fide* economists have written on PMCs. See, for example, J. Brauer, 'An Economic Perspective on Mercenaries, Military Companies, and the Privatisation of Force', *Cambridge Review of International Affairs*, 1999, Vol. 13(1), pp. 130–46; E. Fredland, and A. Kendry, 'The Privatization of Military Force: Economic Virtues, Vices and Government Responsibility', *Cambridge Review of International Affairs*, 1999, Vol. 13(1), pp. 147–64; and E. Fredland, 'Outsourcing Military Force: A Transactions Cost Perspective on the Role of Military Companies', *Defense and Peace Economics*, 2004, Vol. 15(3), pp. 205–19.

5 On the economics of norm-formation, see, for example, K. Binmore, *Natural Justice*, Oxford: Oxford University Press, 2005. Also see George A. Akerlof, 'The Missing Motivation in Macroeconomics', Presidential address, American Economic Association. Chicago, IL. 6 January 2007, www.aeaweb.org/annual_mtg_papers/2007/0106_1640_0101.pdf, accessed 10 January 2007.

6 See, for example, T. Schelling, *Micromotives and Macrobehavior*, New York: W.W. Norton, 1978.

7 A crucial distinction needs to be kept in mind. The theme of this chapter concerns the private or public *provision* of a good, not the public or private *character* of a good: a rival, excludable private good can be publicly provided (e.g. car license plates); similarly, a non-rival, non-excludable public good can be privately provided (e.g. an over-the-air broadcast by a private radio or TV station). On the question of the character of peace and security as public or private goods, see Brauer, 'An Economic Perspective on Mercenaries, Military Companies, and the Privatisation of Force'.

8 Actually, economics is not limited to the human species. As all living beings have to produce, (re)distribute and consume, economics may be viewed as part of biology. See, for example, G.J. Vermeij, *Nature: An Economic History*, Princeton, NJ: Princeton University Press 2004.

9 For convenience, the 'goods and services' phrase is henceforth abbreviated to 'goods' only. But it is always meant to imply both. Goods are tangible items; services are intangibles.

10 This is simplifying for the sake of exposition. For up-to-date research on consumer 'utility maximization', and consistent 'mistakes' people make, see, for example, D. Kahneman, and R.H. Thaler, 'Anomalies: Utility Maximization and Experienced Utility', *Journal of Economic Perspectives*, 2006, Vol. 20(1), pp. 221–34.

11 This statement may surprise but follows from logic. If every contract breaker who ran away were caught, then running away would be futile, and so would contract-breaking. It follows that, on average, contract-breakers must get away at least some of the time. And from this it follows in turn that the combination of benefits derived from trade (exchange) and benefits derived from appropriation (theft) increases the average benefit/cost ratio to contract-breakers, wherefore the incentive is for everyone to break contracts – in which case voluntary trade declines. Thus, contract breakers must be punished, at least

some of the time. To the uninitiated this may seem fanciful but experimental economics – published in no less a journal than *Science* – confirms that (laboratory) societies with punishment mechanisms trade, benefit and prosper at higher levels than those without (see, Ö. Gürerk, B. Irlenbusch and B. Rockenback, 'The Competitive Advantage of Sanctioning Institutions', *Science*, 2006, Vol. 312(5770), pp. 108–11, and J. Henrich, 'Cooperation, Punishment, and the Evolution of Human Institutions', *Science*, 2006, Vol. 312(5770), pp. 60–1, and the literature cited therein).

12  Both law and culture are costly because they require enforcement agencies. Both require resources or opportunities to be given up to fund or sustain law and culture. Both law and culture require further resources to ensure supervision and protection from abuse. Note that small groups such as families or villages do not have law. They have culture. The logic of law requires an exactitude, a measure of nuance, thoughtfulness and impartiality to uphold a standard of fairness and equal treatment under law that culture cannot afford. Law is expensive. It requires a minimum threshold of people to finance it and is suitable only for larger communities such as states. In contrast, culture makes due: it is 'folk-law', good enough until larger structures or purposes require and justify the addition of a formal codex of law. Neither law nor culture necessarily offer justice, which is a different concern altogether.

13  The attempt by a number of PMCs to build a brand name for themselves is, economically, an attempt to provide information while holding themselves 'hostage' to future *lack* of contracts. If PMCs renege on contracted promises, word will spread and future contracts will be harder to get. The value of any brand stems from this quality of addressing customer uncertainty by reassuring potential customers that the supplier will suffer as well if the demander is not satisfied with the good or service provided.

14  One of these failures concerns the public or private *consumption character* of a good. The traditional example of 'national defence' says that once national defence is provided, no citizen can feasibly be excluded from the consumption benefits (i.e., the use) that such defence offers. National defence is a public good. But if a citizen cannot be excluded from receiving the benefit, there is little reason for him or her to contribute to the cost of provision. The citizen becomes a 'free-rider'. And so does every other citizen. Therefore, funds cannot be collected to provide the good in the first place, even if defence is a desirable good to have. Thus, the *private provision* of a *public good* fails, and it must be provided through a coerced payment, for example, taxation by government. That payment, however, addresses only the revenue side: whether government then chooses to expend the funds to raise a 'public' army or to hire private military and security companies is an entirely different issue, one that is the theme of this chapter.

15  In-person sexual services as distinct from, say, telephone sex, printed or audio-visual sexually explicit material.

16  J. Mueller, 'The Obsolescence of Major War', *Bulletin of Peace Proposals*, 1990, Vol. 21(3), pp. 321–8, esp. pp. 322–3.

17  M Olson, 'Dictatorship, Democracy, and Development', *American Political Science Review*, 1993, Vol. 87(3), pp. 567–76. Also see E. Hutchful, 'Understanding the African Security Crisis,' in A.F. Musah and J.K. Fayemi (eds), *Mercenaries: An African Security Dilemma*, London: Pluto, 2000, p. 212, and literature cited there. The public provision of force *can* but not necessarily *must* be as economically desirable as private provision of force. Both (tyranni-cal) empires and (democratic) nation-states need to raise revenue (taxes) but how these are expended – on 'public' or 'private' forces, or a mix thereof – is a

different matter. Either can be efficient or inefficient; there no a priori telling which will be the case.

18 Machiavelli's *The Prince* is frequently referred to, sometimes cited, less read and rarely understood. Brauer and van Tuyll, *How Much Does This Castle Cost? Economics and Military History*, ch. 3 lays out the details.

19 A.K. Sen, *Identity and Violence: The Illusion of Destiny*, New York: W.W. Norton, 2006.

20 For an early piece on this, see Brauer, *How Much Does This Castle Cost?*

21 See, for example, Fredland 'Outsourcing Military Force: A Transactions Cost Perspective on the Role of Military Companies'.

22 This 'trade' can be involuntary and compelled, for instance by conscripting forces. In that case, the benefit/cost ratio for at least some of the conscripted persons is less than one (for if it were greater than one for all conscripts there would be no need to draft them) and hence an inefficient way of organizing force. On conscription, see P. Poutvaara and A. Wagener, 'Conscription: Economic Costs and Political Allure', *The Economics of Peace and Security Journal*, 2007, Vol. 2(1), pp. 6–15.

23 A. Markusen,. 'The Case against Privatizing National Security', *Governance*, 2003, vol. 16(4), pp. 471–501 quoted in Wulf, *Internationalization and Privatizing War and Peace*, p. 59.

24 See, for example, the papers in Mills, Greg and Stremlau, John (eds), *The Privatization of Security in Africa*, Johannesburg: The South African Institute of International Affairs, 1999; also see Deborah Avant, 'The Privatization of Security and Change in the Control of Force', *International Studies Perspectives*, 2004, Vol. 5, pp. 153–7 and Wulf, *Internationalization and Privatizing War and Peace*.

# 8 Ruthless humanitarianism
## Why marginalizing private peacekeeping kills people

*Doug Brooks and Matan Chorev*

A glaring gap exists in the market for humanitarian intervention between the increasing demand for peacekeeping and stability operations and the supply of an appropriate global intervention capacity.[1] The peace and stability industry (PSI), comprised of private companies providing services in hazardous conflict/post-conflict (CPC) environments, has demonstrated its willingness and ability to help shrink this gap and play an ever larger role in ending deadly conflicts. Unfortunately, misguided opposition to private sector utilization from some academics and non-governmental organizations (NGOs) as well as an ideological distaste for for-profit enterprises has prolonged the supply–demand gap and in turn contributed to ongoing humanitarian catastrophes.[2]

The emergence of the private sector in peace operations is a de facto reality of the post-Cold War international system and security environment, and the associated material and ideational changes that accompanied this new reality. The growth in capabilities of the private sector means that impediments to successful peace operations are increasingly artificial. Systemic, strategic and political realities leave no practical alternatives to the inclusion of the private sector in peace operations alongside traditional international efforts, humanitarian organizations and NGOs. Instead of obstruction, energies should focus on ensuring the most ethical, transparent, accountable and effective use of the private companies in the field through standards and regulation. Ultimately, we must decide if the regulatory goal is to harass private companies for helping fill the gap by providing valuable services in areas of conflict, or to exploit their capabilities to truly revolutionize international peace operations.

## 'Westernless' peacekeeping

United Nations (UN) peacekeeping missions have expanded in both size and scale to address the changing nature of the international security environment. Between 1948 and 1990 the UN initiated only eighteen peacekeeping operations, most 'traditional' interventions, which were very narrow in scope and called for little more than monitoring ceasefires and border disengagement agreements. Since 1990, however, the UN has undertaken more than forty new peacekeeping operations with much broader magnitude and scope.[3] UN peacekeepers are now asked to not only monitor borders but also to help reconstruct failing and failed societies, negotiate cease fires and peace agreements, disarm and reintegrate combatants, undertake security sector reform, promote political reconciliation and effective and democratic governance, and operate war crimes trials. UN peacekeeping capacity has not matched the increasingly exacting demands of member nations, and in fact has actually diminished, as Western nations have grown increasingly reluctant to participate.[4] As the United States Institute of Peace (USIP) Task Force on UN Reform concluded, 'current efforts are bedevilled by both limited capacity and operational challenges.'[5]

Despite the inherent problems, there are some important examples of success where the UN has responded fairly effectively to intractable conflicts. Peacekeeping missions in East Timor, Sierra Leone and the Balkans are all considered qualified successes.[6] All of these missions shared four crucial factors for success: a competent and professional force, Western participation, long-term international commitment and adequate resources. These factors are found lacking in the overwhelming majority of missions.

The United Nations Mission in the Democratic Republic of Congo (MONUC) is a prime example of a mission devoid of the imperatives for success. Since 1998, an estimated four million people have died as a result of this conflict, less to directed political violence than to banditry and gangs prowling around the vast lawless regions.[7] The UN, deployed in the DRC since 1999, has lacked the broad international participation required to field and support a credible force. The shameful withdrawal of Western nations from peacekeeping activities in conflicts of limited national interest has left willing, but less capable, militaries to carry out phenomenally difficult military security tasks. Principal contributors to MONUC have come from countries such as Bangladesh, Pakistan, India and Uruguay, without any significant ongoing military contribution from France, Germany, United Kingdom, the United States or other well-trained and equipped 'NATO-class' militaries.[8]

In May 2003, the UN Security Council authorized an emergency international force to support MONUC by securing Bunia, the regional capital of Ituri province. Although painfully limited in scope, it was an important show of Western support, and revealed what could be done given wider international interest. The French-led European Union troops played a crucial role in securing Bunia and providing temporary regional stability, but departed after less than three months.[9] Most disturbing, the United States, with the world's most capable and powerful military, did not contribute even a single military unit to the MONUC mission. MONUC is the quintessential example of the limitations of modern-day peacekeeping and vividly demonstrates the gap in peace operations.

## The peace and stability industry

The PSI is multifaceted and includes a wide variety of for-profit firms offering remarkably diverse capabilities in CPC environments where conditions, infrastructure, legal structures, and above all, levels of risk, can oscillate rapidly. The industry can be broken down into three major categories of CPC service providers:[10]

### *Logistics and support companies (LSCs)*

LSCs are companies that provide crucial services in CPC environments, including logistics, aviation services, construction, unexploded ordnance disposal, water purification, medical services and so on. Employees of these companies are rarely armed, but if they are it is for self-defence, not as part of contracted services. This category makes up well over 90 per cent of the PSI in value and numbers of personnel.[11]

### *Private security companies (PSCs)*

PSCs are security companies that provide protection for people, places or things. In CPC environments their employees are usually, but not always armed. They work under legitimate mandates or contracts provided by governments or international organizations, and their clients are other companies or sometimes governments. PSC security allows other operations to continue in extremely dangerous environments, operations such as humanitarian relief, reconstruction and infrastructure development.

### *Development and security sector reform companies (SSRs)*

SSRs are firms that provide development services, long-term training and security reform to improve the strategic situation permanently. SSRs usually work for governments or international organizations and train militaries, police, border guards or revamp ministries of defence, provide civil-military training and peacekeeping skills.

It is important to note that a number of companies offer services in more than one of these categories, and some of the larger companies cover all three categories. A number of companies operating in Iraq provide both security details and other services such as unexploded ordnance removal, intelligence services or logistics. Such services often require personnel with different expertise and backgrounds, are based on different contracts, and can face quite different regulatory rules and laws both in Iraq and from their home countries.

The industry has a global presence and can be found in virtually every CPC region, but the ongoing conflicts in Afghanistan and Iraq account for over half of the PSI's estimated $20 billion annual value.[12] While there may be as many as 180,000 contracted personnel supporting the stabilization and reconstruction of Iraq, 113,000 of them are Iraqis – it is important to note that whenever possible the PSI utilizes local personnel known as Local Nationals (LNs) or Host Country Nationals (HCNs) for the vast majority of their personnel. This is a pragmatic policy that simplifies legal complications, reduces costs and benefits long-term stability and reconstruction goals. Thus while Western PSCs in Iraq may have as many as 20,000 personnel in country, only between 5,000 and 6,000 are armed non-Iraqi personnel and less than 2,000 are American contractors, mostly the high-end body guards working for the Department of state contract.[13]

Larger Western militaries maintain peace operation capabilities in-house to some degree. Increasingly, however, they are concentrating their shrinking numbers of personnel into the combat arms where they are most valuable for focusing on the traditional core missions. For militaries trying to enhance their effectiveness or stretch their shrinking budgets, the enormous cost-effectiveness, qualitative enhancements and surge capacity of the private sector makes it an obvious choice for many support activities.

The US government, in an effort to limit its future assistance to interventions in non-strategic CPC situations with US military assets, has focused its energies on enhancing regional peace-building capacities. The 2005 *National Defence Strategy of the United States* asserts that, 'one of our military's most effective tools in prosecuting the Global War on Terrorism is to help train indigenous forces.'[14] Among the programmes initiated was the Africa Crisis Response Initiative (ACRI), a programme that trained and supplied African militaries for Chapter VI peacekeeping operations. ACRI's more robust successor, the Africa Contingency Operations and Training Assistance programme (ACOTA) improved on ACRI with Chapter VII peace enforcement training as well as joint training with other African countries to improve interoperability. As part of ACRI, the private sector was able to provide the crucial French-speaking instructors for francophone African states that would otherwise be unavailable if instructors were drawn solely from the ranks of Special Forces.[15] More recently, the Global Peace Operations Initiative (GPOI) has been introduced which vastly expands ACOTA and goes beyond Africa to include global training. The GPOI initiative aims to train and equip 75,000 peacekeeping troops by 2010.

These programmes have taken place in the context of scarce resources allocated towards Africa, which within the current reality are further stretched to meet competing demands in other ongoing conflicts in other parts of the world. As a result, the US State Department and Department of Defense regularly turn to the private sector with demonstrated success.[16] Simply put, critical US support to African militaries for recent peace operations could not have occurred at all without a heavy reliance on the private sector for training, logistical support and technical services. Private firms trained militaries in more than forty-two countries during the 1990s.[17] Unpleasant and dangerous conditions that often deter national militaries are not dissuading the private sector from bidding on contracts. While some pundits have raised the spectre of private companies abandoning a peace or stability operation due to excessive risk, far more often it has been the state militaries that have withdrawn before the contracted companies.

These capacity-building initiatives are capitalizing on past successes and should be supported by the international community. The industry can contribute in a similar manner in other areas and programmes as well. Indeed, peacekeeping troops from poorer countries, no matter how well trained, are inevitably going to lack exactly the sort of 'off-the-shelf' services at which the private sector excels in terms of capability and cost – including aviation, medical services, ordnance disposal and the like. This is not only true for less-developed countries, as European militaries are increasingly finding that they have downsized to the point that they have no choice but to look to the private sector for critical services when they deploy. In fact, *any* Western military that hopes to have any useful expeditionary capability in the future will have to rely on the private sector for support services, although many thus far refuse to admit this unpalatable reality.

## The advantages of the private sector

In short, the private sector offers faster, better and cheaper services. While the peculiarities of mission, situation and of course competition all influence deployment times and costs, if allowed flexibility for innovation the private sector inevitably finds means for greater efficiencies. The truly international nature of the industry allows vastly greater economies of scale that smaller militaries cannot hope to duplicate. The extensive use they make of experienced former military personnel helps to speed deployment, improve quality and reduce costs.

The average deployment time for most regular militaries is around two to four months, while for the UN it is six to eight months. Private sector companies can expect to deploy for similar missions in two to six weeks. A 2003 plan for the disarmament, demobilization and reintegration (DDR) of Liberian paramilitaries proposed by the private sector in conjunction with NGOs offered to be on the ground in two weeks and operational in six weeks. Months later the operation would have been handed over to the UN itself. The UN, uncomfortable with outsourcing DDR activities, announced its own plan, which, to the misfortune of Liberia's nearly 3.5 million residents, took eight months to get into operation. It is unfortunate that the private sector's speed is often compromised by political constraints undermining markets' efficiencies and costing lives.

The far smaller size of private operations minimizes the 'footprint' and negative externalities of large-scale intrusive interventions. For ethical, legal, practical and financial reasons the private sector prefers to utilize local personnel, thereby developing relationships and supporting the economic rehabilitation of the region. By enabling peace operations with substantially fewer international forces, the private sector helps to minimize the occurrence of human rights abuses by peacekeeping forces. The private sector practice of utilizing locals to a far greater degree than regular militaries or the UN also has the advantage of reinforcing indigenous authority as well as boosting the local economy and laying the foundation for the long-term sustainability of reconstruction efforts.

The private sector acts as a force multiplier for all militaries, no matter where they come from. Beyond specialized training, the private sector can provide technical services which otherwise would be prohibitively expensive for many ministries of defence. In addition, expertise in aerial surveillance, helicopter transportation, mine action and the like, enable a smaller force to project its capabilities to a wider geographical area with greater effectiveness. Security sector reform (SSR) programmes are among the latest projects to be outsourced to the private sector. National governments from South America to Africa are using the services of contractors to design and implement military, police, judicial and personnel reforms.

Clever management of the private sector offers a cost-effective alternative to UN or other state forces. A 2003 Government Accountability Office (GAO) report highlights the US military's three principal reasons for outsourcing.[18] The first is to gain specialized technical skills, which might include mine action, logistics and communications expertise. The second is to bypass limits on military personnel that can be deployed to certain regions. The third is that outsourcing should happen in order to ensure that scarce resources are available for other assignments. Implied in these reasons is that outsourcing will be a cost-effective alternative because it will allow the military to be as efficient as possible.

All this explains why the private sector has been used with such frequency in recent conflicts. According to figures presented by Deborah Avant, during the first Gulf War in 1991, the United States deployed about one contractor for every fifty active-duty personnel.[19] The ratio increased to roughly one to ten in the ethnic conflicts in Bosnia and Herzegovina.[20] In the current Iraq conflict, the number of contractors now exceeds that of U.S. active duty personnel. It should be noted that in Vietnam at one point there were 80,000 contractors working in the field with an even higher contractor to soldier ratio, so the value of the private sector has certainly been recognized in the past as well.[21]

## Conceptualizing the debate

The international community is not immune to the law of supply and demand. National governments are now just one of several key actors in the public sphere, sharing core ingredients of sovereignty with businesses, international organizations and non-governmental organizations. In the age of new multilateralism a greater assortment of actors will be called upon with increasing frequency to fill the supply–demand gap, providing logistical and support functions and other services in CPC environments for peace and stability operations. The private sector is just one of the growing number of actors, but the one with the greatest potential.[22]

The increased role of private sector service companies is not solely a result of a preference for a particular political or economic view. Rather, it has grown as a result of rising demands from the new macro realities of the post-Cold War distribution of power, globalization, new security threats and anachronistic international institutions. Governments are the primary customers of private sector operations in CPC environments, where they are seen as a useful tool to facilitate international policies. Governments use the private sector for these activities as a result of pragmatism, 'better government' policies or simple desperation for specialized services to carry out specific international policies in order to achieve broader goals. Too many analysts overlook the fact that it is governments that make policy; private firms are simply hired to carry out the policies, or more often, just selected portions of the policies.[23]

Critics of private sector involvement frequently assume, or imply that the private sector is 'meddling' in CPC environments of its own volition, ignoring the central role of states in the international system. While companies operating in CPC environments may have a variety of motivations, they are inherently for-profit entities that address demand with legitimate services. While some may argue that the extensive support the private sector provides to the US military is at least partially due to private sector lobbying of policy makers, such arguments do not explain the growing presence of private support for the international peace operations that have little or no on-ground Western presence.[24] Despite the lack of private sector representation in the UN General Assembly or on the Security Council, something that could vastly enhance cost-effectiveness and efficiency, every multilateral peace operation conducted by the UN since 1990 included the presence of the private sector.[25] Impressive private sector performance in the field has led Brian Urquhart, the founding father of UN peacekeeping, to recognize that the private sector is a legitimate actor, and that 'some of these private companies could play an extremely useful role. They have quite a good record ... there are all sorts of special tasks which possibly these companies are better trained to perform than a UN force put together at the last minute.'[26]

## Theory and practice

Despite the clear humanitarian benefit of enhanced peace and stability operations, the use of for-profit private sector in peace and stability operations is obviously not without controversy. The debate includes both operational and theoretical aspects of using private, for-profit firms in volatile CPC operations. Since it is quite clear that the private sector will be utilized to an ever greater extent in the future, it is important to raise and address these issues early. We must find solutions that offer the greatest humanitarian benefit while ensuring that the highest standards with the most capable and professional companies continue to provide their services.

The current conflict in Iraq is unique and should not be taken as a model of future operations due to its unusual size, level of risk and policy value. Operations in Iraq have, however, laid to rest many of the negative myths about private companies operating in highly volatile environments.[27] Contractors have a shown robust ability to persevere in even the riskiest environments and carry out their contracted tasks, rivalling the US military itself in terms of risk tolerance. Indeed, despite more than 917 fatalities and more than 12,000 wounded of all nationalities (as of May 2007), private firms in Iraq continue to provide essential security, move convoys and do reconstruction in the face of one of the most ruthless insurgencies in history.[28] This supports evidence from other peace and stability operations, such as Sierra Leone, in which contractors showed greater resilience to risk than regular militaries, and emphasizes the value the private sector brings to international efforts.

Myths spun about contractors not being able to carry out their tasks quickly or effectively in the face of determined armed resistance have largely disappeared in the reality of supply chains that are more sophisticated and better managed than in any conflict in history. The biggest complaint of government procurement officers concerning private sector logistics is not about their unreliability, but that compared to past conflicts, logistics in Iraq is 'too easy', leaving some officers to voice concerns that troops are in fact too well supplied and too comfortable.[29] The US logistics system has been so successful that both the Canadian and UK militaries have adopted similar logistical arrangements with the private sector, and NATO is looking at a similar relationship.

It is also important to address the theoretical issues regarding the long-term consequences of turning to the private sector. For example, theory raises the private sector's role in increasing the government's proclivity for using the military as a diplomatic tool by lowering mobilization hurdles and political costs. Theory also looks at privatization's effects on the future of the military, suggesting that over-reliance on the private sector will cause militaries to give up vital capabilities necessary should they need to operate without private sector support. Anna Leander of the

Copenhagen Business School ominously warns that the private sector 'will crowd out state institutions and hence fuel the spread of violent conflicts which have their roots in the weakness of states.'[30] Theorists have also gone so far as to suggest that these private services threaten democracy itself by making military operations easier to undertake by the executive branch.[31] Of course there are also the larger theoretical questions such as the role of the state in society and whether it should in fact reserve the ultimate monopoly on violence, as well as the reputed negative effects of privatization in general.[32]

Many of these arguments come from an instinctive mistrust in some sectors towards private sector, for-profit entities. The perspective presumes menace while unconsciously (or consciously) ignoring innate incentives and motivations that dilute such misgivings. In fact, the industry is utilized principally by democratic governments in the furtherance of their policies. The industry does indeed make governmental policies easier to implement and improves their quality and cost-effectiveness, but overwhelmingly these polices are public and recognized as being in the interest of the citizens of the state. When companies work for other countries or international organizations, they inevitably require some form of sanction for their operations from their home government through a variety of overt or administrative means. Failure to ensure legal and governmental consent for their operations could easily result in severe financial or legal consequences, and even the termination of the company.

The question of 'crowding out' state institutions in less-developed countries comes from a largely theoretical perspective with little real-world substantiation. The industry is demand driven, meaning services provided for less-developed countries generally do not exist in the first place and private sector firms are more often filling a gap. This is especially true in peace operations in Africa, where peacekeeping militaries from less-developed countries have been bolstered by private sector aviation assets, training, logistics and medical services – all capabilities that are difficult and expensive to maintain in a standing force and thus are rarely available for peace operations. As a result, far from fuelling the spread of war, the PSI has a critical role in helping to end conflicts.

The private sector has certainly been used as a 'stand-in' capability by Western governments that do not see supplying their own military assets as a viable political option. Fortunately, private sector firms used as 'replacements' by averse Western governments have resulted in extremely positive operational results in places such as Darfur, Liberia and Sierra Leone. In such cases, the private sector is not causing the loss of critical capabilities since the capabilities exist and continue to exist, but they are providing a critical humanitarian service that would be politically unviable for regular militaries.

On a similar note, however, some academics have postulated that the use of the private sector to do successful peace operations somehow lets states 'off the hook' – meaning it releases states from their responsibility to support international peace and stability operations. They contend that only the horror of failed peace operations can motivate states to live up to their international responsibilities. Unfortunately, the horrors of four million Congolese who have died as a result of that conflict have apparently done little to stir international consciousness, and it is difficult to see any change no matter the level of carnage.

It is not and should not be the role of the PSI to make policy, but rather to enable it. The industry should focus its energies on working out the operational issues by cooperating with governments and international agencies in moving forward. The two dialogues must happen concurrently, but the opposing poles of the theoretical debate must not hijack the operational issues because, in the end, lives are at stake. Critics of the industry must constructively outline alternatives – simply decrying the industry is insufficient, counterproductive and ultimately inhumane to millions trapped in conflict and relying on the international community for rescue and survival.

## Ensuring the responsible use of the private sector

The private sector, governments and international bodies can do much to ensure that the use of the private sector in CPC environments is ethical, accountable and transparent. It is the ultimate responsibility of states to write laws, carry out criminal proceedings, make policies and draw the ethical boundary lines that need to be drawn. However, it is the private sector that has united and advocated for more rational legislation that will clarify the expectations of the client and will facilitate positive humanitarian outcomes. Recognizing the link between ethical and accountable behaviour and enhanced business opportunities, leading companies in the PSI formed the International Peace Operations Associations (IPOA), a non-profit association of companies providing critical services in conflict/post-conflict environments. This industry recognizes its responsibilities and is one of a few in the world that actively seeks enhanced regulation. The current legal quandary is not due to the prevaricating efforts of the industry but rather due to the tendency of policymakers to avoid honestly and frankly addressing a nuanced and controversial policy issue.

IPOA members have all pledged to abide by a rigorous Code of Conduct – originally written by human rights lawyers, NGOs and activists – that calls for strict rules for the use of force in line with the Universal Declaration of Human Rights. The Code builds on the 'Voluntary Principles on Security and Human Rights', a compact established through a cooperation of NGOs and the extraction industry and maintained by the Fund For Peace.[33] Similar to the Voluntary Principles, IPOA member companies take the Code of Conduct seriously and see it as both an ethical statement and as a badge of quality. Potential clients should pay attention to these codes and principles that responsible companies use to demonstrate their awareness of their ethical responsibilities when operating in CPC environments.

By its very nature the PSI operates in weak and failed states, and initial operations are almost always under international control. As the CPC environment stabilizes, however, there will be an evolution towards local control. The first step to improving the use of the private sector is to encourage and assist client/host countries to clarify their local law. For example, The Private Security Company Association of Iraq (PSCAI) has been more proactive than either the Iraqi government or the Multinational Force Iraq (MNF-I) in calling for companies to register and to aid coordination efforts and increased accountability.[34] As of June 2006 there were forty-three Iraqi security companies registered in Iraq and forty-five pending. The source of delay is the Iraqi government's ongoing consolidation and electoral process, not industry intransigence. Nevertheless, companies fully expect they will be operating under local law at some point in the process.

In the United States, the chief supplier of private sector services in CPC environments, private firms are subject to a group of conflicting and counterproductive laws and regulations. For example, the weapons and services licensing system known as the International Traffic in Arms Regulations (ITAR) can undermine the contracts written by other US federal agencies. Licensing is important, but the process must allow for companies to deploy quickly, especially for humanitarian operations. The Military Extraterritorial Jurisdiction Act (MEJA) provides for US Federal Courts to prosecute contractors of any nationality who committed a felony crime while working in support of Department of Defense missions overseas. While the United States faces various constitutional constraints in drafting such laws, other countries may be able to set up similar or even improved versions of the law to address their own companies and nationals working on these missions.

We should also not ignore the client's key role in ensuring appropriate private sector behaviour. In order to ensure transparency of the operation, the client can build terms into the contract and financial agreements as well as incorporate legal mechanisms in case of violations.[35] Government clients should create a minimum set of standards for companies, ensuring that they pledge to adhere to a Code of Conduct and favouring companies with a good human rights and operational track record.

While outsourcing to the private sector brings efficiencies and advantages, appropriate oversight will maximize value and quality. Oversight mechanisms must be effective, and one of the early complaints from companies operating in Iraq was that the overseeing contract officers were stretched too thin and served for too short a period of time to be truly effective. Good companies benefit from good oversight, and the industry supports an expansion of such oversight and improvements into their operation to ensure that quality companies are recognized as such in future contract bids.

Another way to improve oversight is to allow the presence of independent monitors on operations, especially for humanitarian operations where armed force is authorized. Companies have long been open to independent monitors being included in contracts, and such monitors can also provide a degree of protection for the company against unfounded accusations. The monitors could be from NGOs or humanitarian organizations and ideally would have an appropriate military or law enforcement background to ensure their quality of oversight.

## Conclusion

The systemic factors that drive the international system and define its reaction to the security environment are the core reasons for the re-emergence of private sector involvement in peace operations. The increased demand has, for better or worse, fuelled the market for force and not its multilateral, international institutionalism alternative. The demand for peace and stability operations is unlikely to abate in the near future as millions of lives will continue to require proactive engagement by the international community. Too often policy recommendations are based on idealism and utopian theories. Bad policy recommendations in peace operations, as opposed to most other fields of research, cost lives. Critics of private sector involvement should keep this reality in mind.

We know that peace operations can work, even lacking a robust Western presence. This is fortunate given the political reluctance and real effects of the downsizing of Western militaries. The current situation requires a pragmatic approach that makes the best use of resources, be they governmental, military, NGO or private sector. Ruthless humanitarians argue that peace operations can only be done in one dogmatic fashion allowing unrealistically limited private sector involvement. Real humanitarians utilize all resources available to ensure the best outcome for the people suffering from the conflicts, including those resources that come from the private sector.

This dialogue must mature; our efforts should not be concentrated on brutalizing for-profit companies, striving for utopian peace operation models, or promulgating abstract theory. Ruthless humanitarianism puts too many lives at risk. We should focus on how best to utilize the private sector's astonishing capabilities to revolutionize peace operations.

## Notes

1 Michael O'Hanlon and P.W. Singer, 'The Humanitarian Transformation: Expanding Global Intervention Capacity', *Survival*, 2004, Vol. 46(1), p. 79.
2 Statement of Larry Cox, Executive Director, Amnesty International USA, 23 March 2006.
3 United States Institute of Peace, 'American Interests and UN Reform: Report of the Task Force on the United Nations', 2005, p. 88.
4 No Western nation with a NATO-class military makes the top twenty of nations providing peacekeepers to UN operations. See the DPKO web site: www.un.org/Depts/dpko/dpko/contributors/2005/dec2005_2.pdf, accessed 9 October 2007; IPS, 'Rich Avoid Peacekeeping for the Poor, Says U.N.,' 27 January 2004.
5 Ibid, p. 11.
6 James Dobbins, Seth G. Jones, Keith Crane, Andrew Rathmell, Brett Steele, Richard Teltschik and Anga Timilsina, *The UN's Role in Nation-Building: From the Congo to Iraq*, Santa Monica, CA: RAND Corporation, 2005, www.rand.org/pubs/monographs/2005/RAND_MG304.pdf, accessed 9 October 2007. See also 'Remarks by H.E. Dr Han Seung-soo, President of the United Nations General Assembly, at a Reception for United Nations officials 21 June 2002, Vienna', www.un.org/ga/president/56/speech/020621.htm, accessed 9 October 2007.
7 IRC, 'The Lancet Publishes IRC Mortality Study from DR Congo; 3.9 Million Have Died: 38,000 Die per Month', www.theirc.org/news/page.jsp?itemID=27819067, accessed 9 October 2007.
8 www.monuc.org, accessed 9 October 2007.
9 Victoria Wheeler and Adele Harmer (eds), *Resetting the Rules of Engagement: Trends and Issues in Military–Humanitarian Relations*, Overseas Development Institute Humanitarian Policy Group, Report 22, March 2006, pp. 61–3.
10 In previous articles the International Peace Operations Association (IPOA), a non-profit, non-governmental, association of leading service companies operating in CPC regions, has used the terms 'Nonlethal Service Providers' (NSPs), Private Security Companies (PSCs), and 'Private Military Companies' (PMCs) for the same categories. The categories have remained useful and generally accurate to how companies themselves divide their services, but the terminology needed clarification. Some other models have been well outlined in Deborah Avant, *The Market for Force: The Consequences of Privatizing Security*, Cambridge: Cambridge University Press, 2005, p. 176. The tip-of-the-spear analogy advocated by several analysts works well within Western styles of warfare, but is weak when applied to chaotic CPC environments or guerilla warfare where any firm operating in the theatre can be attacked.
11 Since 2003, the largest of the LSCs, KBR, a subsidiary of Halliburton, has executed $17 billion in logistics and support contracts. The largest PSC contract is less than $100 million per year.
12 While industry numbers as high as $200 billion per year have been cited, such a high estimate would include literally hundreds of companies that have no more than a fringe connection to supporting military operations – for example, counting drycleaners and pizza delivery restaurants as 'indirectly' supporting Pentagon operations.
13 David Isenberg, 'A Fistful of Contractors: The Case for a Pragmatic Assessment of Private Military Companies in Iraq', British American Security Information Council, September 2004, p. 7. Supplemented by IPOA industry research. Estimates of Iraqi-run PSCs run as high as 150,000.
14 The National Defense Strategy of the United States of America, March 2005, p. 15.

15 Deboran Avant, *The Market for Force: The Consequences of Privatizing Security*, p. 123.
16 Theresa Whelan, 'Remarks to IPOA Dinner', Washington D.C., 19 November 2003, http://www.defenselink.mil/policy/sections/policy_offices/isa/africa/IPOA.htm, accessed 11 October 2007.
17 Avant, *The Market for Force: The Consequences of Privatizing Security*, p. 9.
18 GAO-03-574T, 'Sourcing and Acquisition: Challenges Facing the Department of Defense,' 19 March 2003.
19 Lieutenant General W.G. Pagonis states that the US Army drew up, executed and monitored over 70,000 contracts in Gulf War I. See W.G. Pagonis, *Moving Mountains. Lessons in Leadership and Logistics from the Gulf War*, Cambridge, MA: Harvard Business School Press, 1992, p. 2.
20 Christian Miller, 'Private contractors outnumber U.S. troops in Iraq', Los Angeles Times, 4 July 2007.
21 S.J. Zamparelli, 'Competitive Sourcing and Privatization. Contractors on the Battlefield: What Have We Signed up for?', *Air Force Journal of Logistics*, 1999, Vol. 23(3), p. 11. Also, numerous interviews with Vietnam-era contractors.
22 Although their section on the private sector could be updated and enhanced, these actors are discussed in a remarkably insightful article, Michael A. Cohen and Maria Figueroa Küpçü, 'Privatizing Foreign Policy', *World Policy Journal*, 2005, Vol. XXII(3), http://worldpolicy.org/journal/articles/wpj05-3/cohen.html, accessed 6 March 2007.
23 One particularly interesting anti-capitalist perspective arguing strongly that private sector services are merely a powerful enhancement of state power can be found in Dave Whyte, 'Lethal Regulation: State-Corporate Crime and the United Kingdom Government's New Mercenaries', *Journal of Law and Society*, 2003, Vol. 30(4), pp. 575–600.
24 Indeed, arguments often exaggerate the role of lobbying by companies in the PSI. For example, a report by the International Consortium of Investigative Journalists absurdly implied that L3, a gigantic conglomeration of many different companies involved in many different industries, spent its entire lobbying budget on behalf of its MPRI subsidiary. The International Consortium of Investigative Journalists (ICIJ), 'Windfalls of War', www.publicintegrity.org/icij, accessed 9 October 2007.
25 Deborah Avant, *The Market for Force: The Consequences of Privatizing Security*, Cambridge: Cambridge University Press, 2005, p. 7.
26 ABC Lateline, 18 May 2000.
27 The Department of Defense Instruction of October 2005 should be required reading for any military engaging the private sector in the future, as it addresses many of the issues that have arisen in the conflict. US Department of Defense Instruction Number 3020.41, 'Contractor Personnel Authorized to Accompany the U.S. Armed Forces', 3 October 2005.
28 One need only look at the instances where military logistics balked at highly risky missions to realize that the risk tolerance of soldier and contractor are similar. For example, 'US troops "refused Iraq mission"', BBC, 16 October 2004, http://news.bbc.co.uk/2/hi/middle_east/3748390.stm, accessed 9 October 2007.
29 Personal interviews with procurement officers, Army JAG symposium, 6–8 December 2005. For an interesting perspective on the LOGCAP military logistics contract run by KBR in Iraq see Frontline's interview with an expert on contracting, Professor Steve Schooner of George Washington University, www.pbs.org/wgbh/pages/frontline/shows/warriors/interviews/schooner.html, accessed 9 October 2007. While critical of the mission, oversight and the planning, Prof. Schooner credits KBR with doing a superb job in Iraq.

30 Anna Leander, *Global Ungovernance: Mercenaries, States and the Control over Violence*, Copenhagen Peace Research Institute, June 2001, p. 9.
31 Peter W. Singer, 'Outsourcing War', *Foreign Affairs*, March/April 2005.
32 See Avant, *The Market for Force* for a valuable and nuanced discussion on how the market for force affects functional, political and social control of the state. As she shows, the different approaches to the sector and other variables greatly affect different aspects of control – oftentimes increasing one aspect of control while lowering another. A balance is achievable when the sector is used responsibly.
33 http://voluntaryprinciples.org/principles/index.php, accessed 9 October 2007.
34 Interviews with Johann Jones and Lawrence Peter of the PSCAI, interviews with US officials based in Iraq.
35 Laura A. Dickinson, 'Accountability and the Uses of Contracts', *IPOA Quarterly*, newsletter of the International Peace Operations Association, March 2006, p. 5.

# 9 Private security companies and intelligence provision

*Dominick Donald*

Since the beginning of the Global War on Terror (GWOT) in September 2001 there has been a substantial boom in the fortunes of private security companies (PSCs). Much of this boom has been driven by a hugely increased requirement for protective security, above all in Iraq. The sudden profile acquired by many of the firms providing these protective services has focused considerable media, academic and to a lesser degree political interest on the PSC sector as a whole. This interest has tended to revolve around what might be termed the 'sharp end' of PSC activity, namely, the armed men and women working in protective security details (PSDs) and as convoy escorts, and the legal, ethical and political questions thrown up by having armed civilians using lethal force in a high-threat environment where the state's ability to provide those services is limited.

An area which has so far attracted less attention is PSCs' provision of intelligence services. Yet PSCs have been as important to the US military's intelligence function as they have to its training, logistics or equipment maintenance roles. They also appear to be involved in work for US intelligence agencies – work whose scope remains unknown because of the fact that the contracts remain secret. It might also be argued that some of the legal, ethical and political questions thrown up by PSC provision of intelligence services are at least as important as those surrounding PSCs' use of lethal force.[1]

That said, this chapter will neither pose, nor seek to answer, those questions. The purpose instead is to offer an overview of PSCs' work in the intelligence field, a sense of the wider private intelligence market of which those services are a part, and some possible pointers as to where those services might go. My work on the intelligence and analysis side of a PSC provides me with something of an inside view of the subject matter; on the other hand, the fact that I work for a British firm means I am somewhat unsighted on the US market (which, as will be seen, is by far the largest part of PSCs' intelligence work). It is to be hoped that the chapter will strip away some preconceptions about PSCs' intelligence provision, and offer something of a baseline for those better equipped to address the legal, ethical and political questions surrounding those services.

## Definitions

Before addressing any subject matter related to PSCs or the intelligence world, it is advisable to get your definitions in first. Attempts to study the private security sector are often hindered by imprecise and/or incompatible definitions. For instance, the terms 'private military company' (PMC), 'private security company' (PSC), 'private military firm' (PMF) and 'mercenary' are all widely used – in opposition to each other, as rival conceptual grab-alls for the sector as a whole, and as loose synonyms or analogues, often with no clear sense of where one begins and another ends. Even different departments of the British government use PMSC, PM/SC, or PSC almost as the whim takes them.[2] I am going to add to the confusion by offering definitions of my own, largely because existing typologies either fail to reflect contemporary operational reality, or are so excessively dependent on US models that they fail to fit the (admittedly small) British sector in which I work.[3] My typology is based on the armed forces' breakdown of the military spectrum into Combat, Combat Support and Combat Service Support arms.[4] This is because it is government that is the ultimate arbiter of the Western private company's activities in the security sphere; it is government's turf that is gradually being lost to the private sector and it is government that either tacitly or explicitly licenses these companies' activities, either by using them itself, or (where commercial contracts are concerned) making the consequences of unsavoury deals known, before or after the fact. Given that security is predominantly the preserve of the armed forces, it would seem logical to translate a military typology to the commercial domain.

For the purposes of this chapter a PSC, therefore, is a company which provides what the military would term Combat Support or Combat Service Support security functions, for government and/or commercial clients. PSCs do not provide combat services. A PMC is a company which does offer combat services. Combat is the preserve of the PMC in my typology because combat is the core function of armed forces; it would seem illogical to apply the term 'military' to a company which explicitly avoids offering that core service. The mercenary is a freelance soldier, offering combat services to the highest bidder – a PMC or, most probably, either a brass-plate company or a broker, an armed faction or government with no corporate identity at all. I find the term 'private military firm' unhelpful and have dispensed with it.[5]

It is also important to be precise about what one means by the term 'intelligence'. Government and the private sector have different understandings of the word. For government intelligence agencies such as SIS or CIA, intelligence is privileged information not openly available, obtainable only by covert means. For the private sector, intelligence simply means information turned into useful, relevant intelligence by analysis. This is the kind of intelligence that PSCs tend to provide; when the client is the government, this very basic product may be classified. Perhaps a good working definition of the term for the purposes of this chapter is 'superior knowledge at the point of decision making'.

This chapter will therefore focus on companies which provide superior knowledge at the point of decision making as part of a security function, for government and/or commercial clients.[6] I will not touch on PSCs' work for intelligence agencies, in large part because its scale and depth are unknown. The companies referred to will be from the United States and United Kingdom. This is because while the private intelligence market is obviously far greater than those two countries, and while not all PSCs hail from them, the PSCs which dominate their sector's provision of intelligence services are from the United States, and I am best informed on the United Kingdom. But this chapter will also reach beyond companies that consider themselves PSCs, and beyond what government is accustomed to think of as intelligence. This is because of the nature of, and likely changes in, the private intelligence market.

## The private intelligence market

The private intelligence market in the United States and United Kingdom is the creation of two different client bases with different requirements; two different strands of company have emerged to serve those requirements, and each has different origins.

The first client base is government. This is almost entirely the preserve of the US government; the UK government only turns to outside providers for intelligence assistance as part of contracts to protect British diplomatic personnel abroad, while other governments appear to be only in the early stages of their engagement with the sector as whole.

The US government requirement is met almost exclusively by PSCs (as I define them for this chapter). It began as a requirement for specialized technical and systems support, largely in the 1960s, but over time spread to include the provision of translators, analysts and collators, with US military manoeuvre units having specialized contractor personnel embedded in HQs and some subunits. These personnel can be integrated and trusted to a degree outsiders find extraordinary; one former colleague who worked alongside a US division in Iraq in 2004–05 was informed by its commander that he was considered one of the latter's staff officers, and was treated as such.[7] Increasingly, PSCs provide the intelligence support for key elements of the GWOT, often with high levels of clearance. For instance, in Iraq Aegis provides the intelligence capability behind the reconstruction effort, offering all those involved in the reconstruction of up to date information on attack trends, route security and local political developments through the Reconstruction Operations Centre (ROC) system.[8] Outside Washington, SAIC (Science Applications International Corporation) runs a resources centre which handles all Arabic-language military intelligence collected by the Joint Special Operations Command, on behalf of the Defence Intelligence Agency.[9]

This is not the place to rehearse in detail how the US military became so dependent upon PSCs. In broad terms the contractual, conceptual and ideological baseline for widespread privatization of military services had been drawn by the end of the Cold War, a function of the increasing complexity of modern weapons systems and the Reagan administration's interest in outsourcing. During the 1990s the 'peace dividend' – which saw Combat Support and Combat Service Support capabilities cut to a disproportionate degree, to free personnel for the combat arms – and the desire to limit standing force contributions to out-of-area commitments created gaps that PSCs were only too delighted to fill, particularly on operations. By 9/11 contracting and contractors had become part of the US way of war. According to the then Dean of the US Army War College, speaking in March 2002, 'the US cannot go to war without contractors.'[10]

This is as true of intelligence provision as it is of logistics or vehicle maintenance. By 9/11 US military intelligence depended on contractors to provide translators, technical support, and analysts and collators, to fill gaps in expertise and manpower or undertake projects it would be illogical to allocate to military units. It is almost certain that the US intelligence agencies' increasing shift away from human intelligence and towards technical and signals intelligence during the 1990s will also have spurred PSCs' involvement. These services to the military and agencies alike tended to be provided by firms which emerged from, or served, the defence industry, most having their origins in the 1960s or 1970s. In many cases, contractor and military personnel would work in close harmony, with (for instance) military personnel having responsibility for a function largely undertaken by contractors.

The GWOT accelerated this dependence on PSCs for intelligence support. The requirement to maintain substantial forces on operations for protracted periods of time, and in areas of previously low priority for the US intelligence apparatus, has combined with the huge increase in the volume of open-source material engendered by digitized media, to provide a huge boost for companies offering these services. As an example of the requirement thrown up by the GWOT, the US military needed over 8,150 translators in Iraq and Afghanistan over 2006 – a service the military could not possibly provide.[11] More controversially, there has also been a surge in demand for interrogators.[12] As the head of a US intelligence employment website has pointed out, 'the government is desperate for qualified interrogators and intelligence analysts.... Over half the qualified counter-intelligence experts in the field work for contractors like L3.'[13] At the same time, as the number of contractors undertaking government work in operational areas has surged, so has the need for their own support systems; PSCs with US government contracts to protect US diplomatic and military personnel will be supported by their own tactical-level intelligence provision, usually written into the contract.

The period since 9/11 has injected huge dynamism into the PSC sector. Companies have merged and/or changed direction with impressive speed. Again, these developments have been reflected in the sector's intelligence dimension. For many PSCs, intelligence-related work is only a small part of a much wider government dependence; for instance, CACI – which began in 1962 as an information technology (IT) company – has supplemented its substantial technology-based work by providing US forces in Iraq with analysts as well as contractors to screen detainees before interrogation.[14] Firms which are either stretched to fulfil a new contract in an existing area of activity, or which have been awarded a contract in a completely new area of activity, have subcontracted some of the more specialized areas of those contracts to companies which may not have been involved in security-related work at all. This has created new players in the form of companies that may not consider themselves PSCs. For instance, TCS Translations has moved from providing services for the US Department of Justice in the Continental US to a major contract on behalf of the US Army's Intelligence and Security Command (INSCOM) in Afghanistan.[15] Major PSCs have found that the growth in intelligence-linked requirements has given them a new strand of business: Titan – now subsumed in L3 Communications – appears to have had no involvement in the translation world in 2000; in 2003 it received $112 million for US Army translation services, 6 per cent of its revenues.[16] In an excellent example of how demand for intelligence-linked services has mushroomed as a result of the GWOT, the Titan INSCOM contract amounted to $10 million in its first year; in 2006, it earned L3 $840 million.[17] And smaller, more specialized firms have tried to add value to existing provision; SOS International, a long-standing provider of translations to the National Security Agency and the US Army, now provides higher-level analysis for US Strategic Command and Multi National Forces Iraq.[18]

The result is that the government intelligence market is predominantly served by a dynamic PSC sector almost entirely dependent on government for its survival. But the dynamism is more reflected in the alliances and changing fortunes within the sector rather than many of the companies themselves. The reality of this scale of government work is that the contracts are substantial; bidding for, fulfilling and retaining them require structures that make PSCs ponderous and ill-suited to looking for commercial business. One might suggest this does not matter – apart from the fact that margins on government contracts, which are typically 'cost-plus' or fixed-price, are far smaller than those for commercial ones.[19] Often these firms are not specialists in intelligence provision; they are specialists in bidding for government contracts, and rely on their ability to identify and hire appropriate personnel to either win or ensure they can fulfil contracts related to intelligence.

It is important to bear in mind that the bulk of PSC intelligence provision is far removed from what people tend to think of as intelligence. PSCs do not, to my knowledge, recruit or run agents. Much of their work involves repackaging information for wider dissemination, with military Foreign Disclosure Officers sanitizing classified material before releasing it to contractors for collation, analysis and redistribution. PSCs also take much of the burden of sifting huge quantities of raw data, either through the use of technology or translation services. Even when the client is an intelligence agency rather than the US military, the services provided are often technical; Booz Allen Hamilton, the US consultancy firm, has long undertaken work for the US intelligence agencies, including at present the NSA and the National Geospatial-Intelligence Agency (NGA), but the bulk of that work appears to be in IT-related projects.[20] While much of the material seen or generated may be classified, this tends to be a function of the combined military and intelligence desires to classify everything rather than a reflection of the objective value of the material. The reality is that all users in the information business – whether government or private sector – rely predominantly on open-source material. And in the intelligence world, as in all other areas of US security outsourcing, PSCs do not undertake what that world might think of as its core competence; instead they provide the capabilities that enable that core competence – the recruiting and running of agents and the generating of useful, timely product – to be undertaken more effectively. By and large the focus of their efforts is also felt at the tactical, and very occasionally operational, levels; it hardly ever has an impact at the strategic level of command.

The second client base is commercial. Here, typically, the contracts are far smaller, the margins are higher, and the companies fulfilling the requirements began by serving commercial, rather than government, clients. This sector of the private intelligence market is also far less visible than the government sector; potential clients are often unaware of how commercial intelligence providers might help them, providers are often unaware of what potential clients might want, and the contracts that result rarely attract public attention, even if the client is a major company. British PSCs are disproportionately represented in the commercial segment of the market. This is almost certainly because of their commercial beginnings. British PSCs trace their antecedents to firms set up to protect mining and oil companies in the 1970s; British government work was non-existent before 2003, meaning that firms like Control Risks and DSL (now ArmorGroup) had to be agile. US government business so distorts the US PSC sector, on the other hand, that much of it finds itself ill-suited to bidding for commercial work.

Firms dominant in the commercial sector had a variety of beginnings. Some, such as Control Risks Group, began as providers of protective security and/or kidnap and ransom services. Others with substantial starting capital, such as Diligence or Hakluyt, began by offering advanced due diligence (ADD) services – in-depth investigations of the *bona fides* of potential or existing business partners. (This is an expensive service to offer out of the blocks because of the network of informants needed, often in obscure areas.) Firms such as Kroll began by providing investigative services, including background checks. Other companies, such as Oxford Analytica, had their origins as small subscription purveyors of political risk analysis.

Most of the more successful firms have moved beyond their beginnings. Control Risks turned the requirement to provide tactical-level assessments of the threat in operating areas all over the world into a subscription political risk service. Kroll moved into business and political risk and then the provision of protective security; it is now thought to be moving out of the latter. Oxford Analytica has hugely increased the range and depth of its coverage.

As with PSCs' work for government, it is important to bear in mind the prosaic nature of much of the work for commercial clients. None of the work that PSCs do for commercial clients would meet intelligence agencies' definition of 'intelligence'. Even ADD work, which may well involve the use of covert, legal means – typically, the despatch of a number of different contractors to question sources on different elements of the client's question, usually with some kind of cover story – is aimed at discovering information which is not privileged. The analysis offered by PSCs is based on open-source information, with perhaps some confidential, but not privileged, information. The threat-advisory service offered by companies such as Control Risks and SOC-SMG is, again, open-source. Finally the intelligence cells that support PSDs in the field will depend on a combination of declassified military intelligence, contacts with former colleagues and/or local people, and open-source material.

If the work is so prosaic, why do companies providing these services have commercial clients? Often they are providing what government cannot or will not. For instance, while the US State Department and the UK Foreign and Commonwealth Office provide country threat warnings, these tend to be general and reactive, rather than predictive; a firm proposing to operate in, say, Northern Nigeria may not be overly interested in a government threat warning which focuses on recent events in the Niger Delta. Often they are providing an insight the client does not possess. An assessment based on intelligent observation of the news media is likely to lack the detail and context of political- or business-risk specialists can provide, while a client which already has its own intelligence capability may sometimes require a different perspective on a given problem. Sometimes they are answering a legal requirement; the Sarbanes-Oxley Act, for instance, makes Chief Executive and Chief Financial Officers of companies listed in the US individually liable if a plaintiff employee or dependent can show that the company did not take adequate security measures before an incident. At their best, PSCs are offering a service which clients can not only identify as a protection against potential losses; they are also making it possible for the client to do its job better.

Many firms focusing on the commercial sector have never undertaken intelligence work related to security and would not otherwise qualify as PSCs. Yet the reality of the last five years is that companies such as Oxford Analytica find their efforts becoming part of the fabric of the way that commercial clients examine risk. This is because of the shift in the intelligence market.

## The changing intelligence market

I believe that the next few years will see a number of major changes in the private intelligence market. I am going to focus on two which will affect its most capable providers, in large part because they say a considerable amount about wider changes in the intelligence world over that time. It is highly likely that neither will be visible to those watching the PSC sector, but they may well represent a major change in the services the sector provides, and the level at which they are sought.

The first major change is that there is likely to be a fusion of markets at the analytical end of PSCs' intelligence work; commercial and government clients will start looking for the same product. The GWOT is being fought against a globalized enemy with a comparatively sophisticated understanding of the world's financial structures and a desire to use globalized markets and economic targeting against Western states. At the same time the absence of bloc rivalry and comparative global prosperity have helped to create an environment in which comparatively minor acts of violence have the capability to create the perception of instability. The result is that political risk is perceived to be everywhere, and businesses are increasingly subject to that risk. Commercial organizations and governments alike will increasingly demand a sense of how the political and the economic are affecting each other. It is no coincidence that traditional 'guns and trucks' PSCs, as well as companies involved in other areas of intelligence provision, are increasingly trying to improve their political risk capabilities. Astute PSCs should be able to take advantage of this shift.

The second major change is that there may well be a shift in the level at which PSCs' analysis is sought. Hitherto PSCs' intelligence provision has been required primarily at the tactical level, with the odd contract requiring input at the operational level. I believe that government clients in particular are likely to look increasingly for strategic-level input from PSCs' intelligence providers, because of the nature of the GWOT; the changes in government intelligence machinery; and, above all, the crossover of government need and private sector capability.

Western governments' intelligence budgets are increasing out of proportion to other areas of government expenditure. This budget growth is a natural corollary of the GWOT, where the enemy is virtual, networked, self-sustaining, external, internal, imported and home-grown, all at the same time. Successful counter-insurgency is intelligence-driven, and the

GWOT is above all a global counter-insurgency.[21] Western intelligence agencies are faced with the usual structural difficulties that accompany boom spending, and are having to reinforce existing capabilities or acquire new ones. It is only logical to assume that the private sector can help during this period, particularly if it has existing skills that government has yet to work up, and if there is still a gap between increasing capability and the increasing threat.

An obvious area of weakness is in analysis. In the United Kingdom, for instance, SIS has traditionally only collected intelligence, leaving the analysis to others, such as the Cabinet Office Assessments Staff and the Defence Intelligence Staff; and while these can bring exceptional specialized knowledge to bear, the weight given to privileged information because it is privileged means that the analytical outcome can be flawed. Often this undue weight is also a function of workload (there is no time to look at open-source material) and security constraints (for instance, the Internet cannot be accessed on the same desktop as privileged information). In the United States, a particular problem with the current recruitment boom is that 'the intelligence community is saddled with large numbers of new recruits who are, on average, ill equipped to manage the complex analytical demands posed' by an adversary emanating from a context 'alien to the average American'.[22] The CIA is under post-9/11 Presidential guidance to increase its size by 50 per cent, leading George Tenet, then Director, to predict in 2002 that by 2005, 30–40 per cent of its personnel would have less than five years' service.[23] This compounds a long-standing problem identified by a former head of the State Department's Bureau of Intelligence and Research, that of a shift from long-term research (which thirty-five years ago occupied 70–80 per cent of the analytical work force) to current reporting (which now requires 90 per cent of the personnel). This means that analysts 'have no depth of knowledge to determine whether the current intelligence is correct'.[24]

A PSC team may be able to provide better overarching perspective because the private sector is free of policy baggage and so more able to offer assessments which those within government know will be dismissed – perhaps because of institutional rivalries or a lack of trust – and which therefore may not be voiced, particularly if the messenger is likely to become a target. A PSC may well be able to provide decision makers with the analysis that reflects the knowledge base and perspective of different government departments, but without their complex web of institutional positions and obligations; it can tell them what they know already but are unable to say. They may also want to be provided with something that is fast, authoritative and different from their own output, both to keep themselves informed, and to pep up the internal competition. The virtues the PSC sector brings to other areas of activity – speed, agility, imagination and cost-effectiveness – can also be brought to bear in the realm of intelligence.

Both the US and British intelligence agencies are aware of their analytical shortcomings. Reports on the 9/11 attacks and the use of intelligence before the invasion of Iraq have highlighted failings in analytical structures and procedures, as well as in the relevant services' ability to absorb good, relevant analysis, particularly when it contradicts the institution's collective wisdom. This does not mean that they will promptly turn to the private sector to beef up that capability, particularly where privileged information is concerned. But it is widely known that the US government, for instance, is profoundly unhappy with the use it makes – or fails to make – of open-source material.

Governments may also turn to PSCs because of the distortions of the intelligence process. Governments tend to be a hostage to the intelligence requirements system, where different departments identify the specific subjects on which they would like to see intelligence collected over the next year. The collection agencies then try to acquire the intelligence sought, which the originating departments can analyse. The difficulty with this process is that the requirements are very broad (e.g. 'Chinese attitudes towards the future of Taiwan'). Moreover, whole swathes of human activity are not addressed at all, because no department has put in the requirement, or because the requirement has been removed because of limited collection resources. Conversely, governments can be hostage to the intelligence that they do receive. Secret intelligence may be accorded an importance it does not possess simply because it is privileged information, while open-source material risks being ignored because it isn't. PSCs can therefore be used as an analytical trip-wire; to alert government to issues or locations not at present on its radar, or to reinforce open-source analysis.

These problems all provide pointers as to why government should increasingly call on the services of PSCs as intelligence providers. But they also indicate that analysis will be increasingly important at the operational and strategic levels, where their effect can best be felt. Only in the United States is it at all likely that PSCs will be able to provide analysis based on privileged information acquired by intelligence agencies; most PSC analysis – in the United States and elsewhere – is likely to be based on open-source material and come to policymakers through a different (probably open-source-dedicated) silo. Nonetheless, the gap between state will and state capability – the realm occupied by the private security provider down the centuries – exists; and it is almost certain that some PSC intelligence providers have the agility and resources to fill it.

## Conclusion

PSC intelligence providers work in a largely unglamorous market distorted by US government contracts and dominated by tactical-level requirements. For the most part they serve either government (almost by definition,

US government) or commercial clients; the cost of competing for the former often precludes their being competitive for the latter. Yet it is likely that the next few years will see some changes in this picture. The commercial and government markets, above all for analytical product, are likely to merge to some degree, if only because the subject matter will be the same. At the same time, governments are likely to require better, quicker analysis, and at higher levels. The bulk of the private intelligence market will remain unglamorous and driven by tactical-level requirements; but at its more capable end, the next few years are likely to see a considerable, and interesting, shift.

## Notes

1 See, for instance, Max Hastings, 'We Must Lose Our Distaste for Mercenaries', in *The Guardian*, 2 August 2006, for a knee-jerk expression of some of these concerns.
2 The British Government's Green Paper on the sector, published in 2002, is entitled 'Private Military Companies: Options for Regulation'. However, this title was set down by the Foreign Affairs Select Committee when it called for the document; I have heard British government officials, from several different departments, use all of these terms when discussing the issue.
3 For more detail on this argument, see the author's Whitehall Paper No 65, *After the Bubble: British Private Security Companies after Iraq*, London: RUSI, 2006, pp. 1–6.
4 The combat arms are (in Army terms) infantry and armour – those elements of the Army who close with and kill the enemy. Combat support covers those elements who directly help the combat arms close with and kill the enemy; engineers, artillery, air and intelligence fall under this category. Finally, combat-service support encompasses those areas (logistics, signals, medical services and so on) who support the overall military effort.
5 See note 4 above.
6 Some substantial US PSCs have contracts with US intelligence agencies to protect and support their personnel abroad. This is not intelligence provision. Accordingly I will not address this either.
7 Discussion with British contractor, September 2004.
8 For more on the ROC system, see the author's *After the Bubble*, pp. 70–2.
9 'Clearing House for Arab Intelligence', *Intelligence Online*, No. 535, 24 November–7 December 2006, p. 4.
10 Col Kevin Cunningham, statement at panel on 'New Directions in Civil–Military Relations', 2002, International Studies Association meeting, New Orleans, LA; cited in Deborah Avant, *The Market for Force: The Consequences of Privatizing Security*, Cambridge: Cambridge University Press, 2005, p. 115.
11 'Translation a Rich Niche Market', *Intelligence Online*, No. 537, 22 December 2006–11 January 2007, p. 3.
12 Civilian contractors cited in a number of civil and federal suits alleging human rights abuses in Abu Ghraib and Afghanistan appear to have been working as interrogators, although both the Fay and Taguba reports into the former state that the contractors so employed were substantially exceeding their briefs.
13 Bill Golden, Head of IntelligenceCareers.com, quoted in 'Intelligence in Iraq: L3 Supplies Spy Support' by Pratap Chatterjee, *CorpWatch*, 9 August 2006.
14 See www.caci.com, accessed 9 October 2007, for the company's focus on technology and the breadth of its government clients. The CACI contractors' role in

interrogations is based on information from a confidential source. In fact, the CACI contractors had actually been hired under an IT contract. See Ellen McCarthy, 'Contractors Sometimes Stretch Their Deals', *Washington Post*, 31 May 2004.

15 See www.tcstranslations.com. TCS Translations is described as 'the main subcontractor' for a $730 million contract in Afghanistan in 'Cut-Throat Competition on Translation Market', *Intelligence Online*, No. 538, 12–25 January 2007, p. 1.

16 Jonathan Karp, 'As Titan Mutates to Meet Needs of Pentagon, Risks Become Clear', *Wall Street Journal*, 28 June 2004, p. 1.

17 'Translation a Rich Niche Market'.

18 'Cut-Throat Competition.'

19 In 'cost-plus' contracts the PSC is awarded a sum to perform a specific service, and a set profit margin – usually between 5 and 20 per cent – is built into every expenditure towards fulfilling the contract. This can be an incentive for a PSC to spend more than it needs; on the other hand it provides the PSC, in consultation with the client, the contractual freedom to adapt to changing operational circumstances (for instance, by buying more armoured vehicles if the threat level changes). In fixed-price contracts the price is set, the PSC must perform the task and anything left over is profit. During the height of the PSC boom in Iraq in 2003–04, 30–50 per cent margins were commonplace in commercial contracts.

20 See *Washington Technology* magazine's survey of the Top 100 Federal Prime Contractors in the IT field (www.washingtontechnology.com/top-100/2006/9. html, accessed 9 October 2007), which ranks the company at nine, with nearly $1 billion of defence-related revenue in 2006; also 'US Firms Seek Intelligence Market', *Intelligence Online*, No. 537, 22 December 2006–11 January 2007, p. 5.

21 See John Mackinlay, *Defeating Complex Insurgency*, Whitehall Paper No. 64, London: RUSI, 2005.

22 Douglas Hart and Steven Simon, 'Thinking Straight and Talking Straight: Problems of Intelligence Analysis', *Survival*, 2006, Vol. 48(1), p. 37.

23 Ibid., p. 43.

24 Carl Ford, quoted by Rob Johnston, *Analytic Culture in the US Intelligence Community: An Ethnographic Study*, Washington, DC: The Central Intelligence Agency, 2005, p. 15; cited by Hart and Simon, p. 45.

# 10 Private actors and the governance of security in West Africa

*Adedeji Ebo*

The market for non-state means of coercion is booming. Within and between states, the increasing withdrawal of governments from their primary responsibility for maintaining peace and security has left a security vacuum which is being filled by other actors. Such actors are both profit- and non-profit-making, armed and unarmed, internally or externally located. Singularly and collectively, they impact directly and indirectly on security governance. Among these non-state actors, corporate entities – private military companies (PMCs) or private security companies (PSCs) – occupy an ever increasing share of the research agenda and policy debate.

The freelance security industry has transformed from the traditional mercenary outfits into legitimate commercial companies – in some cases blue-chip corporations; the private security business has rapidly become a multi-billion dollar industry. This phenomenon has tended to distract research interest and policy focus away from other non-state actors (NSAs), including civil society organizations and networks, armed groups and traditional security institutions, who play significant roles in security governance within and across state boundaries.

In much of the available literature, the increasing profile of non-state actors in the governance of security is often limited to its corporate dimensions. This chapter identifies and accounts for those actors that, in addition to PMCs, feature prominently in security governance in the West African sub-region. The chapter defines security privatization as the dynamic process by which actors beyond the state increasingly occupy and respond to the expanded and expanding space arising from the state's increasing withdrawal from a monopolized role in the governance of security. It recognizes that while the political economy of post-Cold War global security is largely responsible for the research and policy emphasis on PMCs, the effect has been to overshadow other private (non-state) security actors, shifting attention away from their roles, and narrowing the agenda of non-state security governance to its profit dimension. This chapter however argues that while PMCs may provide short-term responses, they are, at best, tangential, and at times harmful, to promoting democratic control of armed and security forces, based on the principles of accountability, transparency and popular participation.

In West Africa, other actors have played a significant role in the governance of security. The typical West African state has not been a success in the Weberian sense, and has often itself been a major source of insecurity to the populace. Its monopoly of the means of force has always been artificial and limited. A holistic understanding of security governance in West Africa therefore necessarily extends beyond both statutory security institutions and increasingly visible private security contractors. The increasing privatization of security functions can be attributed to a multiplicity of actors at global, regional and sub-state levels, including international non-governmental organizations (INGOs), foreign-based PMCs, armed groups both in opposition to, and in conformity with the government, locally owned private security companies, civil society groups and traditional security mechanisms.

This chapter seeks to paint a broader and more reflective picture of security governance than is currently discernible in much of the available literature. These two post-conflict states highlight the opportunities and challenges confronting NSAs in security governance. In both countries, the vacuum created by the lack of effective democratic governance was eventually filled by armed rebellion and violent power change. The chapter then considers the limits and challenges of PMC regulation, and advocates a more comprehensive governance agenda. The chapter concludes with some specific recommendations for addressing the gaps highlighted by this analysis.

## The political economy of security governance in West Africa

In West Africa, the state has never had a monopoly of legitimate force. Just as West African states have operated dichotomized regimes of formal and informal economies, the security sector has also manifested both formal and informal tracks. While statutory security institutions have been primarily active in the performance of security functions which secure the state and its institutions, large sections of the population have relied on parallel, less-formalized security structures. What is usually referred to as 'state collapse' does not therefore arise from the failure of the state to provide security to its citizens, for it has never performed this function as such. Rather, in its security dimension, state collapse reflects the systemic and systematic failure of the state to maintain control over its statutory security institutions and to use them for the purposes defined by the incumbent regime.

Indeed, citizens seek to ensure their own security against the threats posed by statutory institutions and everyday threats such as armed robbery. Those with the means, particularly large businesses and rich individuals, resort to the services of local security companies. Yet others engage the services of night guards, a widespread practice in urban centres across the West African sub-region. In rural areas, vigilante groups and various forms of militia keep watch over the population. However, the relationship between these informal structures and formal statutory security agents is often an ambivalent one.

In the end, the challenge in some West African states is that state security institutions, while being legal, are far from being legitimate. Other actors have emerged which, while being legitimate in terms of meeting the security needs of the populace, have questionable legal status. The state's inability to meet its security responsibilities, and the attempts by other actors to fill this space, reveals a gap between legitimacy and legality. It is this process by which other actors join the state in the provision and governance of security that is defined here as privatization. It is a dynamic and complex process, in which the state is both a partner and an adversary, and in which non-state actors cooperate with and compete against each other. The following section identifies the various categories of actors beyond the state which are relevant to the governance of security.

## Typology of non-state actors in security governance in West Africa[1]

The role of private (non-state) actors in security governance extends beyond the dimensions of profit, and includes a multiplicity of actors which function as mechanisms and structures for linking security at different territorial levels, from local (sub-state) to global, and which regulate relationships within society. Governance implies the coordination of this multitude of actors.

### International non-governmental organizations (INGOs)

INGOs have become increasingly visible in the West African security landscape, a role largely ignored in current conceptions of security privatization. In post-conflict contexts, INGOs have influenced the policy environment generally, and Security Sector Reform [SSR] particularly. The impact of INGOs in exposing the challenges of post-conflict peace-building in particular contexts often extends beyond the limited organizational objectives which primarily motivate them. For example, even though the International Crisis Group (ICG) simply describes itself as 'an independent, non-profit, non-governmental organization, ... working through field-based analysis and high-level advocacy to prevent and resolve deadly conflict', its various reports have shaped both local and external actors' understanding of the political and security environments in countries which are often so devastated after conflict that a full understanding of internal and external dynamics is problematic.[2] Yet, other INGOs (such as Amnesty International and Human Rights Watch) are motivated by human rights advocacy but the impact of their work extends beyond their immediate concerns, providing valuable information on challenges of security sector reform after conflict. This is a crucial role in security governance in post-conflict contexts, particularly in view of the dearth of local research institutions and think-tanks.

Other INGOs focus on activities which facilitate the SSR processes more directly. For example, the Geneva Centre for Democratic Control of Armed Forces (DCAF) has worked with the Ministry of Justice and the United Nations Mission in Liberia (UNMIL) to facilitate a national dialogue on SSR and with the Governance Reform Commission to support an inclusive SSR programme. DCAF is also directly engaged in research and practical initiatives to promote democratic governance of the security sector within and among states in West Africa, including a working partnership with ECOWAS to develop a West African Code of Conduct for Armed Forces and Security Services.[3]

### *Mercenaries and private military companies (PMCs)*

PMCs are increasingly now being used by supplier governments as tools of foreign policy by proxy, for the provision of logistical and other support services by peacekeeping organizations, by humanitarian agencies, and by extractive commercial ventures. The list of clients includes sovereign governments, the United Nations, the ICRC and a host of other international organizations. Within Africa for example, Military Professional Resources Inc. (MPRI) has, under contract from the US Government, conducted military training in Nigeria, while Pacific Architects and Engineers (PAE) is under contract to provide logistical support for regional peacekeeping in West Africa, with a depot in Freetown, Sierra Leone. UNHCR, UNDP, WFP, UNICEF and ICRC are some of the international organizations which routinely employ the services of PMCs.

### *Local mercenaries*

In addition to the activities of foreign private security outfits, West Africa features indigenous and locally located mercenaries, moving freely from conflict to conflict in the sub-region. Relative to foreign mercenaries, they are more integrated into local societies, generate better intelligence and are better adapted to guerrilla warfare given their superior local knowledge. They also possess a much higher level of resistance to malaria and typhoid fever, often the bane of foreign Western personnel. These mercenaries have been active in virtually all armed conflicts since the end of the Cold War, propelled by widespread poverty and inconclusive

DDR programmes which emphasize disarmament and demobilization at the expense of reintegration and rehabilitation.

## Criminal networks

As already discussed, the West African sub-region is characterized by a vibrant informal sector. In its security dimension, this informal sector centres around cross-border crime. Indeed, transborder criminal networks have played an infamous role in security governance in West Africa, straining relations between and within states, and entrenching a sense of anxiety among the populace. The challenges of transborder crime were articulated in the UN Secretary General's 2005 Report on West Africa.[4]

## Civil society

Several issues arise in considering the role of civil society in security governance in West Africa.

First, protracted military rule and civilian autocracy deprived civil society of the necessary space for participation. Particularly in the security sector, West African governments and military institutions adopted an exclusionary approach. The extent of civil society involvement was often limited to seeking a return of the military to the barracks. As Hutchful has observed, 'the concept of governance itself has only just begun to percolate into the security sector.'[5] Consequently, civil society involvement in security governance is slight.

Second and relatedly, in much of West Africa SSR remains a rather specialized subject on which there is limited expertise and interest. Yet, civil society in West Africa has been vibrant.[6] This can be accounted for by the opening up of the political space enabled by the wave of democratization following the end of the Cold War, the end of military rule in West Africa and the sheer initiative taken by individuals (discussed below) with a commitment and interest in facilitating popular participation in security sector governance. However, civil society is by and large externally dependent financially, which raises questions regarding the extent to which the agenda of civil society is internally generated or may be directed/influenced by donors.

## Domestic private security companies

Beyond imported security services, there has also been a boom in West Africa's local private security services. In Nigeria, it is estimated that there are between 1,500 and 2,000 PSCs, employing in excess of 100,000 personnel.[7] In fact, it has been suggested that 'security is now the second largest source of revenue in Nigeria, surpassed only by oil and gas.'[8]

Across West Africa, the continuing lack of confidence in public security institutions is sustaining a marked and persistent increase in the patronage of commercial security services. The role of domestic private security companies in security governance in Sierra Leone and Liberia are discussed in detail below.

### Non-state armed groups

Particularly since the end of the Cold War, armed NSAs have emerged, either in competition or in cooperation, to share security space with the state. The lack of a consensus and clear policy options on engaging armed NSAs by states and the international community remain a major challenge. In the increasingly arduous task of maintaining control – much less monopoly – over the use of force, several West African states have either had to resist the challenges posed by armed opposition groups[9] or have enjoyed the support of armed actors outside the state's formal control.

### Individuals

Analyses of processes of policy change too often focus on formal state structures and processes. The importance of key individuals who act as 'micro-level sources of influence and change'...playing the role of 'bridges, gateways and routers' is essential but less well recognized.[10] The debate on security governance in West Africa, particularly attempts to generate intellectual debate and policy frameworks for steering security governance in a democratic direction, has benefited from the contributions of some key individuals, whose activities and activism, singularly and collectively, have influenced the prospects for democratic governance of the security sector in West African states and societies. Even though such key individuals usually function under the auspices of particular organizations, their individual contributions extend beyond their official institutional affiliations. In the case of West Africa, key individuals such as Funmi Olonisakin, Eboe Hutchful, Kayode Fayemi, Ishola Williams, Abdoulaye Bathily, Boubacar N'Diaye, to mention a few, have through a combination of activism and scholarship provided leadership and opened the space for advocacy and study of good governance of the security sector.

The following section on Sierra Leone and Liberia identifies the trends and challenges raised by this multiplicity of actors in security governance, particularly in states emerging from years of protracted conflict.

## Sierra Leone and Liberia

A focus on Liberia and Sierra Leone as comparative case studies aptly illustrates the role of private (non-state) actors in security governance in contemporary West Africa. This section examines how various NSAs in the two countries are filling the security gap resulting from the debilitating context of rising insecurity and declining state capacity to respond.

Sierra Leone is, like most other West Africa states, a former colony of a European power. Liberia, on the other hand, stands out as the oldest republic in Africa, having never been formally colonized by a foreign power. However, even though Liberia and Sierra Leone followed different paths to political independence and self-rule, the differences between them are more apparent than real. Founded by freed American slaves in 1822, followed by a declaration of independence in 1844, Liberia has experienced its own form of 'black colonialism'. The Americo-Liberian settlers played the role of colonizers, with a mission to bring 'civilization' and Christianity to the indigenous population who constituted the vast majority (95 per cent) of the population. Liberia manifests the characteristics of the typical post-colonial African state: kleptocracy, nepotism, authoritarianism and the pursuit of regime security as national security. The vacuum created by a lack of good governance in both countries was eventually filled by armed rebellion and violent power change, following protracted civil wars mounted by a critical mass of desperate enemies in opposition to the state. The already-weakened state was unable to respond effectively to the double task of combating armed insurgency and guaranteeing public safety. The legitimate use of force, far from being monopolized by the state, had become shared between the state and a variety of other actors.

In Sierra Leone, the National Provisional Ruling Council (NPRC) government was faced by January 1995 with the challenge that Revolutionary United Front (RUF) rebels had captured the country's three major diamond mines and were making a steady move on the capital, Freetown. By March of that year, the South African company Executive Outcomes (EO) was hired by the government to directly engage the rebels. With support from the ECOWAS Monitoring Group (ECOMOG) and the Kamajor militia, EO was able to drive back the rebels and retake the mining areas. Elections were held in February/March 1996, with Ahmed Tejan Kabbah elected President. RUF insistence at the peace negotiations – signed November 1996 – led to the termination of the EO contract effective 31 January 1997.[11] On 25 May 1997, the Kabbah government was overthrown in a military coup, with the new government forming a coalition with the RUF rebels.

From a governance perspective, EO's operational successes rapidly afforded it a disproportionate and arbitrary influence within the state, raising issues of accountability and conflict of interest. According to Paul Richards, 'Executive Outcomes' influence over strategy was large.... In effect, Executive Outcomes appears to have been making government policy on the war, perhaps mainly to prolong its lucrative contract, or to avoid mineral concessions becoming an issue in peace negotiations.'[12] EO was replaced by London-based Sandline International.[13] With the objective of restoring Kabbah to power, Sandline, allegedly with the knowledge of the British government and in direct violation of UN Security Council Resolution 1132 which imposed an arms embargo on Sierra Leone, imported some 35 tons of assault rifles, ammunition and mortars into the country.[14] This became known in the United Kingdom as the 'Arms to Africa Scandal'. Although the operation to return Kabbah to government was eventually led by ECOMOG troops and the Kamajor militia before the arrival of the illegal weapons imports, the deal showcased the dilemmas of patronizing PMCs. Of particular concern was Kabbah's deal with Sandline, made while in exile in Guinea. In return for an initial $10 million in arms and mercenary support to restore his administration, Kabbah agreed to cede 30 per cent of the country's diamond-ferrous landmass (worth $200 million) to Sandline's mining partners, the Toronto-based British–Canadian company DiamondWorks.[15] In addition, Executive Outcomes' twenty-one-month operation had cost the government $35 million on top of the diamond concessions granted to Branch Energy, a sister company of EO.

In contrast, Liberia's encounter with PMCs has been mostly limited to post-conflict reconstruction, though there are records that MPRI was providing military training to the Liberian Army by 1995.[16] According to the Liberian Comprehensive Peace Agreement (CPA) of August 2003, 'the parties also request that the United States of America play a leading role in organizing this (armed forces) reform programme.'[17] The American government's reluctance to engage directly in non-strategic areas, and the compelling need to not abandon a traditional client state, informed the use of PMCs as tools of foreign policy by proxy.[18] Consequently, the US State Department outsourced American post-conflict involvement in Liberia to two American companies: DynCorp International, responsible for vetting, recruitment and provision of basic training to the new Liberian armed forces, and PAE, responsible for specialized advanced training, equipment, logistics and base services. The $95 million training package is administered by the US State Department.[19]

The demobilization of over 13,000 former-combatants was completed in December 2005. DynCorp has completed the rebuilding of the Barkley Training Centre and, as of 1 June 2006, had considered 4,265 applications for the envisaged 2,000 strong army. By 2007, only 102 new soldiers had been trained. As of the same date, 1,776 applicants had passed the initial screening.[20] PAE is in Phase 2 of a five-phase building process at Camp Schieffellen, with single-soldier housing, ammunition and weapon-storage facilities nearing completion.[21]

In terms of accountability and local participation, Dyncorp publishes names, pictures and records of potential recruits to solicit public information on their human rights records. There is also civilian membership on the Joint Personnel Board that ultimately determines the selection of successful candidates for recruitment.[22] However, governance challenges remain. Liberian civil society has been critical of their lack of involvement in the security sector reform process generally, and in the work of

Dyncorp in particular. A prominent Liberian civil society leader engaged in peace and security issues stated:

> Civil society has not been involved in any meaningful sense in security sector reform in Liberia. In fact, not only is civil society not involved, there is no public debate on these matters. Dyncorp activities is [sic] shrouded in secrecy. We have been trying for almost a year to obtain a copy of the MoU that [brought DynCorp to] Monrovia but so far we cannot get that document, in spite of the high level access we have in government. I guess we are led to believe that since we are not paying for any of these reform undertakings, we cannot participate in the process and we need only be grateful to those who are paying the cost.[23]

Another prominent civil society leader attempted to account for the apparent lack of civil society participation in the military-restructuring process:

> During the early stages of Dyncorp's operations in Liberia, they attempted to engage civil society regarding their mission. However, some civil society organizations had problems regarding Dyncorp's past activities in other countries. Hence, some conflict arose, which I believe could have prompted Dyncorp to marginalize CSOs.[24]

An UNMIL source similarly noted that 'many observers even within UNMIL will raise concerns about how much public information there is on the activities of Dyncorp' but conceded that 'Dyncorp is slowly picking up the message about the need for more openness in the whole reform process.'[25] In this regard, Dyncorp has been making efforts to use some public fora as means of interacting with the Liberian public.[26] There are expectations by Liberians and several interlocutors that the report of the United States-funded security sector review, which was conducted by RAND Corporation, would form the basis of more rigorous public consultation.[27]

The operations of locally owned private security companies have increased dramatically in both Liberia and Sierra Leone as a direct result of protracted conflict. Private security services in Liberia tend to be wholly locally owned. According to Ministry of Justice guidelines, Liberian birth or naturalization is required in order to operate a private security outfit. It is estimated that there were five security companies before the war, eleven during the war, and there are now some fifteen security companies in Liberia. Due perhaps to a more relaxed legal framework, the increase in the private security business in Sierra Leone has been more rapid. There were only two locally registered security companies in Sierra Leone before the war. Official estimates put the number of security companies currently in Sierra Leone at thirty, though there are reputed to be more, employing some 5,000 personnel.[28] In both Liberia and Sierra Leone, security companies serve businesses and affluent residences, international organizations and extraction companies in the mining and logging industry. Also, the evolution of local commercial security entities has been closely related to, and has largely emanated from, the protection of natural resource extraction interests.

While the legislative framework in Liberia seeks to indigenize the security industry, the development of local capacity and participation has been uneven, and the local security industry has largely escaped serious policy attention since the end of the war in both countries. There are no agreed professional standards, and the quality of training varies widely. Sierra Leone's more permissive legal framework – reflected in the National Security and Intelligence Act of 2002 – in principle permits security companies to possess arms, but in practice this is negated by the UN Arms Embargo of 1998.[29] It would seem that the links between locally based and externally located private security businesses and interests are likely to strengthen rather than diminish. As the gospel of marketization takes stronger hold, and African states continue to struggle with even the most minimal security challenges, private security actors will occupy an increasingly strategic and expanding space in security governance.

## Between regulation and governance: towards a more integrated policy framework

The challenge of regulating private actors, particularly PMCs, is multi-faceted and largely context specific. This chapter focuses on post-conflict environments (as illustrated by Liberia and Sierra Leone) where institutional mechanisms are too weak to assert effective authority and oversight over private actors.

The regulation of PMCs, even if plausible, is of marginal significance to a democratic governance framework which is responsive and responsible to the security needs of the states within which PMCs operate. Local governance institutions have no input into contract negotiations, contract monitoring or evaluation. To the extent that they exist, reporting channels lead to home governments' institutions. As was demonstrated in the case of Liberia, civil society participation in the reform and oversight process is often marginal due not simply to incapacity, but to the lack of space for their involvement. Parliamentary oversight has been far from effective, such as in Liberia where the relevant oversight committees have not had access to the relevant contractual documents that form the basis of PMCs' presence in the country. Undoubtedly, therefore, parliamentary capacity and civil society engagement would be two major deficits to be addressed in locating the activities of PMCs effectively within the governance structures of recipient states.

Given their externalities, PMCs are not, and cannot form the basis of democratic governance of security in West Africa. They are externally owned, externally manned and externally based, thus not easily amenable to oversight beyond that of their own shareholders. Their objective role is a function of the length of their contracts, their corporate interests and the dictates of their clients. Given their external orientation, PMCs are neither responsive nor responsible to local governance by the countries and societies in which they operate.

The current debate on regulating PMCs does not place the activities of PMCs within the orbit of control by oversight institutions and mechanisms within the states and societies where they operate. The net contribution of PMCs to democratic governance is negative because they drain resources from public security forces and weaken the incentives for governments to provide security for the local population and to subject themselves to local oversight and control mechanisms within the legislature and civil society. Thus, PMCs undermine the building of state institutions which are essential for both operational efficiency and democratic control in the medium and long term.

Perhaps most significantly, the private sphere of security governance in West Africa includes a multiplicity of actors beyond PMCs. Regulatory regimes for PMCs would therefore be necessary but still insufficient for addressing the challenges of private security governance. The activities of INGOs, for example, are a mass of uncoordinated initiatives by foreign interlocutors. Organizations operating in specific areas such as transitional justice, justice and penal reform, parliamentary capacity-building, or military and police training all approach the reform of the security sector based on individual institutional priorities and cultures. In addition, locally owned private security companies operate largely outside the prevalent oversight mechanisms. With regard to Sierra Leone, for example, neither the Security Sector Review Report nor the draft Sierra Leone Peace Consolidation Strategy addresses the phenomenon of local commercialization of security, despite the increase in their operations. Yet, given the inability of many West African states to fulfil their security functions, and propelled by the global market, these commercial firms are likely to feature more prominently in security governance in the sub-region.

Local mercenaries operate freely across West African borders and remain outside any formal system of control (or even attention). In the absence of transborder mechanisms for controlling the cross-border crime, the role of civil society in particular takes on a strategically important dimension in advocating a consolidated policy approach by West African states. The role of civil society is essential in offering informed policy alternatives which serve the security needs of the populace as well as those of the regime and the state. Civil society therefore has the role of bridging the gap between the state and the society. In much of West Africa,

154   *Adedeji Ebo*

this is a particularly wide gap. Yet, apart from a limited circle of experts and expertise, civil society has only featured marginally in security governance.

With regard to non-state armed groups, the prospects for control of them by the state will be a function of the extent to which governments fulfil their social contract with the populace. The proliferation of armed groups is a direct consequence of governance deficits. Nevertheless, traditional security institutions remain a potential mechanism for addressing accountability deficits and bringing security governance closer to the populace. However, the gap between rural and urban, and between formal and informal structures and processes, may need to be bridged.

The multiplicity of actors engaged in security governance point to a need to re-evaluate the Weberian assumptions underlying the role of the state in security governance. The monopoly of legitimate use of force by the state has been eroded at two levels by the increasing profile of non-state actors. The first, accelerated by the end of the Cold War and the rise of globalization, is the commercialization of security. The second relates to the role of local security governance actors. Particularly in post-conflict states such as Liberia and Sierra Leone, legitimate questions arise regarding the seeming futility of security policy in aiming to establish or re-establish state monopoly of force. In view of the increasing profile of non-state actors in security governance, a more feasible role, particularly for weak states, appears to be that of an umpire and regulator of the competing and conflicting approaches and interests of various security governance actors. This latter role is increasingly being taken on by the state, while prospects for the overall goal of monopoly of legitimate force become increasingly far-fetched.

## Conclusion and recommendations

Based on the political economy of security commercialization, this chapter has argued that commercial security and military services, provided within and between states, is likely to feature more prominently and occupy even more space in security governance in West Africa. Indeed the increasing prominence of the private security industry, featuring both local and foreign businesses, is an offshoot of a global phenomenon reflecting powerful financial and political interests. As West African governments struggle with their security responsibilities, local and foreign actors will continue to emerge to fill the security vacuum left by state incapacity. This gives rise to corresponding sets of governance challenges. With specific regard to PMCs, their externalities infuse them with accountability deficits which can only be partially addressed through regulation. Characteristically, governance institutions in the country of operation do not play a role in the negotiation of the contracts of PMCs. The chapter has argued that PMC oversight is problematic, particularly in regards to oversight mechanisms in their countries of operation. In the final analysis, PMCs hinder the prospects for democratic governance because their ownership and corporate structure is distant from, and thus immune to, governance mechanisms in their countries of operation. The situation is further complicated, and to an extent, explained by the frailty of oversight institutions in post-conflict states.

With about half of West Africans under thirty, the phenomenon of roaming bands of indigenous mercenaries is a direct function of youth unemployment in the sub-region. The widespread informalization of security implies that policy bridges would need to be built between informal security institutions and statutory oversight mechanisms. For example, the widespread use of 'watchmen' and 'guards' needs to be better coordinated and brought under formal control mechanisms. Informal and often illegal local arms fabrication needs to be more effectively monitored and addressed by state security institutions. While PMCs offer operational utility in the short-term, longer-term approaches need to be undertaken to address the root causes of conflict and insecurity. On this basis the following policy recommendations are proposed:

*Support local private security companies*: Given the external location and orientation of international PMCs (usually based in the United States and Europe), and the consequent distance between them and governance mechanisms in the countries of operation, technical assistance and financial support should be directly targeted at developing local and indigenously owned private security companies. Efforts should be geared at creating and enhancing professional associations and setting professional standards to address uneven capacity in the industry.

*Create and enable sub-regional PMCs*: The history of military coups and the resultant early retirements from the military has left the West African sub-region with a wealth of military experience which remains largely unutilized. Senior retired West African military officers should be encouraged and assisted to establish PMCs with a regional area of operation. Their location within the sub-region should contribute to bridging the governance gap and bringing the benefits of security closer to the populace, thus enhancing the prospects of accountability.

*Parliaments and contract oversight*: Parliaments in West Africa should play more direct roles in PMC contract oversight, through the inclusion of details of contractual terms and contract monitoring and evaluation in the bracket of issues covered by parliamentary committees on defence and security. Enhancing the technical and research capacities of parliaments is a necessity.

*Expanding local participation*: In the particular case of Liberia, the Report of the national security review by RAND Corporation should form the basis of extensive public consultation and local participation in the reform process. The report should therefore be disseminated as widely as possible within Liberia.

*Facilitating regional civil society networking*: Donor assistance should be channelled towards building the capacity of civil society to play more active roles in security sector governance, in particular, supporting regional networks and think-tanks that can address issues of security privatization alongside other security governance challenges. Emphasis should be placed on enhancing technical skills for local resource mobilization in order to address dependency on external finance.

*Addressing the 'youth question'*: In order to systemically address the problem of local mercenaries in the sub-region, West African governments should make youth empowerment a deliberate target of policy by developing and adopting a youth policy, and by assessing the impact of government decisions on youth employment. The selective recruitment of former fighters into local PSCs, if handled sensitively, is a useful means of converting the military experience of the youth into a productive economic activity.

*Small Arms Register*: As in the case of EO in Sierra Leone, the movement of arms into and out of zones of conflict occurs outside the existing regional and state arms-control mechanisms. Consideration should be given to the opening of an arms register for PMCs taking part in humanitarian assignments and peacekeeping in any part of West Africa. Thus, the governance of security would be directly linked to small arms control in the sub-region, such as the ECOWAS Small Arms Convention.

*ECOWAS guidelines on PMCs*: ECOWAS should consider articulating guidelines on PMCs for compliance by member states, and other states deploying PMCs for operations in West Africa. Such guidelines should include oversight mechanisms for all PMCs operating in West Africa. For example, with regard to DynCorp operations in Liberia, an oversight committee could comprise ECOWAS, the UN Peacebuilding Commission, ICRC, US Government representatives and DynCorp corporate leadership.

This chapter set out to expand the conceptualization of privatization of security beyond the confines of commercialization. The chapter observed the widespread policy and research focus on PMCs, but argued that privatization of security is more complex and involves a multiplicity of actors beyond PMCs. While non-state actors cannot replace the state, the state also cannot and should not perform on its own the entire range of security functions without the engagement of NSAs in one form or the other.

## Notes

1 Acronyms are spelled out in the list at the beginning of this book.
2 See www.crisisgroup.org/home/index.cfm, accessed 11 October 2007 for various reports on West African conflicts.
3 See www.dcaf.ch/activities/african-programme.cfm?nav1=3, accessed 11 October 2007.

4 Progress Report of the Secretary General on Ways To Combat Sub-regional and Cross-Border Problems in West Africa, S/2005/86, 11 February 2005. According to the report, such challenges include, *inter alia*, the use of child combatants and mercenaries, Small-arms and light-weapons proliferation, impunity for perpetrators of human rights abuses, youth unemployment and corruption.

5 Ibid., p. 35.

6 For example, the African Security Sector Network (ASSN) is a continent-wide network active in research and policy dialogue, with an active sub-regional component in West Africa. In West Africa it facilitates South–South exchanges between parliamentarians, practitioners and scholars. In Liberia, ASSN, in partnership with the University of London and DCAF, has facilitated a National Dialogue on Security Sector Reform and is working with these same partners to lend technical support to the work of the Liberian Governance Reform Commission. The West African Network for Security and Democratic Governance (WANSED), created in 2004, describes its vision as the achievement of democratic governance of the security sector in West Africa. Its activities include research, training, political dialogue and policy advocacy. The West African Action Network on Small Arms (WAANSA) also exists to coordinate and facilitate civil society action in the specific area of small-arms control. In 2003, the West African Civil Society Forum (WACSOF) was established to facilitate civil society interface with ECOWAS, and to further strengthen civil society networking in West Africa.

7 Rita Abrahamsen and Michael Williams, *The Globalization of Private Security, Country Report: Nigeria*, ESRC, January 2005, p. 3.

8 Ibid., p. 3.

9 Caroline Holmqvist has categorized armed NSAs as including 'rebel opposition groups, local militias (ethnically or otherwise based), vigilantes, warlords, civil defence forces and paramilitary groups (when such are clearly beyond state control)'. Caroline Holmqvist, 'Engaging Armed Non-state Actors in Post-conflict Settings', in Alan Bryden and Heiner Hanggi (eds), *Security Governance in Post-conflict Peacebuilding*, Lit Verlag: Munster, 2005. p. 45.

10 Keith Krause, 'Facing the Challenge of Small Arms: The UN and Global Security Governance', in Richard M. Price and Mark W. Zacher (eds), *The United Nations and Global Security*, Houndmills, NY: Palgrave Macmillan, 2004, p. 31.

11 For details, see D.J. Francis, 'Mercenary Intervention in Sierra Leone: Providing National Security or International Exploitation?', *Third World Quarterly*, 1999, Vol. 20(2), pp. 319–38.

12 P. Richards, 'The Return of Great Britain to Sierra Leone', *African Geopolitics*, 2004, No. 15–16, Summer/Fall 2004, availble at: www.african-geopolitics.org/home_english.htm, accessed 11 October 2007.

13 Gerry Cleaver, 'Subcontracting Military Power: The Privatization of Security in Contemporary Sub-Saharan Africa', *Crime, Law and Social Change*, 2000, Vol. 33(1–2), March 2000, p. 143.

14 Ibid. and Richards, 'The Return of Great Britain to Sierra Leone' and Abdel-Fatau Musah, 'Privatization of Security, Arms Proliferation and the Process of State Collapse in Africa', *Development and Change*, 2002, Vol. 33(5), pp. 911–33.

15 See Abdel-Fatau Musah, 'Small Arms: A Time Bomb under West Africa's Democratization Process', *The Brown Journal of World Affairs'*, Spring 2002, Vol. IX I(1), p. 240.

16 'Private Military Companies: Options for Regulation', London, 2002. Annex A, Mercenaries: Africa's Experience 1950s-1990s, p. 33.

17 Article VII (1b).

18 Following the deaths of American troops in Somalia in 1993, a Presidential Directive was signed which provides that US troops would not be sent to hostile environments unless specific national interests are at stake. See Damian Lilly and Michael von Tangen Page (eds), *Security Sector Reform: The Challenges and Opportunities of the Privatisation of Security*, London: International Alert, 2002, p. 16.

19 Nicolas Cook, 'Liberia's Post-war Recovery: Key Issues and Developments', CRS Report for Congress, Updated 5 May 2006, p. 10.

20 Eleventh report of the Secretary general (to the Security Council) on the United Nations Mission in Liberia, S/2006/376, 9 June 2006.

21 Email from UNMIL source, 29 July 2006.

22 Email from UNMIL source, 29 July 2006.

23 Email from civil society source, 26 July 2006.

24 Email from civil society leader, 27 July 2006.

25 Email from UN source, 01 August 2006.

26 Dyncorp's Director of International Peacekeeping made a presentation at the Liberia National Dialogue on Security sector reform, which was convened by UNMIL and the Liberia Ministry of Justice and facilitated by DCAF, Kings College, London, and the African Security Sector Network, held at Corina Hotel, Monrovia on 3–4 August 2005. Dyncorp also participated in the Conference on Security Sector Reform, organized by the Liberia National Law Enforcement Association, in collaboration with the International Centre for Transitional Justice, held in Monrovia, 24–26 January 2006.

27 The RAND Corporation report. 'Making Liberia Safe: Transformation of the National Security Sector', was submitted to the Liberian Government on 16 May 2006. Civil society sources in Liberia indicate that 'RAND is about to release the report and have contacted many civil society organizations for their mailing addresses to be able to furnish them with copies.' Email from civil society source, 27 July 2006.

28 Office of National Security, Freetown.

29 Abrahamsen and Williams, *The Globalization of Private Security, Country Report: Nigeria*, p. 7.

# 11 Private military/security companies

The status of their staff and
their obligations under international
humanitarian law and the
responsibilities of states in
relation to their operations

*Emanuela-Chiara Gillard*

Over the last decade and a half, functions traditionally performed by states' security or military apparatuses have increasingly been contracted out to private military/security companies ('PMCs/PSCs').[1] In view of the increased presence of these relatively new actors, carrying out a range of tasks that is getting increasingly closer to the heart of military operations in situations of armed conflict, including military occupation, and which often puts them in direct contact with persons protected by international humanitarian law, it is natural for the International Committee of the Red Cross ('ICRC') to have commenced a dialogue with these companies and with the states with responsibilities for their operations. The aim of the dialogue is twofold: first, to promote compliance with international humanitarian law by ensuring that PMCs/PSCs and the relevant states are aware of their obligations and, second, to ensure the companies are aware of and understand the ICRC's mandate and its activities with respect to persons affected by armed conflict.

PMCs/PSCs have featured widely in the media in recent months and it is often asserted, both in the popular press and in expert publications, that there is a vacuum in the law when it comes to their operations. In view of this, the ICRC considers it important to emphasize that in situations of armed conflict there is a body of law that regulates both the activities of PMC/PSC staff and the responsibilities of the states that hire them. The states that hire PMCs/PSCs and the staff of PMCs/PSCs have concurrent responsibilities under international humanitarian law. Moreover, states in whose territories such companies are incorporated or operate have a role to play in ensuring respect for international humanitarian law by PMCs/PSCs.

In case of serious violations of international humanitarian law the responsibilities of PMC/PSC staff and of the states that hire them are well-established as a matter of law. However, practical difficulties often arise in bringing proceedings in respect of violations.

There is very limited law in the field of national or international control of the services PMCs/PSCs may provide and the administrative processes, if any, with which they must comply in order to be allowed to operate. Only a handful of states have adopted legislation laying down procedures that PMCs/PSCs based in their territory must comply with in order to be allowed to operate abroad (e.g. South Africa) and equally few regulate the companies operating in their own territory (e.g. Iraq and Sierra Leone)

This chapter briefly outlines the ICRC's position on certain key legal issues raised by PMCs/PSCs operating in situations of armed conflict, namely the status of the staff of these companies, their responsibilities under international humanitarian law, the responsibilities of the states that hire them and the responsibilities of the states in whose territory PMCs/PSCs are incorporated or operate.

It should be noted at the outset that international humanitarian law does not address the lawfulness or legitimacy of PMCs/PSCs or of states' outsourcing to them of certain activities. Rather, its aim is to regulate the activities of these actors if they are operating in situations of armed conflict.

## The status of the staff of PMCs/PSCs under international humanitarian law

It is often stated that PMCs/PSCs do not have a status under international law. From an international humanitarian law point of view this is misleading. The companies themselves do not have a status under international humanitarian law but their staff do. Admittedly, there is no single simple answer applicable to all PMC/PSC employees as their status depends on the nature of the relationship they may have with a state and on the nature of the activities that they perform. It is therefore something that must be determined on a case-by-case basis. However, international humanitarian law contains criteria for determining this status as well as clear consequent rights and obligations.

Before addressing the status of PMC/PSC staff under international humanitarian law a few words are warranted on the question of mercenaries, which, although not central to international humanitarian law, has focalized much of the debate.

### *Mercenaries?*

Discussions of PMCs/PSCs often focus on or at least commence with the politically fraught question of whether their staff are mercenaries.

Mercenaries are the subject of two specific conventions: the 1977 Organization of African Unity Convention for the Elimination of

Mercenarism in Africa and the 1989 United Nations International Convention against the Recruitment, Use, Financing and Training of Mercenaries. The aim of these instruments is to prohibit the use of mercenaries and to criminalize both resort to mercenaries and participation in hostilities as a mercenary.

International humanitarian law tackles the issue of mercenaries from a rather different angle. It does not prohibit the use of mercenaries or criminalize their activities. Instead, it focuses on the *status* to be granted to them if captured. Article 47 of Additional Protocol I of 1977 to the Geneva Conventions lays down a definition of mercenaries – in fact the one subsequently adopted by the two specialized conventions, subject to some minor changes – and provides that persons falling within this definition are not entitled to prisoner-of-war status if captured.[2]

Mercenaries, unlike members of states' armed forces, are thus 'unprivileged combatants' and have the same position, rights and obligations as any civilian who directly participates in hostilities.

What does this mean in practice? Members of the armed forces of a state party to an armed conflict have a right to participate in hostilities. If captured, they are entitled to be treated as prisoners of war and are protected by the Third Geneva Convention of 1949. Moreover, they may not be tried merely for having participated in hostilities.

Mercenaries, on the other hand, are treated in the same way as civilians: they do not have a right to participate directly in hostilities. Should they do so and be captured, they are not entitled to prisoner-of-war status or to the protection of the Third Geneva Convention and may be tried under national law for the mere fact of having participated in hostilities, even though in doing so they did not violate any rules of international humanitarian law.

This does not mean, however, that once captured, mercenaries are not protected by international humanitarian law. Like all civilians who participate in hostilities, they are protected by the Fourth Geneva Convention, which lays down minimum standards to regulate their deprivation of liberty, as well as minimum judicial guarantees to be respected in any criminal proceedings. Moreover, should the person concerned fall within the exceptions to the Fourth Geneva Convention, he or she will nonetheless still be entitled to the fundamental guarantees laid down in Article 75 of Additional Protocol I as well as the customary rules of international humanitarian law applicable in international armed conflicts.

This being said, it should be noted that Article 47 of Additional Protocol I does not prohibit states from giving mercenaries prisoner-of-war status. It merely provides that mercenaries, unlike members of states' armed forces, are not entitled to it as a matter of right.

Article 47 only applies in international armed conflicts, including during military occupation. International humanitarian law is silent as to the position of mercenaries in non-international armed conflicts. Moreover, as prisoner-of-war status does not exist in such conflicts, it is meaningless to say someone is not entitled to it.

Thus, although entitled to the minimum protections laid down in common Article 3 of the Geneva Conventions, Additional Protocol II of 1977 to the Geneva Conventions and the customary rules of international humanitarian law applicable in non-international armed conflict, persons falling within the definition of mercenaries, like anyone other than members of a state's armed forces, may be tried under national law for merely taking part in hostilities, even though they did not violate any rules of international humanitarian law.

### Combatants or civilians?

#### Members of a state's armed forces?

A more central question for the purposes of international humanitarian law, with very immediate practical consequences for the persons involved, is the status of the staff of PMCs/PSCs: are they combatants or are they civilians? If they are combatants, they can be targeted but, if captured, are entitled to prisoner-of-war status. If they are civilians, on the other hand, they may not be attacked. However, if they take direct part in hostilities they will lose this immunity from attack during such participation and, as already noted, if captured, are not entitled to prisoner-of-war status.

The term 'combatant' has a very specific meaning under international humanitarian law, which is not synonymous with the generic term 'fighter'. It is principally members of a state's armed forces that are combatants.[3] Therefore, at risk of stating the obvious, as a preliminary point it should be noted that the question of whether they are combatants only arises in respect of the staff of PMCs/PSCs hired by states.

PMC/PSC employees can only be considered members of a state's armed forces if they form part of these forces. International humanitarian law does not provide specific guidance as to who may be considered a member of the armed forces of a state. The mere fact that a company has been hired to provide assistance to a state's armed forces is not relevant *per se*. Similarly, the nature of their activities, although determinative of whether they are taking a direct part in hostilities for targeting purposes, is also not a key element for determining whether they 'form part' of the armed forces.

The position is thus unclear. This is unfortunate from both a legal and practical point of view. Whether a person is a member of a state's armed forces or not should be a straightforward determination that can easily be made upon capture so that the person concerned can immediately be granted prisoner-of-war status if he or she is entitled to it. This being said, in case of doubt as to the status of a captured person who has taken direct part in hostilities, the Third Geneva Convention requires that person to be treated like a prisoner-of-war pending a decision on his/her status by a competent tribunal.[4]

In any event, as the policy underlying much of the outsourcing of the activities formerly carried out by the armed forces is to reduce numbers of the armed forces and related costs, there are likely to be very few instances in which PMCs/PSCs staff are incorporated into the armed forces to the extent necessary for them to be considered as forming part thereof for the purposes of determination of status under international humanitarian law.

### Civilians accompanying the armed forces

The Third Geneva Convention establishes a narrow exception to the principle that it is only combatants who are entitled to prisoner-of-war status if captured. In addition to the abovementioned members of the armed forces, Article 4(4) includes among those entitled to prisoner-of-war status if captured:

> [p]ersons who accompany the armed forces without actually being members thereof, such as civilian members of military aircraft crews, war correspondents, supply contractors, members of labour units or of services responsible for the welfare of the armed forces, provided that they have received authorization, from the armed forces which they accompany, who shall provide them for that purpose with an identity card similar to the annexed model.

The legal position of persons falling within this category is clear: they are not members of the armed forces and are not combatants but are entitled to prisoner-of-war status if captured.

What is not clear is precisely who falls within this exception. The list of possible activities ('civilian members of military aircraft crews, war correspondents, supply contractors, members of labour units or of services responsible for the welfare of the armed forces') is indicative, not exhaustive. What other activities could fall within it? The non-combatant status of civilians accompanying the armed forces and the nature of the activities listed by way of example in Article 4(4) would indicate that the drafters had intended that this category of people would *not* include those carrying out activities that amount to taking a direct part in hostilities.

In view of this, it is unlikely that *all* PMC/PSC staff hired by states would fall within this category. The matter must be determined on a case-by-case basis, depending on the nature of the activities carried out. While many of the support functions carried out by contractors for the armed forces doubtlessly do fall within Article 4(4) there are also many others, notably those closer to the heart of military operations, which probably do not.

## Civilians

In view of the above, it seems safe to conclude that the majority of PMC/PSC staff hired by states can be considered 'ordinary' civilians. This is also the status of all PMC/PSC staff present in situations of armed conflict hired by entities other than states, such as companies operating in the state in question, inter-governmental organizations, non-governmental organizations and, as this is not an impossibility, organized armed groups participating in a non-international conflict.

As civilians, the staff of PMCs/PSCs must not be the object of attack. However, if they engage in activities that amount to taking a direct part in hostilities, they lose this immunity for the duration of participation. Moreover, as has already been stated, if captured having taken direct part in hostilities, they are not entitled to prisoner-of-war status and may be tried under the national law of the state that is holding them for their participation in hostilities. As already explained in relation to mercenaries, although not protected by the Third Geneva Convention, if they participated in an international armed conflict, such persons would benefit from the protection of the Fourth Geneva Convention, Article 75 of Additional Protocol I and the customary law rules applicable in international conflicts. If they participated in a non-international conflict they would benefit from the protections of common Article 3 of the Geneva Conventions, Additional Protocol II and the customary rules applicable in non-international conflicts.

The question of what activities amount to 'taking a direct part in hostilities' is obviously crucial to determining the protections to which the staff of PMCs/PSCs are entitled. While this is a question central to the whole of international humanitarian law, treaties provide neither a definition nor precise guidance as to the nature of the activities covered. It is generally understood that the commission of acts which, by their nature or purpose may cause actual harm to enemy personnel and *matériel*, amounts to a direct participation in hostilities, while the supply of food and shelter to combatants or generally 'sympathizing' with them does not. A considerable grey zone exists between these two ends of the spectrum.

The answer is the same as for any other civilian and not just one pertinent to PMC/PSC staff. The conclusions of the series of expert meetings on direct participation in hostilities co-hosted by the ICRC should provide useful guidance.[5]

A detailed analysis of the different activities carried out by PMCs/PSCs in recent years to determine whether they amount to direct participation in hostilities is beyond the scope of the present note. Two points nonetheless deserve to be highlighted.

First, in response to the argument often made that PMCs/PSCs are only providing *defensive* services, it should be noted that international humanitarian law does not draw a distinction between offensive or defensive operations. In Iraq PMCs/PSCs have often been retained to protect military installations, such as barracks and military hardware. These are military objectives and defending them amounts to taking direct part in hostilities.

Second, even though the staff of PMCs/PSCs may not in fact be taking a direct part in hostilities, they often work in close proximity to members of the armed forces and other military objectives. This puts them at risk of being objects of permissible 'collateral damage' in case of attacks.

## The responsibilities under international humanitarian law of the staff of PMCs/PSCs

Regardless of their status – that is, combatants, civilians accompanying the armed forces or 'ordinary' civilians – like all actors in a country experiencing armed conflict, the staff of PMCs/PSCs are bound by international humanitarian law and face individual criminal responsibility for any war crimes they may commit.

What steps can be taken by companies to ensure their staff respect international humanitarian law? This is not addressed expressly in any treaty but, as a minimum, the following elements would seem necessary:

- vetting of staff to ensure they have not committed violations of international humanitarian law or relevant criminal offences in the past;
- awareness of international humanitarian law : PMCs/PSCs should provide all their staff with general as well as situation and task-specific training in international humanitarian law. It is not sufficient to rely on training the employees may have received in their previous careers with the armed forces;
- PMC/PSC staff should be issued with standard operating procedures and rules of engagement that comply with the relevant rules of international humanitarian law and
- mechanisms should be established for investigating any alleged violations of international humanitarian law and ensuring appropriate accountability, including by communicating the results of such investigations to the relevant state authority for further investigation, and if warranted, prosecution.

## The responsibilities under international humanitarian law of states that hire PMCs/PSCs

As stated at the outset, the responsibility under international humanitarian law of the staff of PMCs/PSCs exists alongside that of the states that hire them. While some aspects or consequences of this parallel responsibility are expressly addressed in international humanitarian law treaties, the provisions for doing so are just a specific expression of the rules relating to the responsibility of states for the acts of their agents under general public international law.

### States cannot absolve themselves of their obligations under international humanitarian law by hiring PMCs/PSCs

Generally international humanitarian law does not preclude states from hiring PMCs/PSCs to carry out certain activities. It is clear that if and when they do so, they remain responsible for meeting their obligations under international humanitarian law. A failure by a company to comply with the state's obligations will not absolve the latter of its responsibilities.

So if, for example, a state hires a PMC/PSC to run a prisoner-of-war camp, the state must still ensure the standards of internment and treatment laid down in the Third Geneva Convention are met, and cannot avoid responsibility by claiming the company was responsible for the operations.

### States must ensure respect for international humanitarian law by the PMCs/PSCs they hire

As is the case for their armed forces and anyone acting on their behalf, states must ensure that the staff of PMCs/PSCs they hire respect international humanitarian law.

What steps can a state take to meet this obligation? Possible measures could include

- requiring that the staff of PMCs/PSCs they hire be properly trained in international humanitarian law. Indeed, this is expressly foreseen in the Third and Fourth Geneva Conventions for persons who assume responsibilities in respect of prisoners of war and protected persons during occupation, respectively;[6] and
- requiring that companies' standard operating procedures/rules of engagement comply with international humanitarian law.

### States may be responsible for violations of international humanitarian law committed by the PMCs/PSCs they hire

States are responsible for violations of international humanitarian law that can be attributed to them. These include those committed by:

- their agents, including members of their armed forces;
- persons or entities empowered to exercise elements of governmental authority; and
- persons acting on the instructions of a state or under its direction or control.

This is a generally accepted principle of international law, recently re-stated in the International Law Commission's Articles on the Responsibility of States for Internationally Wrongful Acts of 2001.[7] To the extent that the activities of the staff of a PMC/PSC hired by a state can be attributed to the latter on one of these bases, the state will bear responsibility thereof. This responsibility of the state exists alongside the responsibility of the PMC/PSC staff and that of the companies themselves.

While this responsibility of states is well-established as a matter of law, it is often difficult to enforce as a matter of practice, both before international tribunals, because of the absence of a body with compulsory jurisdiction and the unlikelihood that another state would commence proceedings, and before national courts, where proceedings may be thwarted by the non-self-executing nature of international humanitarian law in certain states or assertions of sovereign immunity.

*States must investigate, and if warranted, prosecute serious violations of international humanitarian law alleged to have been committed by the staff of PMCs/PSCs they hire*

The four Geneva Conventions require states to take measures necessary for the suppression of all acts contrary to the Conventions as well as to search for and bring before their courts persons alleged to have committed grave breaches.[8] Effectively, this requires states to grant their courts universal jurisdiction over grave breaches. This obligation exists for *all* persons and applies *a fortiori* in respect of persons hired by a state. Accordingly, states must establish mechanisms for holding the staff of PMCs/PSCs accountable should they commit violations of international humanitarian law.

This being said, while the criminal responsibility of individuals is well-established, its enforcement in practice has proved problematic for the following reasons:

- PMCs/PSCs and their staff are often given immunity in country where they operate (this was the case in Iraq, for example, by means of CPA Order 17);
- the courts in the countries where the PMCs/PSCs are operating and the alleged violation took place may not be functioning because of the conflict;
- the state hiring the PMC/PSC – or, indeed, any third state, including that of nationality of the company – may be unable or unwilling to exercise extraterritorial jurisdiction over the PMCs/PSCs in civil matters or criminally over their staff;
- even where the courts of the state hiring the PMC/PSC – or any state on the basis of universal jurisdiction – can and will exercise

jurisdiction, much of the evidence and witnesses are in the country where the violations took place, making prosecutions and proceedings complicated.

Problems also arise with regard to the responsibilities of the PMCs/PSCs themselves, as opposed to their staff. First, it is questionable whether PMCs/PSCs are directly bound by international humanitarian law, in the same way as states and individuals. Second, apart from this question, few states recognize the criminal responsibility of companies. In practice this means that the most likely form of proceedings against PMCs/PSCs are civil rather than criminal actions, which raises a third problem: the fact that while many national courts have extraterritorial criminal jurisdiction, extraterritorial *civil* jurisdiction is rare.

## The responsibilities under international humanitarian law of the states of nationality of PMCs/PSCs or where they operate

The previous section addressed the obligations of states engaged in armed conflict that hire PMCs/PSCs. Those states have direct obligations and responsibilities. While their responsibilities are evident and clear-cut, other states also have a role to play in ensuring compliance with international humanitarian law by the staff of PMCs/PSCs operating in situations of armed conflict.

Common Article 1 of the Geneva Conventions requires *all* states to take steps to ensure respect for international humanitarian law. The states of nationality of PMCs/PSCs and those in whose territory they operate are in a particularly favourable position to affect their behaviour.

One way for the state of nationality to exercise some control and oversight on a PMC could be by establishing a licensing or regulatory system. A review of existing regulatory systems and of possible elements is beyond the scope of this chapter, which will limit itself to outlining possible key elements of a regulatory system. These basic elements could include

- a prohibition to perform certain activities (e.g. direct participation in hostilities unless incorporated in the armed forces of the hiring state);
- a requirement that PMCs/PSCs obtain operating licences based on meeting certain criteria, including, for the purpose of ensuring compliance with international humanitarian law, requirements that the companies

  - train their staff in international humanitarian law
  - adopt standard operating procedures/rules of engagement that respect international humanitarian law
  - adopt appropriate disciplinary measures;

- a requirement for authorization for every contract depending on the nature of the proposed activities and the situation in the country where the contract will be executed and
- sanctions for operating without having obtained the necessary authorizations or in violation thereof (e.g. withdrawal of operating licence, loss of bond, criminal sanction).

Such a regulatory system should be complemented by a functioning system for bringing to justice persons accused of having committed violations of international humanitarian law, including the staff of PMCs/PSCs and, possibly, the PMCs/PSCs themselves in civil proceedings.

Similarly, states in whose territory PMCs/PSCs operate may not only have hired them themselves but may also be 'hosting' the PMCs/PSCs hired by others – for example, in Iraq today there are PMCs/PSCs hired by the United States which is a party to the conflict, by third states not involved in the hostilities, by private companies and by inter-governmental organizations. The points made above with regard to the responsibility of the states of nationality of PMCs/PSCs are applicable to the 'host' state: it too has a responsibility to ensure the respect of international humanitarian law and accountability for violations.

Accordingly, such states could also establish a mechanism for registration or licensing of the PMCs/PSCs operating on their territory, setting out similar requirements, with possibly certain more specific ones, for example, relating to the type of weapons that can be employed, and also take measures to punish violations of international humanitarian law that may be committed.

## Notes

A fuller article on the present topic appears in Emanuela-Chiara Gillard, 'Business Goes to War: Private Military/Security Companies and International Humanitarian Law', *International Review of the Red Cross*, September 2006, Vol. 88(863), pp. 525–572.

1 This article reflects the views of the author alone and not necessarily those of the ICRC.
2 Article 47 of Additional Protocol I provides as follows:

   1    A mercenary shall not have the right to be a combatant or a prisoner of war.
   2    A mercenary is any person who:

      a    is specially recruited locally or abroad in order to fight in an armed conflict;
      b    does, in fact, take a direct part in the hostilities;
      c    is motivated to take part in the hostilities essentially by the desire for private gain and, in fact, is promised, by or on behalf of a party to the conflict, material compensation substantially in excess of that promised or paid to combatants of similar ranks and functions in the armed forces of that party;

      d    is neither a national of a party to the conflict nor a resident of territory
           controlled by a party to the conflict;
      e    is not a member of the armed forces of a party to the conflict and
      f    has not been sent by a state which is not a party to the conflict on offi-
           cial duty as a member of its armed forces.

3  Pursuant to Articles 4A(1) and (2) of the Third Geneva Convention members of
the armed forces of a state party to an armed conflict or members of militias
or volunteer corps forming part of such forces and members of other militias
and of other volunteer corps, including those of organized resistance movements,
belonging to a state party to an armed conflict, who meet certain conditions
may also be considered combatants. For a discussion of whether the staff of
PMCs/PSCs may fall within these categories see Gillard, 'Business Goes to War.'

4  Third Geneva Convention, Article 5.

5  In an effort to address the challenging issues raise by the concept of 'direct
participation in hostilities', the ICRC, in cooperation with the TMC Asser
Institute, initiated a process aimed at clarifying this notion. In the framework of
this process, four informal Expert Meetings entitled 'Direct Participation in
Hostilities under International Humanitarian Law' have been held in The
Hague (2 June 2003 and 25–26 October 2004) and Geneva (23–25 October 2005
and 27–28 November 2006), which brought together around forty legal experts
representing military, governmental and academic circles, as well as
international and non-governmental organizations. The reports of the first
three meetings held to date are available at www.icrc.org/web/eng/
siteeng0.nsf/html/participation-hostilities-ihl-311205, accessed 9 November
2007.

6  Articles 39 and 129 of the Third Geneva Convention and Articles 99 and 143 of
the Fourth Geneva Convention.

7  Draft Articles on Responsibility of States for Internationally Wrongful Acts,
adopted by the International Law Commission at its fifty-third session, and
Commentaries thereto, 'Report of the International Law Commission on the
work of its Fifty-third session (2001)', *Official Records of the General Assembly,
Fifty-sixth Session, Supplement No. 10*, (UN Doc A/56/10) Chapter IV.E.1. Articles
4, 5, 7 and 8, that set out certain rules for attribution are particularly relevant for
present purposes.

8  See Article 49 of the First Geneva Convention, Article 50 of the Second Geneva
Convention, Article 129 of the Third Geneva Convention, Article 146 of the
Fourth Geneva Convention and Article 85 of Additional Protocol I.

# 12 Regulating private military and security companies

## The US approach

*Marina Caparini*

Commercial companies that offer military- and security-related services transnationally in conflict- or crisis-ridden environments have proliferated since the end of the Cold War, especially since the onset of the US-led interventions in Afghanistan and Iraq. Although it is frequently asserted that such companies exist in a legal vacuum, this claim is somewhat exaggerated. While no overarching international regulatory framework yet exists, pockets of applicable regulation can be found both in international law and international humanitarian law,[1] and in the national legislation of certain key source states and contracting states. This patchwork quality remains unsatisfactory and has raised concerns about the legal accountability and oversight of private military and security companies (PMSCs), their employees, as well as those who engage their services.

Given the constraints of space, this chapter explores only a few selected aspects of the regulatory approach of a key source and contracting state of PMSCs – the United States. The chapter begins by examining three key factors that support regulation, then turns to some relevant legislation and recent efforts to improve regulation, ending with challenges to the enforcement of legislation. This chapter does not discuss the merits or disadvantages of outsourcing or privatizing military and security functions to private contractors, which have been addressed extensively elsewhere in the literature.[2] This chapter proceeds from the assumption that such outsourcing is already a well-entrenched dimension of US policy and practice, and that commercial firms are used extensively to support US forces and policy objectives abroad. The question that is asked here is why there is a perceived need for regulation of private security contractors, what are some current legal means of holding them to account and what obstacles have impeded the sector from being adequately regulated?

## Why regulate?

There are three primary arguments in support of developing and improving the national regulation of private military and security services. The first relates to the lack of clarity as to which laws foreign

PMSC personnel currently fall under, particularly in crisis or conflict zones. This uncertainty exists among PMSC companies and employees, as well as the spectrum of actors who deal with them, including contracting parties, military commanders, and populations of host states, or those who look to exercise oversight of their activities.

International law has a (flawed) definition of mercenarism, but has yet to define the status of private military and security contractors. Normally an individual's crimes would fall under the laws of the state where the crime has been committed and thus private military and security contractors would be subject to the laws of the state on whose territory they are operating. However, PMSCs often operate in failed states or conflict zones where the law enforcement, legal and judicial systems of the host state do not function properly. In such circumstances foreign civilian contractors may be granted immunity from the jurisdiction of local courts. The responsibility then falls to the home state of the contractor to prosecute crimes committed by the contractor. But because the acts were committed abroad, the application of home state law is problematic and experience has shown that enforcement of the law faces significant obstacles.

Thus, in June 2004 the Coalition Provisional Authority or CPA – the US-led occupation government of Iraq – granted foreign (non-Iraqi) contractors immunity from jurisdiction of Iraqi legal system and subjects the contractors to the jurisdiction of the 'sending state', or the state that provided personnel, consultants, services and so on.[3] CPA Order 17 stemmed from concern about the condition of the Iraqi justice system, which still cannot guarantee either the safety of individuals of foreign nations detained in Iraq or due process, but also stemmed from the acknowledgement that no reconstruction would go forward in the deteriorating security environment without the armed protection provided by either coalition forces or PMSCs. CPA Order 17 also allows for the waiving of immunity of a contractor by the sending state.[4] However, the key sending country, the United States, has declined to waive immunity of foreign contractors and this provision remains moot. Although US security contractor employees can be prosecuted under US criminal law, to date the Department of Justice has generally not pursued prosecutions for serious crimes by security contractors relating to the use of undue force in Iraq.

According to the US House of Representatives' Committee on Oversight and Government Reform, 'The conduct of private security contractor personnel has not been subject to a clearly defined and practically effective legal regime.'[5] US private military and security company personnel have been subject to a shifting and ambiguous set of legal rules that is different to those constraining the deployed US forces they are often working to support, although recent changes have introduced the possibility that in certain circumstances contractors may be subject to the Uniform Code of Military Justice. The extension remains ambiguous, contested, and so far, hypothetical. Some laws, such as the Military Extraterritorial Jurisdiction Act (MEJA), clearly apply to contractors and have been on the books for numerous years, but have very rarely been used.

A second factor in support of greater regulation of PMSCs relates to the need to clarify protections with regard to the safety and wellbeing of their employees in the performance of their functions. Some private military and security companies are alleged to have failed to adequately equip, train and protect their personnel. Along these lines, the families of the four Blackwater employees killed in Falluja in 2004 have launched a civil suit seeking redress and compensation for wrongful death, claiming that the company sent the four employees into hostile territory unprepared.[6] Blackwater's legal defence in this case, which is being closely watched by PMSCs, is based on the argument that the services it provides are integral to the US armed forces and as such they enjoy the same immunity from liability and damages as the government.

PMSCs are also increasingly hiring third-country nationals (TCNs) from developing states as sources of cheaper labour than their Western counterparts. PMSC recruitment has been undertaken in countries such as Fiji, El Salvador, Honduras, Chile, Colombia, Philippines, Nepal, India and Uganda. Representatives of some private security firms claim that recruitment of cheap TCN labour is 'standard business practice' and that they merely 'pay what the market will bear', however, some human rights groups have accused security contracting firms from developed states of exploiting TCN recruits by inadequately training them, providing insufficient protective clothing or weapons, and failing to provide promised health and insurance coverage. Peruvian authorities, for example, have accused several US-based PMSCs of requiring their locally recruited employees to sign contracts that lack the normal legal protections stipulated in the country's labour laws and exempt the US government, the hiring company and all subsidiaries from any claims, losses, damages or injuries that may occur to the signatory.[7] It can thus be argued that more regulation is needed to ensure that employees of PMSCs are assured of certain protections and obligations of their employer in terms of providing duty of care, adequate safety measures, instructions that do not contravene the law and compensation in case of injury.[8]

A third factor supporting stronger efforts to regulate private military and security service providers is suggested by periodic media reports of the alleged involvement of the companies or individual employees in a serious misconduct causing injury to or death of Afghan and Iraqi civilians.[9] Despite regular credible allegations of human rights violations and undue use of lethal force by foreign security contractors, there has been a general failure to prosecute those implicated and hold them legally accountable.[10] The lack of oversight and accountability has sustained widespread perceptions that security contractors in zones of crisis and conflict enjoy *de facto* legal impunity.[11]

There are a significant number of foreign private security contractors present in Afghanistan and Iraq – estimates for Iraq vary between 5000 and 30,000 or more[12] – many of whom are heavily armed to fulfil their functions in a volatile high-risk environment where the host state's central authority is uncertain and they enjoy immunity from local prosecution. Within this context, very few security contractors have been prosecuted for crimes by US authorities since 2001 in Afghanistan and 2004 in Iraq. Although at least twenty alleged incidents of abuse by civilians are known to have been forwarded by the Department of Defense and the Central Intelligence Agency to the Department of Justice by 2006 for prosecution, only one civilian contractor has been indicted, two have been dismissed and seventeen remain open.[13] That single contractor was subsequently prosecuted and jailed for assaulting an Afghan detainee during interrogation who later died of his injuries.[14] No civilian contractor is known to have been prosecuted for a crime against an Iraqi, although one US contractor was indicted for assaulting another foreign contractor,[15] and various contractors have been prosecuted for other crimes, such as possession of child porn[16] and defrauding the US government.[17]

Several of the ongoing investigations concern alleged (and in at least one case, self-confessed)[18] involvement of several civilian contract interrogators and interpreters in detainee abuse at Abu Ghraib prison. In the investigations surrounding detainee abuse, collecting evidence is claimed to have been particularly problematic, impeding prosecutions.[19] Yet while the implicated civilian contractors have yet to be held accountable due to problems collecting evidence, nine US military personnel (all enlisted soldiers, no commanding officers) working alongside the civilian contractors and implicated in the abuse at Abu Ghraib have already been prosecuted under the Uniform Code of Military Justice.[20] Observers who are closely following the investigations are sceptical that any prosecutions of the civilian contractors will result.[21]

In some instances, allegations of severe misconduct of PMSC personnel have emerged from lawsuits by former employees of such firms. For example, two former employees of the US firm Triple Canopy are suing the company for wrongful dismissal and wrongful interference with their professional future, claiming they were fired for filing a report on their supervisor whom they accused of shooting at Iraqi vehicles and civilians without provocation, and that they were subsequently 'blacklisted' and prevented from finding work with other PMSCs operating in Iraq. The case has revealed that the only investigation of the alleged incidents was conducted by the company itself, which found it was unable to establish the circumstances around the shootings since no deaths were recorded by Iraqi or US authorities.[22]

Where investigations of alleged security contractor misconduct are known to have occurred, they have been quietly undertaken and opaque, releasing little or no information into the public realm.[23] Several contractors in Iraq have reportedly been relieved of their duties for shooting without cause, but 'actions taken against contractors are generally carried out quietly and rarely, if ever, disclosed.'[24] The US State Department claims to investigate all shooting incidents involving State Department security contractors. In response to queries about an incident in which private security contractors allegedly shot two passengers in a taxi in February 2006 in Kirkuk, a State Department official noted that 'as is also standard, the results of such federal investigations are not made public. So we're not about to share any investigation results.'[25] While valid security or proprietary reasons may prevent the release of critical details relating to the duties of the security contractors or security procedures, the failure to more fully explain the findings of investigations serves to reinforce public perceptions of the reckless behaviour and legal impunity of security contractors.

Even where investigations by state authorities have cleared PMSC employees of misconduct, they have remained highly opaque and release minimal, if any, information. One particularly controversial incident involved a video released in late November 2005 and which spread rapidly via the Internet. The 'trophy' video was comprised of a series of edited scenes of security contractors shooting into civilian vehicles in Iraq, set to the music of Elvis Presley's 'Mystery Train'. Released by a disgruntled employee of the PMSC Aegis Defence Services, the video triggered a firestorm of condemnation. After conducting an investigation into the events captured on the video, the US Army Criminal Investigation Division made a departure from its usual procedure of not commenting on such investigations in stating that 'the review determined that no further investigative effort on the part of Army CID was warranted.'[26] The statement exonerated the firm's employees of any suspicion of criminal conduct, implicitly confirming the findings of the firm's own investigation that the recorded shootings were legitimate operations and occurred within the established Rules for the Use of Force by civilian personnel.[27] However, by offering no information about the investigation or the grounds on which the firm's employees were cleared, the Army CID arguably failed to allay public concerns about the behaviour of the implicated PMSC personnel and their company, missing an opportunity to help dispel public distrust and misperceptions about an industry on which the United States now relies extensively.

## Selected aspects of US regulation of PMSCs

The United States is an obvious choice for a study of national-level regulation of PMSCs, being both a main source of private military and security firms, and through its various government departments and agencies, heavily reliant on their services at home and abroad. The United States has numerous laws that can be applied to contractors. These include the War Crimes Act of 1996; the Alien Tort Claims Act; the Victims of Trafficking and Violence Protection Act of 2000; the Anti-torture Statute; the McCain Amendment to the 2006 Department of Defense Appropriations Bill; the Defense Trade Controls Act (DTCA); the Arms Export Control Act (AECA); the Gun Control Act; the Export Administration Regulations; ITAR (International Traffic in Arms Regulations); the Defense Base Act; the Foreign Corrupt Practices Act; General Orders of the Central Command, Multinational Corps – Iraq and Combined Joint Task Force.[28] Regulation may also take place through orders, policy and instructions as is found in the Defense Federal Acquisition Regulation Supplement (DFARS), and various Department of Defense instructions and guidances that would apply to DoD personnel and contractors, including Instruction 3020.41 'Contractor Personnel Authorized to Accompany the US Armed Forces' in October 2005; Directive 3115.09 that establishes standards for humane treatment of detainees and requirements for reporting violations of the policy; and Directive 2311.01E, which requires that international law regulating armed conflict, such as the Geneva Conventions, be observed and enforced by the DoD and its civilian contractors.

Discussions of regulating the US PMSC sector often focus on the existing regime for controlling the export of commercial military and security services, which is derived from the ITAR, AECA and DTCA. This regime establishes a dual system for controlling exports of the types of services that PMSCs provide. While the licensed (ITAR) and non-licensed (Foreign Military Sales) regimes provide an effective means of controlling which commercial military and security services can be contracted by foreign buyers, an export control regime constitutes only one dimension of a comprehensive regulatory approach.[29] The following section will briefly examine another regulatory dimension, that of the US legislation that could be used to prosecute PMSC personnel for serious crimes such as human rights violations.

### USA PATRIOT ACT amendment on SMTJ

The recent conviction of civilian contract interrogator David Passaro, and his sentencing to eight years in prison for assaulting an Afghan prisoner who died after four days of interrogation, highlighted a new vector for regulation of PMSC personnel. Passaro was convicted under a provision of the USA PATRIOT ACT that extends the jurisdiction of US federal courts to crimes committed by or against any US national on lands or facilities designated for use by the US government, including military or diplomatic facilities anywhere in the world, classified as the special maritime and territorial jurisdiction (SMTJ) of the United States.[30] The federal criminal statutes that apply within the SMTJ include those for maiming, assault, kidnapping, murder and manslaughter.[31] While applauding this rare instance of enforcing contractor accountability, human rights groups criticize the prosecution and conviction of Passaro on assault charges rather than for torture and homicide, which carry life sentences under US federal law, as well as the failure to prosecute any other individual who was present with Passaro.[32]

## *Alien Tort Claims Act (ATCA)*

A further law that may be relevant for holding private military and security companies accountable, whether directly or through the client they were contracted to work for, is the Alien Tort Claims Act of 1789. The ATCA allows foreign nationals to sue non-state actors including corporations in the US courts for certain violations of the law of nations.[33] By 2006, some thirty-six cases had been brought against corporations under the ATCA, with twenty dismissed, three settled out of court and thirteen ongoing.[34] The application of the ATCA to PMSCs is currently being tested through a lawsuit recently launched by the American Civil Liberties Union (ACLU) against Boeing subsidiary Jeppesen Dataplan, a company that provided logistics support for CIA rendition activities and other federal agencies in the war against terror, facilitating the disappearance, torture and inhumane treatment of three suspected Al Qaeda militants.[35] Observers maintain that even if ATCA does not result in winning cases against contractors and corporations, the bad publicity and embarrassment such lawsuits bring for firms accused of complicity with human rights abuses may be enough to compel them to change their behaviour.[36]

## *War Crimes Act*

The US War Crimes Act of 1996 (WCA) made it a felony under US law for anyone to commit grave breaches of the Geneva Conventions if the crime was committed by or against a US national or a member of the US Armed Forces.[37] Bringing prosecutions under the WCA was doubtful, however, because its provisions were seen as lacking sufficient specificity to support a successful criminal prosecution in US courts.[38] To date no one has been prosecuted under the WCA. However, the advent of the permissive environment engendered by the war on terror has engendered a number of legislative developments that have 'opened up soldiers, interrogators, commanders, and contractors to potential criminal liability', including under the now-amended WCA.[39]

The landmark Supreme Court decision in *Hamdan v. Rumsfeld* on 29 June 2006 rejected the administration's argument that common

Article 3 of the Geneva Conventions did not apply to the conflict with Al Qaeda, and made it clear that the abusive interrogation techniques used by the CIA violated US obligations under international law and that CIA operatives could be held criminally liable for such abuses.[40] In quick response to *Hamdan*, and with the ostensible goal of bringing greater clarity to the WCA, the Bush administration developed the Military Commissions Act of 2006 (MCA), passed by Congress on 28 September 2006. In addition to establishing procedures for military tribunals of foreign terrorist suspects, the MCA contains several provisions that may impact the legal accountability of private security contractors as well as the US officials who hire and direct their actions. By redefining 'war crimes' into a series of specific chargeable offences and prohibiting eight specific types of 'grave breaches', the net result is to limit the extent to which criminal sanctions under the WCA can be applied to violations of common Article 3.[41]

Although all DOD military and civilian personnel, including DOD contractors, are clearly bound to fully comply with the entirety of the Geneva Conventions according to the directive issued by the new Army Field Manual of September 2006,[42] the amended War Crimes Act makes it more difficult to prosecute questionable techniques and practices not defined as grave breaches in the US courts. It thus creates legal scope for civilian officials and personnel of the CIA, including private contractors, to employ practices short of the most extreme constituting torture in the treatment of detainees.[43] Further, the amendment introduced retroactive immunity to 1997 for government officials and civilians, such as CIA operatives or contractors, or those who may have authorized, ordered or participated in harsh tactics in interrogations of detainees that amounted to torture or abuse.[44]

The Military Commissions Act may have other effects on contractors, such as through its redefinition of 'combatant' through its expansion of the meaning of 'unlawful enemy combatant', which carries the potential to inflict a 'legal boomerang' on the status of US civilians and contractors who accompany and support US operations. The Department of Defense has maintained a rigorous effort to distinguish such contractors from combatants, and has sought to prevent them from becoming too closely involved with major combat operations. Such contractors would lose civilian immunity against attacks if they directly participate in hostilities. The expansion of the definition of combatant in the MCA,[45] however, raises the possibility that civilian contractors could be defined as actively or directly participating in hostilities. Thus the amended War Crimes Act now offers both lowered capacity to hold civilian contractors involved in intelligence and interrogation to account for torture, although the most extreme forms of it remain prohibited; provides retroactive immunity for those who committed war crimes in the past; and potentially affecting the status of private military and security personnel as non-combatants.

*Uniform Code of Military Justice*

The Uniform Code of Military Justice (UCMJ), or court martial system, has recently been broadened to apply to private contractors and other civilians supporting US forces in declared wars and contingency operations. Previously civilians could be tried under the UCMJ only during a war. Since the US Congress has not declared a war since 1942 and is not likely to in the sorts of contingencies and interventions that the United States has become involved in since that time, there was little that a military officer could do when confronted by contractor misconduct aside from requesting that the firm employing the individual remove or fire him, or possibly report the individual to the civilian authorities if it was suspected that a crime had been committed. The impunity of contractors who have committed crimes in conflict zones has contrasted with the constraints of the military justice system on the US troops, and this discrepancy can have detrimental effects on the morale, good order and discipline of the military forces who work alongside the civilian personnel.[46]

The recent amendment to UCMJ supposedly would allow application of the UCMJ to accompanying civilians also during a 'contingency operation', such as Afghanistan and Iraq. It is too soon to tell what impact the UCMJ amendment will have on PMSC accountability, as military lawyers are still examining the ramifications of the amendment and how UCMJ jurisdiction can be managed in the future. Moreover, there is reason to believe that the effort to hold civilians to the same standards as US troops will be challenged on constitutional grounds:

> Civilians prosecuted in a military court do not receive a grand jury hearing and are tried by members of the military rather than by a jury of their peers. The US Supreme Court has struck down civilian convictions under military law, and no conviction of a civilian under the UCMJ has been upheld in more than half a century.[47]

*Military Extraterritorial Jurisdiction Act*

The Military Extraterritorial Jurisdiction Act (MEJA) of 2000 (Public Law 106–778) was intended to address a long-standing problem of how to deal with civilians who had committed crimes while accompanying military forces overseas. As noted above, the US federal criminal jurisdiction normally ends at the US border and crimes committed abroad by its citizens are dealt with by the state in which the crime took place. However, in the US military experience, host nations often declined to prosecute contractors or dependents who had committed crimes there, even when it concerned serious crimes.[48] Moreover, in fragile or post-conflict states, there is often no functioning government or criminal justice system to bring prosecutions and as a result the crimes have gone unprosecuted. In order to correct this problem, the MEJA established Federal jurisdiction over offences committed outside the United States by persons employed by or accompanying the armed forces as well as former members of the US armed forces.

MEJA allows for the prosecution in federal courts of any individual employed by or accompanying the military on deployments overseas who engages in conduct that if committed in the United States would constitute a federal criminal offence punishable by imprisonment for more than one year. MEJA empowers the Secretary of Defense to authorize the military police to arrest the individual and deliver him or her to the US civilian law enforcement authorities for removal to the United States for judicial proceedings, or to the authorities of the state where the alleged offence took place if so requested by those authorities and where such delivery is covered by a treaty to international agreement to which the United States is party.

However, MEJA has so far been applied only once to a contractor.[49] The Department of Defense initially delayed issuing the necessary implementing regulations, which only took effect on 29 September 2004. Further, a major loophole in MEJA soon became visible with the large-scale deployment of private contractors to Iraq under a variety of agreements. MEJA applies only to contractors employed directly by the Department of Defense.[50] This limitation may have, in theory, prevented it from being used to prosecute the contractors implicated in detainee abuse at the Abu Ghraib prison in Iraq, since their contracts were not with DoD but with the Interior Department.

In an effort to plug this loophole, Congress moved to amend MEJA in its FY 2005 DOD Authorization Act to apply to civilian employees and contractors of 'any other Federal agency, or any provisional authority, to the extent such employment relates to supporting the mission of the Department of Defense overseas'.[51] However, the phrasing of the amendment is imprecise and problematic, leaving undefined how broadly 'supporting' and 'mission' should be interpreted. The term 'mission' could be interpreted very narrowly to identifiable missions, such as those given a name like 'Operation Iraqi Freedom', or very broadly to apply to all of DoD's regular day-to-day operations. Similarly, how can one determine at what point another agency's activities constitutes support of the DoD mission? In the view of one expert, as drafted, the MEJA amendment would apply to employees of the CIA, which shares some intelligence with DoD.[52] Another problem is raised by extending the provisions to include 'any provisional authority'. While the phrase was clearly meant to apply to entities such as the Coalition Provisional Authority (CPA) in Iraq, it is unclear what is the US government's view of the CPA and its legal status. The CPA has variously been described by the US government as a USG entity, a multinational coalition, an interim government, and an international, UN-created entity. In the latter two cases, the conduct of contractors working for another government's agencies or an international agency would fall beyond the scope of the MEJA. Thus, although an effort was made to close the loophole in MEJA revealed by the events involving civilian contractors at Abu Ghraib, the amendment's imprecise language and the lack of legislative guidance for interpreting the language used could make it difficult to enforce.[53]

In another effort to strengthen the MEJA, US Representative David E. Price introduced legislation in early 2007 that would extend the reach of the MEJA to allow prosecution in civilian courts of any contractor employed under contract or subcontract by any department or agency where such work is carried out where the US military is conducting a contingency operation.[54] The Transparency and Accountability in Security Contracting Act proposes expanding the Military Extraterritorial Jurisdiction Act (MEJA) to apply to contractors working on any US government contract in an area where the US military is deployed in contingency operations.[55] Specifically, in response to the reluctance of federal prosecutors to pursue criminal prosecutions against contractors for acts committed abroad, the draft bill also proposes the establishment of FBI Theatre Investigative Unit for each contingency operation where contract personnel are carrying out functions. The unit would be funded by the FBI and responsible for carrying out investigations of alleged criminal misconduct by contract personnel, and referring the case to the Attorney General for further action as appropriate.[56] However, this initiative has attracted controversy, including criticism from one of the strongest proponents for rigorous regulation, Jeremy Scahill, who sees it as both practically unfeasible in proposing to monitor the more than 100,000 contractors on the ground in Iraq and have FBI investigators collect evidence in a war zone, and well as handing the private security industry 'a tremendous PR victory' because they could claim once it is passed as legislation that they are legally accountable.[57]

## Enforcement: a problem of resources, will or politics?

As described in the preceding section, the United States has various laws that could be applied to those individuals and firms who provide transnational commercial military and security services and who commit grave violations of human rights or other serious crimes. Enforcement of these laws, however, has been deeply problematic to date and the United States has, with very few exceptions, generally failed to prosecute civilian security contractors who are suspected to have committed serious crimes and human rights abuses. That failure has been attributed to legal ambiguities, some of which have been outlined above, and continuing uncertainties as to which laws are applicable, as well as the difficulties of collecting evidence in investigations that would support a prosecution.

Fault may lie with the national prosecuting authority's failure to undertake prosecution due to a lack of resources or a belief that the effort is unjustified or has a lower priority than other matters. In this sense, the United States existing regulatory framework has been built upon the questionable presumption of interest, ability, resources and opportunities of domestic prosecutors to investigate, gather evidence and prosecute nationals who have allegedly committed crimes in conflict zones when working as contractors. Peter W. Singer claims that when MEJA was created, it was underpinned by the assumption that civilian prosecutors back in the United States would be able to make determinations of what is proper and improper behaviour in conflicts, gather evidence, carry out depositions in the middle of war zones, and then be willing and able to prosecute them to juries back home. 'The reality is that no US Attorney likes to waste limited budgets on such messy, complex cases 9,000 miles outside their district, even if they were fortunate enough to have the evidence at hand.'[58]

The failure to enforce legislation and prosecute security contractors for severe misconduct may also stem from the recognition that contractors are an essential component of the stabilization and reconstruction effort in Iraq and Afghanistan, and that instances of severe misconduct are considered relatively uncommon, or perhaps less deserving of attention than other issues, given the context in which they occur. For example, a DoD investigation of detainee abuse at Abu Ghraib found that 'notwithstanding the highly publicized involvement of some contractors in abuse at Abu Ghraib, we found very few instances of abuse involving contractors.'[59] Moreover, in the context of an insurgency that increasingly approaches civil war, military officials have more pressing concerns than what could be considered overzealous behaviour of PSC personnel while performing their duties.

Nevertheless, a deliberate and wilful tendency to ignore evidence of contractor malfeasance has been noted by industry representatives. Even when alerted by the management of a private security company that one of its employees may have committed a crime, contracting state authorities have reportedly been reluctant to investigate or prosecute private security contractors. One PMSC executive has pointed to the reluctance of the US, the UK and the Iraqi government authorities to demonstrate resolve to take action in Iraq, where the firm has operations. Thus even in situations where the firm 'had itself raised concerns about the actions of some of its employees, it had found great difficulty getting the authorities to act'.[60]

Political interference has also been suggested as a reason lying behind the general failure to prosecute civilian contractors, and specifically those civilian contractors implicated in detainee abuse. A specific memorandum of agreement by the then head of the Criminal Division of DoJ, Michael Chertoff, between the Department of Justice, DoD and CIA established that no prosecutions for death, dismemberment or assaults of detainees would be undertaken by the DoJ as long as certain interrogation techniques were employed. The practice of drafting memos describing which torture techniques would be legally defensible has been ascribed to the political subservience of Justice Department lawyers.[61] This would seem to apply also to the failure to prosecute implicated PMSC employees.

Further, the consistent failure to prosecute alleged fraud and corruption in security and reconstruction contracts in Iraq uncovered through whistle-blower suits filed under the False Claims Act has similarly triggered accusations of political interference. According to the False Claims Act, whistle-blower cases filed against contractors alleged to have defrauded the US government must be brought under seal, during which the Administration has sixty days to investigate. Critics have charged the government with seeking repeated extensions for court-ordered seals, which have the effect of keeping the cases hidden from public view.[62] If the Justice Department decides against joining a whistle-blower case under the FCA, which it has done in at least ten such whistle-blower cases alleging fraud and corruption in government reconstruction and security in Iraq, the whistle-blower's challenge is more difficult and he or she may end up dropping the case.[63] Although it has conducted investigations spanning several years, it has yet to recover any of the money that was misused or misspent in Iraq. In its defence, the Justice Department points to the difficulty of collecting evidence in Iraq to prove that there was fraud and corruption.

## Conclusion

While some have argued that 'the absence of prosecution reflects an absence of regulation,'[64] it is suggested here that this is only a partial explanation for the prevailing lack of legal accountability of PMSCs and their employees. For example, the US regulatory problem has been less an absence of the applicable law, and more one of the gaps, ambiguities and complexities present in a rapidly changing legislative framework, along with insufficient incentive and will to enforce an existing law that could be applied, as well as politicization of decisions whether or not to enforce the law.

Efforts to make civilian contractors legally accountable for human rights violations are highly significant given evidence of the central role that private contractors have played in interrogation and abuse of detainees both at Abu Ghraib and at Guantanamo Bay.[65] More generally, a recent estimate by the CIA indicates that more than 70 per cent of its classified intelligence budget is spent on private contracts, and other reports establish that contractors comprise between 60 and 70 per cent of the employees at the National Counterterrorism Centre and the Pentagon's Counter-intelligence Field Activity office.[66] However, recent developments in the United States law, discussed above, risk creating a double standard whereby the US military personnel and contractors are bound to respect a complete prohibition on torture, while civilians and contract employees will be held to a less-rigorous set of rules.

While it is essential that there be effective legal means to hold security contractors accountable for serious misconduct and human rights abuses, it is also important to not lose sight of higher-level accountability issues. For example, aside from the failure to prosecute civilian contractors implicated in the detainee abuse scandals at Abu Ghraib, there is evidence that the abuse by military and civilians occurred as a result of a policy sanctioned by high-level military and political officials.[67] That is, while being actors in their own right and responsible for acting lawfully, private military and security contractors are also instruments of those who hire their services, and may function as implementers of government policy. In focusing on holding individual contractors or firms accountable for their actions, we must not lose sight of the need to hold their 'principals', i.e. clients-contracting states, accountable, whether on a technical level for failing to set out contract requirements adequately, to set the necessary qualifications and training requirements of contract personnel, or to conduct effective oversight and management of the work that contractors do for them, or on a more fundamental normative and political level, for explicitly or tacitly endorsing approaches that knowingly contravene international and national law, including fundamental human rights.

## Notes

1 For the application of international law to PMSCs, see Andrew Clapham, 'Human Rights Obligations of Non-state Actors in Conflict Situations', *International Review of the Red Cross*, September 2006, vol.88(863), pp. 513–22. The application of international humanitarian law to PMSCs is discussed in the chapter by Emanuela-Chiara Gillard, this volume.
2 Deborah D. Avant, *The Market for Force: The Consequences of Privatizing Security*, Cambridge: Cambridge University Press, 2005; Peter F. Singer, *Corporate Warriors: The Rise of the Privatized Military Industry*, Ithaca, NY: Cornell University Press, 2003.
3 Coalition Provisional Authority (CPA) Order 17 (revised), www.cpa-iraq. org/regulations/20040627_CPAORD_17_Status_of_Coalition__Rev__with_ Annex_A.pdf, accessed 9 October 2007.
4 CPA Order 17, Section 5 'Waiver of Legal Immunity and Jurisdiction'.

5 US Congress, House of Representatives Committee on Oversight and Government Reform, 110th Congress, Memorandum to the Members of the Committee from the Majority Staff, 7 February 2007.

6 See Jeremy Scahill, 'Blood Is Thicker than Blackwater', *The Nation*, 8 May 2006.

7 Cesar Uco, 'Latin American Mercenaries Guarding Baghdad's Green Zone', World Socialist Website, 28 December 2005, available online at: www.wsws.org/articles/2005/dec2005/merc-d28.shtml, accessed 11 October 2007.

8 T. Christian Miller, 'War-scarred Contractors Battle Red Tape', *Los Angeles Times*, 17 June 2007.

9 For example, Steve Fainrau and Saad Al-Izzi, 'U.S. Security Contractors Open Fire in Baghdad', *Washington Post*, 27 May 2007, p. A01.

10 For example, see Amnesty International, Fact Sheet on 'Outsourcing Abuses in the "War on Terror"'.

11 In 2005, for example, four military veterans who had been employed as security contractors for the firm Custer Battles accused the firm of condoning the use of brutal tactics by its employees against unarmed Iraqi civilians, including children. Although two unrelated cases brought against the firm have been brought (and subsequently overturned or dismissed), there is no evidence of charges against the firm or its employees for brutalization and similar offences against Iraqi civilians. See Lisa Myers, 'U.S. Contractors in Iraq Allege Abuses', MSNBC.com, 17 February 2005. On the dismissed fraud charges, see Renae Merle, 'Verdict against Iraq Contractor Overturned', *Washington Post*, 19 August 2006, p. D01 and Dana Hedgpeth, 'Judge Clears Contractor of Fraud in Iraq', *Washington Post*, 9 February 2007, p. D01.

12 T. Christian Miller, 'Private Contractors Outnumber U.S. troops in Iraq', *Los Angeles Times*, 4 July 2007.

13 Amnesty International, 'Outsourcing Facilitating Human Rights Violations', *Annual Report*, 2006.

14 David Passaro, a contractor for the CIA, has been the only person associated with the CIA to be prosecuted for prisoner abuse, despite more than twenty cases of CIA personnel and civilians alleged to have been involved in prisoner abuse being forwarded to the Justice Department. Passaro received a sentence of eight years and four months in prison. See Andrea Weigl, 'Passaro Will Serve 8 Years for Beating', *News & Observer* (North Carolina), 14 February 2007.

15 One US national working for Kellogg Brown and Root was indicted for stabbing an Indian fellow contractor. US Department of Justice, Press Release, 'Military Contractor Charged with Assaulting Woman on U.S. Military Base in Iraq', 1 March 2007.

16 A US contractor working for L-3 Communications Holdings Inc. at Abu Ghraib prison was sentenced to more than three years in prison for having images of child pornography on his computer. US Attorney's Office Eastern District of Virginia, Press Release, 'Contractor Pleads Guilty to Possession of Child Pornography in Baghdad', 20 February 2007; and Matthew Barakat, 'Abu Ghraib Contractor Sentenced for Child Porn', *Associated Press*, 25 May 2007.

17 A third US citizen was sentenced to forty-six months in jail for a bid-rigging scam and paying bribes, kickbacks and gratuities to American Coalition Provisional Authority officials in Iraq in exchange for reconstruction contracts for his firm, Global Business Group. Several of his various co-conspirators have also been investigated and sentenced. US Department of Justice, Press Release, 'U.S. Contractor Sentenced in Case Involving Bribery, Fraud and Money Laundering Scheme in Al-Hillah, Iraq', 16 February 2007.

18 Eric Fair, 'An Interrogator's Nightmare', *Washington Post*, 9 February 2007, p. A19; see also Dan Ephron, 'Aftermath: Eric Fair's Abu Ghraib Confession', *Newsweek*, 18 June 2007.

19 Following the revelations of the torture of detainees at Abu Ghraib, the Justice Department established a team of six federal prosecutors in June 2004 to investigate abuse of detainees by civilian government employees, but collecting evidence has been problematic and has impeded prosecution of both civilian government employees and civilian contractors in Iraq and Afghanistan. See David Johnston, 'U.S. Inquiry Falters on Civilians Accused of Abusing Detainees', *New York Times*, 19 December 2006.
20 Salon, 'Prosecutions and Convictions', The Abu Ghraib Files, 14 March 2006, www.salon.com/news/abu_ghraib/2006/03/14/prosecutions_convictions/index.html, accessed 9 October 2007.
21 Tara McKelvey, 'Contractors Rarely Face Disciplinary Action in Iraq', Ask This, Niemen Watchdog, 15 May 2007, Niemen Foundation for Journalism at Harvard University, www.niemanwatchdog.org/index.cfm?fuseaction=ask_this.view&askthisid=269, accessed 9 October 2007.
22 Steve Fainrau, 'Hired Guns Are Wild Cards in Iraq War', *Chicago Tribune*, 16 April 2007; and Tom Jackman, 'U.S. Contractor Fired on Iraqi Vehicles for Sport, Suit Alleges', *Washington Post*, 17 November 2006, p. A20.
23 For example an Iraqi security officer was allegedly killed on Christmas eve 2006 by a US Blackwater security contractor in Baghdad's Green Zone. The contractor was immediately repatriated by the company following the incident. While an investigation was launched by the Justice Department and the Federal Bureau of Investigation, six months after the alleged shooting no charges had yet been laid against the contractor. See Yochi Dreazen, 'New Scrutiny for Iraq Contractors', *Wall Street Journal*, 14 May 2007, p. A4.
24 Jonathan Finer, 'Contractors Cleared in Videotaped Attacks', *Washington Post*, 11 June 2006, p. A18.
25 Finer, 'Contractors Cleared'.
26 Finer, 'Contractors Cleared'.
27 AEGIS Defence Services, ' "Trophy Video" Allegation', Press Release, no date, available at 5, www.aegisworld.com/article.aspx?artID=5, accessed 9 October 2007.
28 David Isenberg, 'Challenges of Security Privatisation in Iraq' in Alan Bryden and Marina Caparini (eds), *Private Actors and Security Governance*, Zurich and Münster: LIT Verlag, 2007, p. 159.
29 See Marina Caparini, 'Domestic Regulation: Licensing Regimes for the Export of Military Goods and Services', in Simon Chesterman and Chia Lehnardt (eds), *From Mercenaries to Market: The Rise and Regulation of Private Military Companies*, Oxford: OUP, 2007, pp. 158–178.
30 See Section 804 of the USA PATRIOT Act, P.L. 107–56, title VIII, 26 October 2001, 115 Stat. 377, subsequently codified as 18 USC Section 7(9).
31 Congressional Research Service, 'Private Security Contractors in Iraq: Background, Legal Status, and Other Issues', by Jenniefer K. Elsea and Nina M. Serafino, updated 21 June 2007, RL32419.
32 Human Rights Watch, 'US: Failure to Provide Justice for Afghan Victims', 15 February 2007.
33 Andrew Clapham, 'Human Rights Obligations of Non-state Actors in Conflict Situations', *International Review of the Red Cross*, September 2006, Vol. 88(863), pp. 514–16.
34 Bill Baue, 'Win or Lose in Court', *Business Ethics*, Summer 2006, pp. 12.
35 Bart Mongoven, 'The Alien Tort Claims Act: An Activist Tool for Change', Stratfor.com, 7 June 2007.
36 Baue, 'Win or Lose in Court'.
37 See 18 U.S.C. Section 2441.

38 See comments of David Rivkin, 'Fearing Prosecution, Bush Admin Tries to Change War Crimes Act', *Democracy Now!*, 16 February 2006, transcript, www.democracynow.org, accessed 9 October 2007.
39 David Crane, 'Narrowing US War Crimes Law: Having Our Cake and Eating It Too?', *Jurist*, 4 August 2006.
40 David Cole, 'Why the Court Said No', *New York Review of Books*, 10 August 2006, Vol. 53(13). Online edition, avaliable at: www.nybooks.com/articles/ 19212, accessed 11 October 2007.
41 Michael J. Matheson, 'The Amendment of the War Crimes Act', *The American Journal of International Law*, 2007, Vol. 101, pp. 51–2.
42 US Department of the Army, 'Human Intelligence Collector Operations', Field Manual 34–52, September 2005. See Appendix M, 'Humane Treatment', M-15 and M16.
43 Matheson, pp. 52–4.
44 P.L. 109–366 (Military Commission Act of 2006, 17 October 2006).
45 The MCA broadened the concept of combatancy by redefining the term 'unlawful enemy combatant' to include a person directly engaged in hostilities against the United States as well as a person who has purposefully and materially supported hostilities against the United States or its co-belligerents who is not a lawful enemy combatant. The definition thus 'removes any requirements for proximity to the battlefield itself'. See Jack M. Beard, 'The Geneva Boomerang: The Military Commissions Act of 2006 and U.S. Counterterror Operations', *The American Journal of International Law*, 2007, Vol. 101, p. 59.
46 Kevan F. Jacobson, 'Restoring UCMJ Jurisdiction over Civilian Employees During Armed Hostilities', USAWC Strategy Research Project, US Army War College, Carlisle Barracks, Pennsylvania, 14 March 2006, p. 1.
47 Griff Witte, 'New Law Could Subject Civilians to Military Trial', *Washington Post*, 15 January 2007, p. 1.
48 Glenn R. Schmitt, 'Amending the Military Extraterritorial Jurisdiction Act of 2000: rushing to close an unforeseen loophole', *Army Lawyer*, June 2005.
49 MEJA has only been used to date to bring the case against the contractor found with child porn on his work computer at Abu Ghraib. See note 14 above.
50 See MEJA, §3267 'Definitions'.
51 18 United States Code, Section 3267 (1)(A)
52 Schmitt, 'Amending the Military Extraterritorial Jurisdiction Act of 2000'.
53 Schmitt, 'Amending the Military Extraterritorial Jurisdiction Act of 2000'.
54 See Section 4, para 3 of H.R. 369 'To require accountability for personnel performing private security functions under Federal contracts, and for other purposes', 10 January 2007.
55 S.674 Transparency and Accountability in Military and Security Contracting Act of 2007, Section 7 Legal Status of Contract Personnel.
56 S.674 Transparency and Accountability Act, Section 8 Federal Bureau of Investigation Investigative Unit for Contingency Operations.
57 Jeremy Scahill, 'Who Will Stop the U.S. Shadow Army in Iraq?, 30 April 2007, www.antiwar.com, accessed 11 October 2007.
58 Peter W. Singer, 'Law Catches up to Private Militaries', *Defense Tech*, 4 January 2007.
59 Office of the Inspector General of the Department of Defense, *Review of DoD-Directed Investigations of Detainee Abuse (U)*, Report No. 06-INTEL-10, 25 August 2006, p. 68.
60 Stephen Fiddler and Demetri Sevastopulo, 'Civilian Workers Could Face Court Martial', *Financial Times*, 10 January 2007.

61 Scott Horton, 'When Lawyers Are War Criminals', Remarks delivered at the ASIL Centennial Conference on The Nuremberg War Crimes Trial, Bowling Green, Ohio, 7 October 2006.
62 Alan Grayson, 'An Oversight Hearing on Accountability for Contracting Abuses in Iraq', Senate Democratic Policy Committee Hearing, 18 September 2006.
63 Farah Stockman, 'Justice Dept. Opts Out of Whistle-Blower Suits', *Boston Globe*, 20 June 2007, p. 1.
64 Sarah Percy, 'Regulating the Private Security Industry', Adelphi Paper 384, London: Routledge for International Institute for Strategic Studies, 2006, p. 8.
65 Griff Witte and Renae Merle, 'Contractors are Cited in Abuses at Guantanamo', *Washington Post*, 4 January 2007, p. D01.
66 Tim Shorrock, 'The Corporate Takeover of U.S. Intelligence', *Salon*, 1 June 2007.
67 Seymour M. Hersh, 'The General's Report', *New Yorker*, 25 June 2007.

# Part III
# Civil–military relations

# 13 Privatization of security, international interventions and the democratic control of armed forces

*Herbert Wulf*

This chapter addresses two separate but interrelated issues of democratic control of military force. They are connected to contemporary violent conflicts and wars and to the reactions by the international community.[1]

First, the boom in the activities of private military firms is the result of various factors, among them a purposefully planned outsourcing of traditional military functions by governments to enhance their military capabilities. These companies are deeply engaged in numerous conflicts, tasked by besieged governments, international organizations, humanitarian groups, governments which intervene in foreign conflicts and so on. Tasking private firms with military jobs complicates the democratic control of the instruments of the state monopoly of force or might even make their control impossible in certain situations.

And second, interventions in today's conflicts are usually undertaken by armed forces from a number of different countries, typically so in UN peacekeeping, peace enforcement and peace-building operations. While these armed forces operate under a joint command, their control is grounded on various national rules. The democratic control of such internationalized armed forces is more complex than of national forces and no unified, democratically legitimized control authority exists.[2]

The regulation and the strict legal control of private military companies, the reform of parliamentary control of the armed forces to overcome the democratic deficit in international interventions, and the improvement and development of the monopoly of violence beyond the nation-state are of great importance in helping the international community to cope with increased calls for intervention and to establish accepted norms and rules under which force might be applied.

## Privatization of violence from below and above

Privatization of military and security services embraces a wide variety of different concepts and developments. Privatization, occasionally also called commercialization or outsourcing, includes delegating state authority in exercising the monopoly of violence. I differentiate between two principally different types of privatization of power or violence.[3]

The first type, bottom-up privatization, which could also be categorized as pre-modern, describes activities of non-state actors who use violence for their own political or economic gain. Usually, these actors operate without authorization of state authorities or even against their explicit wishes, but occasionally representatives of the state system are accomplices. The police and military forces are too weak, too corrupt or unwilling to exercise the rule of law and the state monopoly of violence. The armed non-state actors, who can also be classified as violence entrepreneurs, create a situation of insidious insecurity.[4] They are often the cause for chaotic or lawless situations or even the collapse or failure of states and are directly responsible for the loss of the state monopoly of violence. In many cases where the UN intervened, such as in Liberia, Sierra Leone, Democratic Republic of Congo, East Timor, Kosovo, Haiti and Afghanistan, these non-statutory armed forces were (and in some instances remain) the cause of the violent conflict. It is typical of such situations that the state cannot guarantee the security of its citizens and that a state monopoly of force does not exist. This does not mean that security is completely absent; often competing groups, sometimes called violence oligopolies,[5] try to establish a level of security in the areas under their control. Almost by definition, democratic control of the agents of force is totally absent.

The second type of privatization, top-down or post-modern privatization, is purposely planned and implemented by governments. The aim is to outsource traditional military and state functions to private companies. These companies offer a wide range of services: they provide not only logistics for armed forces on the battlefield, but also protection for non-state institutions such as international agencies and humanitarian organizations in post-conflict societies, for governments in their fight against rebels or insurgents, as well as for multinational companies.

Current debate about the activities of these private military firms, for example, in the conflicts in Africa or the Middle East, sometimes creates the impression that this is an entirely new phenomenon, rather than a trend that has developed with ups and downs over centuries. The state monopoly of violence, however, as it is ideally defined in theory, has never been fully accomplished, and governments have long entrusted companies or other private actors with diverse military tasks. The most prominent example is weapons manufacturing, which has been privatized in most countries during the last century.

Today, some defence ministries privatize not only logistical services, training or military planning but increasingly also the infrastructure of the armed forces as well. Companies have been entrusted with the management of military installations, especially military bases, including the servicing of military barracks, management of fleets of vehicles, purchase and stocking of uniforms, running of canteens and so on. A few companies operate alongside the armed forces, close to or on the battlefield.

## Causes and motives for outsourcing

The causes and motives that lead to the demand for services from private military companies are manifold and sometimes overlapping.[6] Several military, economic, political and ideological reasons for commercialization or privatization can be identified:

1 *The availability of qualified military personnel*: On the supply side, there are vast quantities of highly qualified military experts in many countries of the world who are no longer used in the armed forces and are now hired by the newly emerged military companies.

2 *Over-burdened armed forces*: The flipside of this development are over-burdened armed forces which are deployed in numerous military interventions abroad. Outsourcing of military missions is a reaction to bottlenecks in the availability of troops.

3 *Modern war fighting*: Armed forces tend to use ever more specialized and sophisticated equipment. As the armed forces themselves, however, are no longer in a position to use and maintain all the systems pertaining to this modern equipment, they depend on the services of companies.

4 *Demand by weak or besieged governments*: Several governments have hired private military firms with fighting capabilities when they feared being overrun by rebels.[7] Some companies have established themselves as a serious alternative to insufficiently trained, equipped or trustworthy state armed forces.[8]

5 *The intensified demand for international interventions and emergency aid*: The increasing number of war refugees, ethnic cleansing and genocide, and the fact that civilians are becoming primary targets has intensified the perception in the international community of the need to intervene in conflicts, even with the use of military power. The demand for UN peace missions was always larger than the troops and other resources offered by member states for such missions. This situation has strengthened the demand for the services of private security and military companies to support or even replace the state troops.

6 *The intensified demand for armed forces in the 'war against terror'*: Threat perceptions have completely changed since 9/11. This has affected the armed forces as they are tasked with new and additional missions.

7 *Public opinion*: For some governments it is more politically attractive to task military firms rather than the armed forces. Public awareness and criticism when 'body bags' return home have an effect on government decision-making. It is less controversial to send contractors than uniformed soldiers.

8 *The concept of a 'lean state'*: The relatively new and rapidly growing market for privately supplied security has developed into a subset of a systematic scheme to privatize state functions. The concept of a lean state is central to this development. Many state functions – civilian as well as military – are outsourced in order to find market solutions that are more cost-effective. Deployment of private military companies is seen as an effective free market method of meeting the demands for military services. Outsourcing and public–private partnership are no longer alien terms in the military.

In weak or failing states private services are generally demanded to protect or defend the government, to stabilize a society or to re-establish law and order. In some cases, certainly, military companies can indeed deliver services efficiently. Privately organized security can contribute to avoiding anarchy or chaos or other local security problems.[9] They are seen as an alternative in keeping public order if the state has insufficient security forces at its disposal. In addition, private actors are attractive to the government since they are only paid for the services they deliver; a standing regular army consumes scarce resources on a continuing basis.

In defending or promoting outsourcing of military functions the most common argument used is economic. According to the dominant economic theory, the market is better qualified to handle these functions and carry them out more efficiently than the armed forces themselves. But the private sector still needs to produce the empirical evidence that it can contribute to solving some of the budgetary difficulties of the defence sector. The economic success of privatization depends on the following three minimum conditions.[10] The service to be contracted by the public sector must be open to true and sustained competition. Real competition is essential to prevent companies from maximizing their profit-seeking strategies. But in reality this competition is often lacking. Furthermore, the client himself must have a clear understanding of what kind of services are expected and he must be able to articulate his demand. If the definition of the contract is vague, the supply of the services can be expected to be inadequate. Finally, the client must be in a position to control and verify the services delivered. Success in outsourcing requires management and control by the public sector authorities. The actual economic results of privatization of military functions in the United States and in the United Kingdom put a damper on the enthusiasm for privatization.[11] Experience shows that often more gains in efficiency are promised or hoped for than are actually delivered.

## The public good 'security' and the democratic control of the monopoly of violence

The policy of outsourcing military functions is an effort to create more efficient armed forces. But this notion also has an inherent danger since a central function of the state, the monopoly of violence, could be damaged or endangered. Privatization is not by definition a total renunciation of state functions or their controls, but rather the *delegation* of public services to non-state organizations. In many developing countries a proper and efficient state monopoly of force has never existed. And the long-term historical trend shows that the nation-state that exercises a monopoly of force is actually an exception. Despite the fact that the norm of the state monopoly of force is not questioned in principle, it is being restricted or undermined in practice.

Deployment of private military companies is not without tension, because of the friction generated by the interaction of two partially competing processes, namely the delegation of the state's guarantee of security to contractors versus the contractors' prime motive of maximizing the economic gain of their company. The public good 'security' and the private good 'economic gain' can be in competition with each other or even be contradictory. Therefore, in privatizing public goods, certain limitations should be observed. Although these private military companies might offer specialized services, they might nevertheless be reluctant to engage in providing security or preventing war by military means if too high a risk exists of losing the companies' assets in such conflicts. Is this risk-avoidance strategy of private companies possibly a new and completely unexpected barrier to the engagement in fighting? Or is the profit motif of the companies a conflict accelerator?

Deployment of private companies has a profound impact on how the state monopoly of violence is exercised and controlled. An important consideration must be that these companies are presently not accountable to parliament or the public. While the government is held accountable by parliament, private companies are responsible only to their shareholders and clients. This is precisely the reason why some governments find private companies attractive.

Contracting private companies might result in mutual dependencies between client and contractor, and conflicts might be extended in the bilateral interest of such contracts. In such a situation it is not clear which state tasks can be implemented, who decides upon them, and if decisions are taken as to the way in which the monopoly of violence (which, strictly speaking, is no longer a monopoly) is carried out. Contractors seem to create their own demand or at least have influence on shaping the demand for security services when security is purchased commercially.

There are presently no indicators that the privatization trend is being reversed or that countervailing forces are in the making. While companies might contribute to security if they are properly regulated and monitored, and many people rely on them for their everyday security, they have also become a source of insecurity in many countries. The privatization of violence is a trend of great concern since it questions the public good security and transforms it into a commercial and marketable product. Experts capable of performing almost any military job wait to be called.

Economic power can now be more quickly transformed into military power than before.

The extent of the currently existing regulation of these violence actors is inadequate. National laws have been introduced in only a few countries; international law and the regulation of mercenary activities are deficient or do not apply. To ensure a public monopoly of force, steps need to be taken to improve regulation of the private security and military companies at the international and global level. The significant difference between outsourcing postal, railway or utility services and outsourcing military, police or judicial functions is of a qualitative nature, the defining aspect of this difference being that they involve an erosion of the public monopoly of force. The combination of privatization (including privatization of violence) and globalization can give rise to a process that is almost the reverse of the process through which modern states were constructed.

## The changed role of the military

Globalization and the ensuing erosion of the nation-state are a fundamental challenge to the efficacy of state-oriented monopoly of force inasmuch as that globalization leads to de-nationalization and promotes the relocation of authority, from the nation-state to supranational actors. Globalization has not only changed the conditions for the model of the nation-state, but the consequences of globalization and the reaction to international military interventions has also another long-term effect, namely it calls into question the concept of nationally organized and orientated armies. Precisely because the military possesses the instruments of ultimate power, it is highly important to regulate its legitimacy, civilian control and accountability. Yet it is exactly owing to military requirements that the military is the least democratically structured organization in most countries; the conduct of the military in situations of armed conflict and its command structure collide directly with the concepts of liberty and individuality.[12]

Expert studies offer a plethora of systematic analyses of the institutionalization of democracy in nation-states. Likewise, the literature on global governance hosts many future-oriented publications. Yet, the democratic control of the armed forces and the question of responsibility in international operations are poorly researched.

Whereas nation-states possess elaborate and systematic doctrines for military operations containing clear delimitations of competences and responsibilities, similar regimes on the international level are almost completely lacking for UN peacekeeping missions. Specifically, the UN peacekeeping infrastructure lacks adequate institutional guidance concerning the civilian control of military operations and responsibilities for norm compliance.[13] For military operations conducted under the auspices of the UN the requirement prevails that military commanders are responsible to civilian authorities – mostly the UN Secretary General. The Security Council authorizes missions, yet the armed forces are responsible to their respective national civilian authorities. Moreover, it has become common practice that those units operating under UN command touch base regularly with their national superiors. Ku and Jacobson[14] conclude: 'It is highly implausible that these commanders have ever followed an order given in the international chain of command to which their national authorities have not at least acquiesced, if not given their approval.' It is fair to assume that international military operations have been altered by national instructions with respect to both planning and conduct. In this game of mixed competences and responsibilities, questions regarding who has the final say and what are the clear delimitations of competence are not answered.

At the national level especially, many norms with respect to the conduct of soldiers in war and conflict situations have been developed. However, not until 1999 was it decided that armed forces under the command of the UN are subject to the Geneva Conventions. The issue of crimes committed by peacekeepers only became regulated with the establishment of the International Criminal Court (with important exceptions, particularly that of the self-imposed exclusion of the United States).

The intensification of international interventions and their increasingly military nature are a challenge for the armed forces since they are confronted with new types of missions, requiring a new organization and new doctrines. To cope with these new challenges international co-operation and an international orientation of the military organization are vital. This development requires that the armed forces are reformed and restructured if they are to prevent conflict for humanitarian reasons or to react to the new wars.[15] Three changes are important in this regard: A major new development is the change in the military purpose from fighting wars to missions that would not be considered military in the traditional sense, namely peace building which includes post-conflict reconstruction tasks. Another change, mentioned above, is that the military forces are used more in international missions authorized by entities beyond the nation-state. A third change is the internationalization of military forces themselves.

International democratic control of the armed forces has not developed in parallel to changes in the nature of international military interventions and the consequent reorganization of the forces. A culture of accountability of the decision makers is glaringly absent. Democratic control, if exercised at all, takes place at the national level as in the past but not internationally.

Accountability and democratic control of internationally implemented interventions is – as a rule – more complex and complicated than national deployments. When conducting international interventions the desire of democratic decision makers for efficient control is stronger, because the risk for the troops is larger, the missions last longer and the success of a military action is less likely.

The question is, whether the exclusively nationally oriented democratic control of the armed forces – conceptually as well as practically – serves the purpose of multinational missions or if this control is no longer sufficient and needs to be reformed? But truly internationalized military institutions and structures are still not very common; however a beginning of this development can be seen in the efforts of the European Union to create a rapid reaction force.

The debates on civil–military relations indicate how complex the democratic control of the armed forces is at the national level in democratic countries.[16] The engagement of private military companies and their growing activities in recent years is an additional complication to upholding the delicate civil–military balance. The relationship between the military and private military firms is not without a certain degree of tension that affects the operations of the armed forces. But more important is the fact that neither the executive government nor parliament has effective control over these new actors on the battlefield.

The obviously insufficient democratic controls of the armed forces and of private military companies at the national level are even more visible and distinct on the international plane. The evolution of new types of civil–military relations at the national and more so on the international level is both a challenge and an opportunity. However, the international community is far from establishing the accepted national democratic practices of civil–military relations with regard to international interventions.[17]

The major impact of privatizing and internationalizing military functions is a fundamental change in the role of the military in its relation to the nation-state and the long-term effects for the state monopoly of force. Globalization has changed the basic concept of the nation-state. Even the concept of nationally organized and oriented armies is questioned. In most cases, national governments can no longer take unilateral decisions regarding war and the use of force.

## Conclusion

Though the two trends of privatizing military force and internationalizing the armed forces are separate developments, they are nevertheless interconnected. Both outsourcing military functions to private contractors and the absence of strict parliamentary controls in international military operations have undesirable effects on exercising the monopoly of violence as long as this monopoly remains with the nation-state. Therefore, reforms are required in the two interrelated areas; in the regulation of private military companies and in the restructuring of nationally oriented armed forces which are increasingly deployed internationally.

1   *Regulation of private military companies*: There is a real danger that the state instruments of force may fall into the hands of non-state actors such as criminal gangs, insurgents, militias and rebels, or they will be handed over to privately operating companies. Efficient rules are urgently required to uphold the public monopoly of violence, especially in weak states.

Three principally different approaches to deal with the increasing but unregulated practices of private military companies are possible: prohibition, reliance on self-regulation of companies and national and international legally binding regulations. A comprehensive prohibition of private military companies would be the most direct control, but there are a number of reasons that make this an impracticable solution, not the least of which is that it would be difficult to implement this prohibition extraterritorially on the basis of national laws. To ignore the problem and to hope for the self-regulation of the companies, as has been suggested by company and industry representatives, seems inadequate given that companies cannot be forced to abide by certain behaviour or to accept the code of conduct of an industry association. In any case, the 'black sheep' within the industry would not observe the self-regulation mechanism. In some areas, industry codes have improved the situation and some of the illegal and unfair practices have been stopped. Self-regulatory initiatives by companies and industry associations are positive, but they are not sufficient since neither the problematic cases in the grey zone between legal and illegal activities nor what are clearly illegal excesses can be prevented or prosecuted. A whole range of different, partly complementary options for national and international regulation are available, reaching from the expansion or reformulation of the Geneva Conventions, to establishing a government-controlled licensing system, to national registration, to international registration and verification.[18] Lessons for regulations and their shortcomings can be learned from the history and practice of arms-transfer regulation. Reforms of parliamentary control of the tools of violence need not only take the new realities of increased international interventions of the military into account, but should also recognize that the operation of private actors close to or on the battlefield has become common practice in recent years. Since the privatization of military force is not likely to be reversed, there is a requirement to keep those private military actors under control and make them accountable.

2   *The role of parliaments in authorizing interventions*: The role of parliaments in authorizing military interventions, such as peace operations, and their implementation varies greatly in different countries. Parliaments in only a few countries have the constitutional right to make decisions concerning the deployment of national troops in war and crises. Moreover, there is hardly any parliamentary role anywhere regarding as to when private military companies are contracted to perform military services. National parliaments are in some cases part of the decision making process when international interventions are planned, but in most

cases the parliamentary role is marginal, and not sufficient to facilitate the creation of democratic standards and norms at the international level. Damrosch[19] concludes that parliaments have in recent years played a more intensified role in deployment decisions. But even in those countries with more explicit parliamentary decision making, tensions exist between parliamentary control and the internationally relevant decisions of the executive and their accountability *vis-à-vis* parliament and the public.[20]

Beyond the legislative function the parliament can use its budgetary powers as a key function and effective instrument to strengthen the role of parliament to be able to influence or prevent the executive decisions. Nevertheless, while this is not uncommon with regard to the deployment of troops, contracts with military firms and the deployment of contract personnel are hardly on the agenda of parliaments. So far parliaments have not realized that they need to play a role in controlling the executive in this area too. To be fully effective improved parliamentary oversight of peace operations would imply making private military companies as accountable as the armed forces.

Constitutions were not designed originally with a view to cover UN peacekeeping or peace enforcement operations. Given the large number and permanence of such international missions and relief programs, constitutional amendments might be necessary in some countries. Inadequate parliamentary and democratic control, however, is not only a result of constitutional gaps. It is important not only to strengthen the various parliamentary functions but also to shore up the willingness of parliamentarians and their ability to engage in such issues.[21] Parliaments must attempt to find the middle road between the present widespread absence of controls on the one hand and an overemphasis of parliamentary intervention on the other.

An additional area in need of democratic reform, which is not discussed here in detail, is the international level and the future of the monopoly of violence. At the global level the monopoly of violence is a completely open question. The established, although often inadequate, control mechanisms at the national level are complicated when international missions are decided upon and the national control instruments are often unsatisfactory for this purpose.[22] Increasing internationalization and globalization results in some erosion of sovereignty and requires co-operation among nations. The nation-state alone can no longer effectively exercise the monopoly of force in such a changed environment. At the same time, the lack of legitimacy and the democratic deficit at the international level becomes more and more evident. The more decisions are transferred from the national to the international sphere the more difficult the situation will be for the elected national parliaments. A system beyond the nation-state with overlapping authorities entitled to exercise the monopoly of violence is required. Given that the assault on Westphalian nation-state system is so far-reaching such alternatives need to be considered, even though they might appear utopian at first sight.

## Notes

1 This chapter is based on a recent book publication of the author, Herbert Wulf, *Internationalization and Privatizing War and Peace*, New York: Palgrave Macmillan, 2005.

2 A third area of lacking democratic control, the decisions of the UN Security Council to intervene, is not addressed here.

3 Robert Mandel, 'The Privatization of Security', *Armed Forces & Society*, 2001, Vol. 28(1), pp. 129–51.

4 Georg Elwert et al. (Hg): '*Dynamics of Violence: Processes of Escalation and De-escalation in Violent Group Conflicts*. Sociologus Beiheft 1. Berlin: Duncker and Humblot Verlag, pp. 119–32.

5 Andreas Mehler, 'Dezentralisierung, Machtteilung und Krisenprävention', in Tobias Debiel (ed.), *Der zerbrechliche Frieden*, Bonn: Dietz Verlag, 2002, pp. 121–40.

6 Peter W. Singer, *Corporate Warriors: The Rise of the Privatized Military Industry*, Ithaca, NY: Cornell University Press, 2003.

7 Abdel-Fatau Musah, and J.K. Fayemi (eds), *Mercenaries: An African Security Dilemma*, London: Pluto, 2000; and Damian Lilly and Michael von Tangen Page (eds), *Security Sector Reform: The Challenges and Opportunities of the Privatisation of Security*, London: International Alert, 2002.

8 Stefan Mair and Die Rolle von, 'Private Military Companies in Gewaltkonflikten' in Sabine Kurtenbach and Peter Lock (eds), *Kriege als (Über)Lebenswelten*, Bonn: Dietz Verlag, 2004, pp. 260–73.

9 Mandel, 'The Privatization of Security'.

10 A. Markusen, 'The Case against Privatizing National Security', *Governance* 2003, Vol. 16(4), pp. 472–8.

11 Wulf, *Internationalization and Privatizing War and Peace*, pp. 185–92.

12 Richard H. Kohn, 'How Democracies Control the Military', *Journal of Democracy* 1997, Vol. 8(4), p. 141.

13 Charlotte Ku and Harold K. Jacobson, 'Using Military Forces under International Auspices and Democratic Accountability', *International Relations of the Asia-Pacific* 2001, Vol. 1, p. 35.

14 Ibid., p. 45.

15 Charles C. Moskos, John Allen Williams and David R. Segal (eds), *The Postmodern Military*, Oxford: Oxford University Press, 2000, pp. 1–5.

16 Peter D. Feaver, Richard H. Kohn and Lindsay P. Cohn, 'The Gap between Military and Civilian in the United States Perspective' in Peter D. Feaver and Richard H. Kohn (eds), *Soldiers and Civilians: The Civil–Military Gap and American National Security*, Cambridge, MA: MIT Press, 2001, p. 1.

17 Hans Born and Heiner Hänggi, (eds) *The Double Democratic Deficit*, Aldershot: Ashgate 2004 correctly points out not only a democratic deficit in international and regional organizations but also in the national context. The authors write of a 'double democratic deficit' in decisions about war and peace – nationally and internationally.

18 Fred Schreier and Marina Caparini, *Law, Practice and Governance of Private Military and Security Companies*, Occasional Paper No. 6, Geneva: Geneva Centre for the Democratic Control of the Armed Forces, March 2005; and Wulf, *Internationalization and Privatizing War and Peace*.

19 Lori Fisler Damrosch, 'The Interface of National Constitutional Systems with International Law and Institutions on Using Military Forces: Changing Trends in Executive and Legislative Powers' in Charlotte Ku and Harold K. Jacobson (eds), *Democratic Accountability and the Use of Force in International Law,* Cambridge: Cambridge University Press, 2003, pp. 39–60.
20 Hans Born and Marlene Urscheler, 'Parliamentary Accountability of Multinational Peace Support Operations: A Comparative Perspective', in Hans Born and Heiner Hänggi (eds), *The Double Democratic Deficit*, Aldershot: Ashgate, 2004, p. 63.
21 Heiner Hänggi, 'The Use of Force under International Auspices: Parliamentary Accountability and "Democratic Deficits"' in Hans Born and Heiner Hänggi (eds), *The Double Democratic Deficit*, pp. 12–15.
22 Herbert Wulf, *Good Governance beyond Borders: Creating a Multi-level Public Monopoly of Legitimate Force*, Occasional Paper No. 10, Geneva Centre for the Democratic Control of Armed Forces, April, 2006.

# 14 Privatized peace?

## Assessing the interplay between states, humanitarians and private security companies

*Christopher Spearin*

During the course of the 1990s, a number of supply and demand arguments suggested the desired necessity of 'privatized peace', meaning that private security companies (PSCs), through their application and management of violence, should become involved in peacebuilding, peacekeeping and peace enforcement activities. Former Soviet bloc countries no longer possessed the interest or capacity to come to the aid of their Cold War clients in the developing world. Similarly, many Western states did not see the geostrategic imperative to become involved in dangerous environments that could lead to casualties. Developing world countries did sometimes conduct interventions under UN sanction, but their troops frequently lacked the appropriate equipment, training and professionalism. In light of these limitations, the Brahimi report on peace operations asserted that '[n]o amount of good intentions can substitute for the fundamental ability to project credible force.'[1] PSCs, therefore, were a possibility in filling the void left by states in countering intra-state strife.

At a deeper or more fundamental level, the notion of privatized peace ostensibly reinforces a larger shift in how international affairs are conducted and in how the international environment is populated. First, many analyses, starting in the late 1980s, take the tone that the state is no longer the primary actor in world politics, or that the state has lost its authority or capacity to act in certain realms, or that the state must have to compete against, cooperate with, or live alongside non-state actors of growing prominence. These arguments reveal, *vis-à-vis* states, a degree of freedom and independence held by non-state actors, such as humanitarian non-governmental organizations (NGOs), not evident since pre-Westphalian times. In addition, with respect to PSCs specifically, they suggest that, in a zero-sum sense, all states decline and suffer in terms of their utility and as social constructs because they are no longer the sole containers of violence in the Weberian sense. Second, the seeming success of PSCs, especially Executive Outcomes (EO) of South Africa, in quelling violence that was not only morally repugnant, especially given the ethnic cleansing and genocidal events in the 1990s which the community of states would not or could not counter, but also reveals a possible avenue for non-state providers of violence to regain their legitimacy and acceptance in the international milieu. In this vein, the promotion of human security seemingly advances the important role to be played by non-state actors of whatever stripe. Overall then, for analysts such as Doug Brooks, PSCs offer a basic solution in countering post-Cold War violence: 'Write a cheque, end a war'.[2] This cheque writing would not only serve international needs; but it would also reinforce significant changes in international affairs and enhance the stature of the PSC industry.

Yet in the now post-9/11 environment, the cheques have still not yet been written for PSCs to apply and manage violence to bring about privatized peace in any substantial or independent way. This chapter's objective, therefore, is to consider how the aforementioned dynamics between states and non-state actors have not evolved as some expected. To make this case, the chapter first considers more closely these arguments and then contends that the privatization of security does not affect all states in the same way; it presents unique possibilities for powerful states. With particular respect to the United States, as the world's only super-power, it has the ability to structure the PSC marketplace and provide a significant amount of opportunity that draws upon globally sourced security sector expertise. As a result, PSCs help to substantiate US power, but in so doing, they lose some of their independence and freedom of action in return for continued remuneration and legitimacy granted by the global hegemon. This in turn sets limitations on the PSC industry itself. As for humanitarian non-governmental organizations (NGOs), they have not developed relationships with PSCs so that together these non-state actors could operate with a substantial degree of independence from states. This stems from the hesitancy of NGOs regarding violence generally and PSCs specifically and from the important, and largely subservient, relationships they have developed with states. On the whole, the inter-national dynamics of privatized security have not developed in a vacuum such that all cases and clients are equal; the state, and especially powerful states, structure the marketplace for security sector expertise.

## Arguments of state decline and the rise of the non-state actor

A broad brushstroke survey of the relevant literature, dating back to the late 1980s, finds a number of factors leading to why the centralized nation-state, dominant for the past three and a half centuries, may be in the process of decline.[3] The growth of the world economy permits the easy movement of people, products, services and ideas across borders, often at the expense of state control. The proliferation of computing and communications technologies empowers individuals and groups and facilitates their ability to organize effectively. It also allows for allegiances, loyalties and communities to flourish that are not necessarily contained within the state. Similarly, global market pressures frequently lead states to embrace neoliberal thinking and privatization, a cumulative process that promotes the retreat of state presence. Also, complex cross-border challenges exist, such as environmental degradation, the spread of disease and refugee movements that no one state can manage and that require the growing expertise held by non-state actors. For instance, the early 1990s marked the start of the 'NGOization of politics', a process recognized by then UN Secretary General Boutros Boutros Ghali when he stressed the specific expertise of NGOs in the fields of advocacy, conflict prevention, aid delivery and post-conflict peacebuilding.[4] Not only, therefore, are non-state actors empowered through cross-border activism and economic activity, but they have also entered the state domain of peace and security policy.[5]

This line of argument, cumulatively, does not suggest that the state is to disappear from the world stage anytime soon, but it is increasingly clear that its dominance on the international stage is questionable. This shift is described by James Rosenau as requiring the state to 'compete, conflict, cooperate, or otherwise interact' with the growing array of non-state actors.[6] Such is the makeup of this state/non-state interaction that, for Lawrence Freedman, the very nature of statecraft as traditionally understood is in question:

> [A]ny grand strategy for a status quo state in the twenty-first century may not so much be about protecting its international position *vis-à-vis* other more radical states, but *vis-à-vis* these more fundamental shifts in the system that contest the very idea of the state.[7]

Another challenge is that, despite the emphasis placed on them in international affairs, many states in the post-colonial or post-communist contexts lack the ability to provide for their citizenries and to ensure their security as assumed in the Hobbesian bargain. The advent of human security, therefore, points towards readjusting the balance between ends and means such that individuals are treated more as the former and states as the later. In this regard, Caroline Thomas asserts that, 'it is helpful to understand their significance [states] in terms of their contribution to human security and not simply for their own sake.'[8] As spelled out in the UN's *1994 Human Development Report*, this means that human security is necessarily a wide-ranging concept: 'It is concerned with how people live and breathe in a society, how freely they exercise their many choices, how much access they have to market and social opportunities – and whether they live in conflict or peace.'[9]

This is not to contend that human security entails anti-statism. States with the appropriate resources are encouraged to promote human security domestically, their apparent *raison d'être*. As well, the promotion of human security is not meant to bring about different political forms;

its promotion can assist weak states in developing strengths, competencies and good governance. However, given the wide range of problems and their considerable spread across the globe, it is clear that states cannot be alone in this task. Certainly, the International Commission on Intervention and State Sovereignty acknowledges the scope of the concept given that human security has a universal and indivisible application: 'Human security means the security of people – their physical safety, their economic and social well-being, respect for their dignity and worth as human beings, and the protection of their basic human rights and fundamental freedoms.'[10]

In addition to the functional requirements regarding human security promotion, ethical requirements, whether they relate to humanism or cosmopolitanism, raise the concept's purview beyond state-centrism. When a state, due to its lack of empirical attributes or the systematic abuse of its citizenry, becomes a problematic instrument in the promotion of human security, other actors should respond. As a result, the promotion of human security is a 'diffused responsibility' as described by Emma Rothschild, one that extends: (1) downwards to the individual; (2) upwards to the international system and the natural environment; (3) horizontally to other entities in order to cover all the threats posed to human security and (4) in all these directions in terms of political responsibility. On the latter point, this covers expansion that is 'upwards towards international institutions, downwards to regional or local government, and sideways to non-governmental organizations, to public opinion and the press, and to the abstract forces of nature or of the market'.[11]

These trends regarding non-state actors and human security arguably came together in the context of EO and its operations in Angola and Sierra Leone in the mid-1990s. From one standpoint, EO, with its use of force, revealed that its client states did not possess a monopoly on internal violence nor did South Africa, EO's home state, possess a monopoly over violence emanating from its borders. Therefore, EO's operations, those of a private, non-state actor, stood in sharp contrast to two of the tradition-ally assumed characteristics of statehood.[12] EO's expertise, transnational reach and lack of national allegiance seemingly suggested a new, unique and independent form of power in international affairs. PSCs could apparently determine for whom they worked and what skills they passed on to clients such that the Westphalian architecture of state security and international relations was now in question.

From another standpoint, although EO's activities were not without criticism, this PSC is often credited with developing the conditions that contributed to the human security of Angolans and Sierra Leonians. Proponents of EO contend that it terminated the fighting, forced the respective rebel movements in each country to the bargaining table, ended the atrocities committed by rebels, helped with the repatriation of child soldiers, interacted with NGOs to facilitate the delivery of humanitarian assistance and contributed to the reinvigoration of normal economic activity and democratic development.[13] Moreover, it brought about these successes that outside states and the UN alike failed to achieve both before and after EO's contracts.

In light of the relevance of non-state actors, human security and the apparent characteristics and successes of EO, it is surprising that there have not been further private interventions in the likes of EO's activities in Angola and Sierra Leone. This is despite the fact that a prominent lobby group for PSCs in the United States is the International *Peace Operations* Association (italics added). The term 'peace operations' brings to mind the UN and suggests a certain role to play and a certain marketplace to serve. Why, then, has the industry not evolved in the way suggested in earlier analysis? What can be garnered by looking at the actual relationships between states and non-states? It is to answering these questions that the chapter now turns.

## US unipolarity, military requirements and the draw of private security sector expertise

First, a caveat: the privatization of security has had a profound impact upon the management and ownership of security sector expertise such that state centralization and good governance have not necessarily been the outcomes of the private presence. The state, especially in the developing world context, has arguably declined or retreated in many cases.[14] However, the effects and implications of private security have not been even or the same the world over. In fact, for developed world states and especially for the United States, while PSCs do present ramifications stemming from the private management and ownership of security sector expertise, PSCs are increasingly not seen as 'rogue' actors in the sense of possessing independent initiative at the strategic level. Instead, one can argue that many PSCs are the tools of developed world statecraft. This falls in line with realism's contentions as espoused by the likes of Hans Morgenthau, Kenneth Waltz and John Mearsheimer that powerful states in the international system are not only affected by global phenomena differently, but they can also to a certain extent shape these phenomena to their benefit.[15] Thus, Norrin Ripsman and T.V. Paul assert that it 'is not whether the new challenges of globalization will overwhelm the state but in what ways will they alter the state and what mechanisms will the state use to adapt to global social forces while retaining its centrality'.[16] How, therefore, has the United States in particular, as the unipolar power, managed to draw in private security sector expertise such that strategic independence, the likes of which was exercised by EO to advance privatized peace, has largely been eschewed by, or denied to, the private sector?

To help frame the answer to this question, one can note a truism in international affairs: a hegemonic power possesses unique responsibilities and faces unique challenges that demand an assertive posture, if not presence, internationally. Moreover, with respect to the United States specifically, the attacks of 11 September 2001 and the consequent 'War on Terror' serve to reinforce this general sense of activism. Given that at least 20,000 private security personnel are operating in Iraq alone, making them collectively the largest force in the country save the US military and Iraqi security sector institutions, it is clear that PSCs are thriving in an international marketplace influenced heavily by the United States.

Troop limitations, in part, create the US demand for private security sector expertise. Since the first Gulf War in 1990–91, the US military decreased in size by 35 per cent. Specifically, the active strength of the US Army fell from 711,000 personnel to the current number of 487,000. This reduction contributed to insufficient numbers of 'boots on the ground' to conduct policing, counterinsurgency or nation-building activities. In turn, this limited force faces a high operational tempo, a factor that has implications for readiness, recruitment and retention. Whereas US politicians are wary about reinstituting the draft, Department of Defense (DoD) officials are wary of increasing the size of the active force because of the extra costs required for training, benefits, medical care and pensions.

Moreover, any extra costs here would likely take away from the US military's transformation towards the 'new American way of war', a way that emphasizes a reliance upon high technology, precision-guided munitions, air power and special operations forces.[17] The expense of additional personnel costs, as expressed by former Defence Secretary Donald Rumsfeld, could be detrimental: 'I am very reluctant to increase end strength... Resources are always finite, and the question is, would we be better off increasing manpower or increasing capability and lethality?'[18] Clearly, however, the challenges here are circular, because not all of the components of this new way directly support the aforementioned activities related to 'boots on the ground'. Private boots, therefore, permit for the new way to evolve while at the same time allowing for sufficient strength on the ground without the long-term costs associated with expanding the ranks of those in uniform.

The US demand is also, in part, made real by international political factors. In the past, traditional US allies, such as countries in Western Europe, have provided the personnel for numerous types of ground operations. On the one hand, this has caused resentment in some circles such that Europe is viewed as 'the cleaning lady to American intervention'.[19] On the other hand, this does lead arguably to a military division of labour within NATO and it recognizes the difficulties Europe has faced in terms of catching up technologically with the United States to ensure sufficient interoperability in all types of operations. Even with the first-ever evocation of NATO's Article 5 in 2001, the volume of military assets offered by alliance members in the context of Afghanistan operations was 'underwhelming'.[20]

But in addition to capability arguments, while the international political legitimacy provided by a formal alliance is appealing, it can also serve to overly bind the United States. For many, this was made clear in earlier operations in the Balkans.[21] As such, important guiding documents for the US military do not emphasize reliance upon military allies.[22] PSCs, therefore, can provide the flexibility wished for by the United States because it need not develop consensus decisions or follow the lowest common denominator as is often the case with alliance politicking.

As a result, there is less of a need for a PSC to assert independent and far-searching initiative because with the hegemon as the client – a client with worldwide responsibilities – contractual opportunities will continue to arise, and lucrative ones at that. Note, for instance, the shift made by Tim Spicer, the public face of the now-defunct Sandline International, a firm that offered similar services to EO. Mr Spicer is currently Chief Executive of Aegis Defence Services Limited, the PSC hired by Washington for US$293 million to coordinate the actions of the other PSCs operating in Iraq. Consider also that in Iraq, the US Government Accountability Office reported in July 2005 that with US$60 billion directed towards reconstruction, for some projects the costs of security equated to a considerable 36 per cent.[23]

Moreover, while the 'Baghdad bubble' may eventually burst, the US demand for private security sector services will likely not decline. The manpower issues mentioned above will continue to exist. As well, the US strategy of preventative war requires that Washington have access to a sufficient manpower pool to conduct operations overseas and serve in reserve as a deterrent to rogue states and terrorist organizations. Should the United States become bogged down in any particular operation such that its military manpower becomes overly strained, US credibility and Washington's ability to deter will both suffer. The rise of China, India and/or a resurgent Russia as potential peer competitors, the prevention of which is also a component of Washington's grand strategy to ensure US primacy, also highlights capability issues. Taken together, US geostrategic posture, whether in the war on terror or in preventing hegemonic decline, presents considerable opportunities to PSCs and significantly lessens the requirement for them to exercise their assumed freedom as non-state actors and strike out in search of other wide-ranging opportunities the world over.

Finally, beyond the matter of financial remuneration, the heavy reliance of the world's hegemon upon PSCs provides them with long sought-after assets – legitimacy and acceptance. With respect to Iraq, US military operations were launched against insurgents in the wake of the killings of PSC personnel.[24] US officials have praised the work of private US personnel, they have publicly mourned their deaths, and they have attended their funerals back in the United States. Highly public and influential exposure removes some of the pejorative tone that has been cast on the word 'mercenary' over the past two centuries. It also lessens the need for PSCs to promote what they could offer in terms of peacekeeping or the promotion of human security. While advertising services meant to independently counter intra-state violence in the 1990s at a time when the UN and states alike faced difficulties in responding may have been a way for PSCs to ingratiate themselves, the international context and the private security industry itself have evolved such that this emphasis is no longer necessary.[25]

In sum, because of the qualitative and quantitative characteristics of the relationship the United States has with PSCs, and will likely have with them over the longer term, this suggests, using the language of game theory, that the relationship will be an iterative game and should not be viewed as a simple, one-time arrangement between a principal and agent. Given the increasing US proclivity to rely upon the PSC industry, the majority of the prominent PSCs are now based in the United States. PSCs in other prominent supplier states, such as the United Kingdom, are also increasingly geared to serve the hegemon's marketplace. This terminates any lingering concerns that, as a transnational business actor, these PSCs either would, in an independent sense, act in ways contrary to the interests of prominent state clients (let alone switch sides in search of higher reward). Not only would this have the PSCs potentially face the wrath of powerful states in the international system, but also it would likely close down the lucrative market opportunities upon which they heavily rely. US influence over the PSC industry cannot be understated because the United States 'has chosen to play a large consumer role in the market and its choices have therefore had a large impact on the market's ecology'.[26] While reliance upon PSCs will surely have a long-standing impact on how the US projects security sector expertise beyond its borders, the United States will in turn be able to inform and structure, in large part, the nature of the global private security industry itself.

## Non-state humanitarian interaction

In light of the aforementioned 'NGOization of politics' in the post-Cold War setting, one might have expected greater interaction between the NGOs and PSCs given the contexts in which they operate and the independence from states they presumably hold. Analysts such as Paul Ghils view NGOs, amongst their different activities, as critical of states, in competition with states, and acting autonomously of states.[27] In the 1990s, the worldwide presence of NGOs and their expertise seemingly not possessed by state actors permitted their delivery of assistance in a number of intra-state conflicts, conflicts in which developed world states did not wish to intervene. However, this considerable level of NGO involvement led to attacks against NGO personnel and a hindrance of NGO activities. In part, this was because NGOs were getting caught in the crossfire in conflict-torn countries. But it was also the case that even if NGOs followed the humanitarian ethic's principles of neutrality, impartiality and humanity, the effects of their assistance had negative implications on the ground. Therefore, stopping humanitarian assistance or manipulating its delivery was often a goal of warring parties. Similarly, many of these groups did not respect the presumed sanctity of humanitarian assistance and purposely targeted NGOs out of greed. As a result, in the 1990s, the personnel of ICRC, CARE USA, Caritas, Save the Children, Norwegian Peoples Aid, German Agro Action, Médecins du Monde and Médecins Sans Frontières were all subject to threats, kidnappings and/or the murder of their personnel.

NGO/PSC interaction seemingly presents the possibility for humanitarian assistance to be delivered and for NGO personnel to operate unmolested in conflict environments. For PSCs, this interaction offers greater legitimacy for their services given the prominence of NGOs and the hoped-for positive nature of NGO work. In this way, PSCs might hitch themselves to a general humanitarian trend explained by Michael Barnett: 'Humanitarianism became so popular that everyone wanted to be a humanitarian and to label their activities as humanitarian. The result was that humanitarianism became caught...in broader activities and practices.'[28] What is more, because of the global need and the level of NGO involvement in humanitarian affairs, the interaction between NGOs and PSCs ostensibly offers lucrative opportunities for PSCs well into the future.

This scale of interaction, however, has not materialized. While some NGOs are more pragmatic than others, and while PSCs differ substantially from the soldiers of fortune, many NGO leaders are concerned that their involvement with PSCs would legitimize mercenarism (in its most pejorative sense), hamper the image of their particular organization, and/ or tarnish humanitarianism generally.[29] Greg Nakano and Chris Seiple, for instance, contend that NGOs have to face up to the implications posed by their interaction with PSCs: 'Aid agencies need to consider how they might be contributing...to this trend and how this squares with their humanitarian goal of relieving human suffering.'[30] Another concern is how interaction would impact upon the humanitarian ethic because of the desire to deliver assistance free from the influence and normative framework of armed actors, whatever their nature.

Moreover, in the cases in which PSCs and NGOs did interact, the independence from states implied in the NGO–PSC relationship is frequently not forthcoming. To explain, Howard Lentner asserts that we need to look at the links NGOs hold with states: '[T]he immense growth of NGO activities in international politics...results from political decisions and a framework that has been put into place by the leading powers.'[31] Because NGOs increasingly receive considerable amounts of their funding from states, NGOs can be seen as the privatized arm of state foreign policy. By serving in this manner, NGO activities, as described by Larry Minear, contribute to the 'humanitarian alibi', meaning action that avoids essential political measures made by states concerning non-strategic areas.[32] In fact, to substantiate the humanitarian alibi, it has been the case that states often pressure NGOs to purchase PSC services.[33] This opens the possibility for state funds funnelled to NGOs to then pay for the presence of PSCs, hardly a sign of independent non-state initiative. Likewise, because the humanitarian sector is described as 'fiercely competitive', this sees many NGOs attentive to the concerns of their major donors – states – and thus raises the possibility of NGOs operating in line with state wishes with PSCs following in tow.[34]

The dynamics found in the Iraq case draw interaction between PSCs and NGOs even closer to state influence, namely that exercised by the United States. As occurred in other strife-plagued regions in the 1990s, NGO personnel face considerable dangers and work-inhibiting violence in Iraq. But here, of course, the humanitarian alibi is moot because of the large scale US military presence. Non-state actors are instead part of the state-led 'peace consolidation strategy'.[35] In this light, many PSCs have multiple clients, some of them state organizations, some of them rebuilding Iraq with the aid of US funding and some of them NGOs. Interaction across the state/non-state divide such as this is not lost on Iraqis. As many contend, the Iraqi insurgency, whether domestic or foreign in nature, links *all* foreign activity to the US intervening presence.[36]

In sum, the state, and in the Iraqi case the United States, the world's unipolar power, is closely implicated in the activities of these two non-state actors; they do not operate in a void left by the state.

## Conclusion

The goal of this chapter was not to debunk all the arguments pertaining to the salience and independence of non-state actor activity. Indeed, the chapter's focus largely on PSCs is a relatively narrow one. Instead, the goal here has been to argue that PSCs, despite their transnational status, do not affect or interact with all states in the same way. They can be the tools of state policy beyond a state's borders. As a result, PSCs, in search of remuneration and legitimacy and acceptance, need not necessarily wed themselves to serving a peace support marketplace or developing marketing approaches that emphasize the independence and freedom of action presumably held by non-state actors. The resulting effect on the industry is transformative. In fact, the United States, given its position in the world and the marketplace it presents, has considerable control over PSCs at the strategic level. In short, this chapter provides nuance to the arguments regarding non-state actors and transnationalism by examining the power dynamics that underlie these phenomena. In turn, the chapter also asserts that the world will not experience 'privatized peace' in the near future; considerable forces impact upon and ultimately structure frameworks that constrain PSCs strategically.

Though PSCs may not possess the degree of freedom to act globally, PSCs nevertheless pose ramifications for international security through their contractual relationships with powerful states. As such, this chapter points to important issues that will likely be the focus of further study. One point concerns the freedom of action granted to the United States through its employment of PSCs. As has been argued elsewhere, one of the apparent advantages of this form of outsourcing is that the deaths of contracted personnel do not have the same political saliency as those of uniformed personnel.[37] As a result, the US government can achieve its policy goals and maintain public support for operations overseas. However, as outlined above, if contractors are increasingly praised and their deaths receive public exposure, does this mean that PSCs acquire enhanced legitimacy and acceptance, but that the flexibility provided to the United States by PSCs will diminish? How will this impact upon the hegemon's global posture or its strategy of preventative war? For the PSC industry itself, will this see a move towards hiring individuals not from the United States, or the developed world generally, but rather from the developing world, for reasons related both to cost and to the saliency of their potential deaths? If so, how will treating individuals from the developing world as 'cannon fodder' impact upon US relations with many countries?

A second point is that if the United States influences heavily the strategic horizons of the PSC industry, then it will be interesting to see if future effort is directed at developing international regulation. Should analysts turn their attention somewhat away from the industry's regulation at the global level, conducted by the UN or another body, and instead consider how the United States, as the world's hegemon, will likely attempt to mould the industry to its liking and how PSCs will respond? Put differently, if the United States now determines more often where and in what contexts PSCs operate, can its determinations as to how PSCs should operate at the operational and tactical levels be far behind? Such shifts would certainly further instil the PSC presence on the world stage while at the same time further limit their independence and freedom of action as non-state actors.

## Notes

For this chapter, the term private security company (PSC), rather than private military company, is employed because companies conduct a hybrid of policing and military tasks. This is in light of the environments in which these companies are frequently employed (conflict- and violence-prone weak states in the developing world) and the actual effects the companies may have in these environments. Moreover, the main goal in all cases is to make something or someone more secure. As such, the term PSC is more appropriate in the cumulative sense.

1 Cited in Marc Lacey, 'U.N. Forces Using Tougher Tactics to Secure Peace,' *New York Times*, 23 May 2005, www.nytimes.com/2005/05/23/international/africa/23congo.html, accessed 10 October 2007.
2 Doug Brooks, 'Write a Cheque, End a War: Using Private Military Companies to End African Conflicts', *Conflict Trends*, Vol. 1(6), June 2000, pp. 33–35.
3 See Rodney Bruce Hall and Thomas J. Biersteker (eds), *The Emergence of Private Authority in Global Governance*, Cambridge: Cambridge University Press, 2002; James N. Rosenau, *Turbulence in World Politics: A Theory of Change and Continuity*, Princeton, NJ: Princeton University Press, 1999; Susan Strange, *The Retreat of the State: The Diffusion of Power in the World Economy*, Cambridge: Cambridge University Press, 1996, pp. xvii, 218.
4 Anna Leander, 'Conditional Legitimacy, Reinterpreted Monopolies: Globalisation and the Evolving State Monopoly on Legitimate Violence', CIAO Working Paper, March 2002, p. 18; Loramy Conradi Gerstbauer, 'The New Conflict Managers: Peacebuilding NGOs and State Agendas', in Elke Krahmann (ed.), *New Threats and New Actors in International Security*, New York: Palgrave Macmillan, 2005, p. 27.
5 Bjørn Møller, 'Privatisation of Conflict, Security and War', DIIS Working Paper no. 2005/2, p. 7.
6 James N. Rosenau, 'Armed Force and Armed Forces in a Turbulent World', in James Burk (ed.), *The Adaptive Military: Armed Forces in a Turbulent World*, Second Edition, New Brunswick: Transaction Publishers, 1998, p. 59.
7 Lawrence Freedman, 'Grand Strategy in the Twenty-First Century', *Defence Studies*, Spring 2001, Vol. 1(1), p. 11.
8 Rodney Bruce Hall and Thomas J. Biersteker (eds), *The Emergence of Private Authority in Global Governance*, Cambridge: Cambridge University Press, 2002, p. 1.
9 United Nations Development Program, 'Redefining Security: The Human Dimension,' in Mark Charlton (ed.) *Crosscurrents: International Relations in the Post-Cold War Era*, Second Edition, Scarborough: Nelson, 1999, p. 257.
10 International Commission on Intervention and State Sovereignty, *The Responsibility to Protect: Report of the International Commission on Intervention and State Sovereignty*, Ottawa: International Development Research Centre, 2001, p. 15.
11 Emma Rothschild, 'What is Security?' *Daedalus*, Summer 1995, Vol. 124(3), p. 55.
12 For a consideration of these two monopolies, see Janice E. Thomson, *Mercenaries, Pirates, and Sovereigns: State Building and Extraterritorial Violence in Early Modern Europe*, Princeton, NJ: Princeton University Press, 1996.
13 See, for instance, Doug Brooks, 'Messiahs or Mercenaries? The Future of International Private Military Services', in Adekeye Adebajo and Chandra Lekha Siram (eds), *Managing Armed Conflicts in the 21st Century*, London: Frank Cass & Co. Ltd., 2001, pp. 129–44; K. O'Brien, 'Military-Advisory Groups and African Security: Privatized Peacekeeping?', *International Peacekeeping*, 1998, Vol. 5(3), pp. 78–105; Herbert M. Howe, 'Private Security Forces and African Stability: The Case of Executive Outcomes', *Journal of Modern African Studies*, 1998, Vol. 36(2), pp. 307–31.
14 See, for instance, Anna Leander, 'The Commodification of Violence, Private Military Companies, and African States', Copenhagen Peace Research Institute Working Paper, June 2003, available at www.ciaonet.org/wps/lea10/lea10.pdf, accessed 11 October 2007.

15 Hans J. Morgenthau, *Politics among Nations: The Struggle for Power and Peace*. Seventh Edition, Montreal: McGraw-Hill Higher Education, 2006; Kenneth N. Waltz, *Theory of International Politics* (Reading: Addison-Wesley Publishers, 1979); John J. Mearsheimer, *The Tragedy of Great Power Politics*, New York: Norton, 2001.
16 Norrin M. Ripsman and T.V. Paul, 'Globalization and the National Security State: A Framework for Analysis', *International Studies Review*, 2005, Vol. 7(2), p. 224.
17 See Jeffrey Record, 'Collapsed Countries, Casualty Dread, and the New American Way of War', *Parameters*, 2002, Vol. 32(2), pp. 4–23.
18 Cited in Ann Scott Tyson, 'Wider Mission Stretches Military,' *Christian Science Monitor*, 2 May 2002, p. 1.
19 Rachel Bronson, 'When Soldiers Become Cops', *Foreign Affairs*, 2002, Vol. 81(6), p. 126.
20 R.L. Russell, 'NATO's European Members: Partners or Dependents?', *Naval War College Review*, 2003, Vol. 56(1), pp. 35–7.
21 See Richard K. Betts, 'Compromised Command: Inside NATO's First War', *Foreign Affairs*, 2001, Vol. 80(4), pp.126–32; Michael Mandelbaum, 'A Perfect Failure – NATO's War against Yugoslavia', *Foreign Affairs*, 1999, Vol. 78(5), pp. 2–8; Peter W. Rodman, 'The Fallout from Kosovo', *Foreign Affairs*, 1999, Vol. 78(4), pp. 45–51.
22 Noted in David King, 'We Need a Romanow Commission for Defence and Foreign Policy', *Policy Options*, Vol. 23(3), April 2002, p. 8.
23 Renae Merle and Griff Witte, 'Security Costs Slow Iraq Reconstruction,' *Washington Post*, 29 July 2005, p. A01.
24 The US military's April 2004 attack on Falluja was in part precipitated by the deaths of four Blackwater USA personnel on 31 March 2004.
25 The goal here is not to imply that PSCs working in the context of the US marketplace do not promote human security or 'peace' endeavours. Rather it is to suggest that many PSCs do not have to market themselves as security providers in this specific regard or search the globe for clients in dire need of assistance.
26 Deborah Avant, *The Market for Force: The Consequences of Privatizing Security*, Cambridge: Cambridge University Press, 2005, p. 220.
27 Paul Ghils, 'International Civil Society: International Non-governmental Organizations in the International System', *International Social Science Journal*, 1992, Vol. 133(3), pp. 417–29.
28 Michael Barnett, 'What is the Future of Humanitarianism?', *Global Governance*, 2003, Vol. 9(3), p. 415.
29 See Christopher Spearin, 'Private Security Companies and Humanitarians: A Corporate Solution to Securing Humanitarian Spaces?', *International Peacekeeping*, 2001, Vol. 8(1), pp. 20–43.
30 Tony Vaux, Chris Sieple, Greg Nakano and Konrad Van Brabant, *Humanitarian Action and Private Security Companies: Opening the Debate*, London: International Alert, 2002, p. 3.
31 Howard H. Lentner, *Power and Politics in Globalization: The Indispensable State*, New York: Routledge, 2004, p. 157.
32 Larry Minear, 'Humanitarian Action and Peacekeeping Operations', *Journal of Humanitarian Assistance*,1997, www.jha.ac/articles/a018.htm, accessed 10 October 2007.
33 The contention that NGOs are often pressured is made in Vaux, *et al.*, *Humanitarian Action and Private Security Companies: Opening the Debate*, p. 10.
34 This description is made in Roger MacGinty, 'The pre-war reconstruction of post-war Iraq,' *Third World Quarterly*, 2003, Vol. 24(4), p. 612.

35 This term is found in Kjell Bjork and Richard Jones, 'Overcoming Dilemmas Created by the 21st Century Mercenaries: Conceptualising the Use of Private Security Companies in Iraq', *Third World Quarterly*, 2005, Vol. 26, p. 791.
36 For instance, see Anthony H. Cordesman, 'US Policy in Iraq: A "Realist" Approach to its Challenges and Opportunities', Center for Strategic and International Studies, 6 August 2004, pp. 6 and 28.
37 Deborah Avant, 'Privatizing Military Training', *Foreign Policy In Focus*, 2002, Vol. 7(6), pp. 1–3.

## 15 The military and the community
### Comparing national military forces and private military companies

*Jessica Wolfendale*

I will begin this chapter by rewriting some of Australia's military history. Suppose that during World War I the Australian Government employed a private company, Australasian Military Resources Inc., to fight the Gallipoli campaign. So, on 25 April 1915 the brave men racing up the beach at Gallipoli to be mown down by the Turkish army were not Australian soldiers who enlisted to serve their country – were not the brave Aussie diggers of the ANZAC legend – but were employees of a private military company.

If this had been the case, would Australia celebrate ANZAC day? I suspect not. No matter how brave or resourceful the employees of AMR Inc. were and no matter how well or how badly they fought, it is unlikely that they would be honoured by war memorials or days of remembrance. This is because the real ANZAC soldiers, unlike the employees of AMR Inc., were part of the Australian Defence Force and members of the Australian community – they were representative of the community in a way that employees of a private military company could not be. Using private military companies instead of national military forces would undermine the connection between the military and the community and would probably spell the end of national war memorials, days of remembrance and other commemorations of a nation's military history.[1]

In this chapter, I explore the meaning and value of the connection between the military and the community. There are two questions I address. First, what is valuable about the relationship between military and community and second, does the connection between national military forces and the community mark a significant moral difference between private military companies and national military forces? I argue that while the mythology of war is often used for morally problematic purposes, maintaining the connection between the community and the military is important for two interrelated reasons. It means that governments must justify the use of military to the public and it means that governments do not have complete control over the public's perception of and reaction to a war. I show how national memorials, images of war, veterans and casualties all play a role in altering public perceptions of a war and in putting pressure on a government's justification for using military force. If a government uses a private military company, there will be little reason for the government to justify how and when force is used and the public will have little direct access to the experience of war. Private military companies are not representative of the community they serve, and this is a morally significant difference between these companies and national military forces and provides the strongest moral reason for preferring national military forces.[2]

## Mercenary motives

It may be objected at this point that the obvious difference between private military companies and national military forces lies in their motivations for fighting. Perhaps the reason we would not raise memorials to the dead employees of AMR Inc. is simply because they fought for money, not for love of country or to protect their homeland. We honour the Diggers because they died in the service of their country; they died to protect a way of life and a set of values that were threatened by the war in Europe. The employees of AMR Inc., on the other hand, died in the service of a contract – their deaths count as the moral equivalent of a foreseeable death in a particularly risky workplace.

This purported moral difference between military personnel and employees of a private military company has been discussed by Tony Lynch and A.J. Walsh in 'The Good Mercenary?' Walsh and Lynch argue that the motives of individual military personnel might be just as mercenary as those of an employee of a private military company. As they point out, many military personnel join the army not out of love of country or a desire to serve the state but simply because the military provides a guaranteed income.[3] Looking at the motives of individual military personnel and mercenaries cannot provide a sound way to distinguish morally between them – some military personnel might be motivated solely by the desire for financial security and some mercenaries might be motivated by more noble aims than mere money, such as the protection of human rights.[4]

Walsh and Lynch are correct in their contention that there is no *prima facie* moral difference between individual military personnel and mercenaries based on their motivations for fighting. However, by focussing only on the motives of *individual* military personnel, they fail to recognize a crucial distinction between private military companies and national military forces. While the motives of some individual military personnel may be straightforwardly dominated by the desire for financial gain, the national military *as an institution* is not governed by mercenary motives. In a democratic state the national military force is created to protect the nation's interests at the behest of the civilian government; it is the servant of the government. The importance of the military's subordination to the civilian government is evident from the many safeguards that are in place to ensure that the military has little or no influence on politics and remains under civilian control.[5] Unlike a private military company therefore a national military force is not subject to market issues such as supply and demand; they cannot charge for their services and they cannot pick and choose who they fight for or who they fight against. While private military companies can (and some do) set voluntary limits on who they will work for, those limits are not intrinsic to the institution of private military company itself and do not form the guiding motivation of the company. National military forces, however, by their very nature serve what Samuel Huntington calls a 'single corporate client' – the state.[6] Serving the state is the *raison d'être* of the institution.

Yet clarifying the difference between the guiding institutional motivations of private military companies and national military forces does not tell us whether this difference is *morally* significant.

## Protecting the nation or fulfilling a contract?

The military profession claims to be a morally justified institution because the existence of competing nation-states justifies the need for effective means of national defence. But in order for the difference in institutional motivations to ground a moral difference between private military companies and national military forces, protecting the nation-state must count as a moral good or at the very least a morally preferable goal to the pursuit of profit. Yet it is not immediately obvious that protecting the nation-state is such a moral good. As Lynch and Walsh point out: 'it is unclear why – Realpolitik aside – the nation-state makes all or any difference.'[7] Can an argument be made for the intrinsic moral superiority of national military forces based on the value of national defence?

## The military profession and national defence[8]

A state's right or at least its moral permission to maintain a military force is derivative of the right to national defence. In international law and traditional Just War Theory – and indeed from the perspective of everyday morality – it is generally accepted that states have the right to defend themselves and others against aggression.[9] However, it is unclear that this connection between a state's right to national defence and the moral standing of a national military force provides national military forces with a *prima facie* moral advantage over private military companies. To see this, we must consider the goal that the military exists to serve. We must distinguish the nation from the state.

In 'Just War and Human Rights', David Luban argues that 'nation' and 'state' are not equivalent, although the meanings of the terms are often conflated.[10] He argues that 'nation' indicates a political community, while 'state' refers to 'an on-going institution of rule over, or government of, its nation'.[11] Thus, the *nation* of Australia refers to the community of Australian citizens, whereas the *state* of Australia refers to the current system of government. Luban introduces this distinction to discuss the definition of wars of aggression in Just War Theory. He argues that the common appeal to 'state's rights' as a reason for not interfering in another country's affairs confuses the concept of the nation with that of the state. A state is legitimate only so long as it has the consent of the nation and it is only the legitimate states that can be said to have rights that could be infringed by outside military interference from other countries.[12] To an extent, Michael Walzer shares this view. He argues that 'The moral standing of any particular state depends upon the reality of the common life it protects.'[13] However, unlike Luban, Walzer distinguishes a state's legitimacy 'at home' from its legitimacy in the eyes of the international community. The international community may believe that a particular state is tyrannical or otherwise illegitimate, but as long as the government of that state 'actually represents the political life of its people' then intervention is not justified.[14] This means that even if a state is illegitimate it should have 'presumptive legitimacy' in the eyes of the international community.[15] Only the citizens of that state have the right to rebel or overthrow their government if the government no longer represents them or defends their common life.[16] However, there are occasions when foreign intervention may be justified. Foreign states could intervene to overthrow the government of an illegitimate state when it is radically clear that the government does not represent or 'fit' with the community it claims to represent, when, for example:

> the violation of human rights within a set of boundaries is so terrible that it makes talk of community or self-determination or 'arduous struggle' seem cynical and irrelevant, that is, in cases of enslavement or massacre.[17]

This distinction between nation and state has important implications for our discussion about the end of the military profession. The end of national defence is the protection of the nation – the community of citizens. It is possible to argue that defending the nation is a moral good in and of itself although, as David Rodin argues in *War and Self-defence*, it is not easy to do this in a way that successfully grounds states' rights to national defence.[18] Even so, commonsense morality, international law and Just War Theory all operate on the assumption that the defence of the national community is defence of something morally valuable. So if the primary role of the military is to protect the nation, it would be plausible to claim that such an end was both morally valuable and morally superior to the pursuit of profit. However, the end of the military institution is not simply national defence.

There is no doubt that the military does protect the nation, but it does so by obeying the state. The military is the agent of the state and exists to carry out the policies of the state. The guiding motivation of the military, as an institution, is to serve the civilian government regardless of the justness of the government's defence policies. This means that the end of the military profession is not national defence *per se* but national defence as determined by the civilian government of the state – the military does not and should not decide for itself when and how to defend the nation. Most writers on professional military ethics agree that the military's subordination to the civilian authority – the state, in other words – is of crucial importance. It is no part of the military's role to make foreign and domestic policy. Instead, its role is to implement those policies at the will of the civilian authority. The military profession is duty bound to protect and further the security of the nation-state but *only* as interpreted by the civilian government of that nation.

Given that it is possible for the state's interests to be distinct from, and in some cases counter to, the nation's interests, there is the possibility of conflict between the military's role as agent of the state and the end of national defence. This would most obviously occur in cases where an illegitimate government used the military to enforce tyrannical policies against the population but it is also possible that a particular government policy (when the government itself is legitimate) might run counter to what could be construed as the best interests of the nation. In such a case, where should the loyalty of the military lie?

If the state is no longer serving the interests of the nation then there could be occasions when protecting the nation would require disobeying the state. In extreme cases this could take the form of a military coup, where the military not only disobeys but also overthrows the current civilian leadership and assumes control of the nation. Military dictatorships often arise out of the military's belief that they could protect national interests better than the current civilian government. As such, military coups seem to be based on an extreme version of the belief that the primary, most fundamental, duty of the military is to the well-being of the nation, not the state. However, the military's adoption of ultimate power is a clear case of the formation of an illegitimate state; one formed without the consent of the governed, and so such coups cannot be considered justified instances of military disobedience.

Yet it seems plausible that there might be a mean between the military blindly obeying the state regardless of the moral or even military wisdom of the state's orders, and the military taking over the state. There is one recent example of a nation's military forces refusing to obey the civilian authority. During 1989 the Romanian military, after having previously obeyed orders to fire on protestors in several regions, refused outright to obey Nicolae Ceausescu's orders and went on to play a central role in his downfall.[19] However, this example is the exception that, if anything, proves the rule. In countries with democratically elected governments such disobedience and subsequent political manoeuvring by the military is unknown and would be considered well beyond the acceptable role of a national military force. The military institution is and should be subordinate to the civilian authority. This means that the concerns of *jus ad bellum* – the conditions that specify when a state is justified in using military force – are outside the military's jurisdiction. The decision to go to war is made by the civilian authority and the military profession is subordinate to that authority.

The upshot of the military's role as the agent of the state as opposed to the protector of the nation is that the moral standing of the military is conditional on two things: the legitimacy of the state and on how that state uses military force. The military serves the state and there is no reason to suppose that defending the state (as opposed to defending the nation) is a morally valuable end in and of itself. The military force is not morally valuable in and of itself because the end that it serves is not intrinsically morally valuable.[20] Similarly, private military companies do not possess a moral value independent from who hires them and how they are used. The only difference is that, unlike a national military force, a private military company is not dependent on the state for its existence and is free to work for more than one state and for non-state actors.

If there is no intrinsic moral difference between private military companies and national military forces based on who uses them and when, is there any moral difference between them? If the use of military force is justified in certain circumstances – in defence of legitimate states, in defence of others and in certain kinds of humanitarian interventions, then does it matter, morally speaking, whether a national military force or a private military company is used? In the next section I show that there is one important reason why national military forces are morally valuable: military personnel in national military forces are members of the community.

## Citizens and employees[21]

Regardless of their motives for joining the military, military personnel in national military forces are usually members of the community that they defend. In Australia, for example, military personnel must be permanent residents or citizens of Australia, the UK requires that new recruits be UK nationals or holders of dual citizenship of the UK and another country and the United States requires that new recruits be citizens of the United States, have a US background, hold a green card or (if they are not citizens) apply for naturalisation once they have joined the military. In liberal democracies with all-volunteer forces, therefore, the national military is a physical manifestation of citizens' willingness to defend their common life and the common life they share with their allies. In 'The New Mercenaries and the Privatization of Conflict' Thomas K. Adams points out that the fact that a national military force is composed of volunteers consenting to defend their nation can be taken to legitimize that nation's government.[22] Even in conscript armies, military personnel are still representative of the community even if their participation cannot be interpreted as willingness to defend their country.[23] As a result, national military forces have both a literal relationship with the community – the majority of military personnel are physically drawn from the community – and a symbolic relationship – as part of the national military force, military personnel represent 'all of us' and 'the nation' in the field of battle.[24] As will become apparent, both the literal and the symbolic aspects of the relationship are morally significant.

While members of a private military company might be members of the community and thus have a literal relationship with the community, they are not part of an institution that is representative of the community and so the symbolic relationship is missing. National military forces have a two-fold relationship with the community and it is this relationship – particularly the symbolic relationship – that is recognized by war memorials, days of remembrance and other commemorative rituals.[25] A government who used private military companies instead of maintaining a national military would undermine the relationship between the military and the community. This is clearly a loss, but is it a loss we should mourn? What is valuable about the relationship between the community and the military?

## National military forces and national mythology

For many nations, military history plays an important role in the conception of national identity and national mythology. Narratives of wars won and lost, of lives sacrificed in the name of national glory or national liberation and comparisons with other nations' military exploits all play a role in public characterizations and displays of national identity.[26] For example, Independence Day in the United States is a deeply symbolic celebration linked to ideas about national character and national independence. In Australia ANZAC day is far more than a public recognition of the soldiers who died at Gallipoli. ANZAC day now commemorates all Australian military personnel who have fought in Australia's military engagements. In political and military rhetoric and indeed for many ordinary people, ANZAC day symbolizes a set of traits taken to be characteristically and uniquely Australian. In the words of the historian Charles Bean; 'ANZAC stood and still stands for reckless valour in a good cause, for enterprise, resourcefulness, fidelity, comradeship and endurance that will never admit defeat.'[27] References to Australia's brave soldiers and rhetoric about the ANZAC spirit is often used to foster uncritical patriotism in order to generate public support for the government's defence policies, but this does not change the fact that ANZAC day carries immense emotional and social significance for a great number of Australians. Furthermore such uncritical patriotism is far from the single or most common response to ANZAC day. Every year, ANZAC day provokes intense debate about Australia's current and past military engagements. This is evident from the amount of media coverage that ANZAC day receives. In 2005, in just one newspaper (*The Age* in Melbourne) there were over 250 articles and letters that referred to ANZAC day and debated its meaning.[28]

ANZAC day is emotionally and symbolically significant primarily because the soldiers who fought were Australian citizens. These soldiers' deaths and the large numbers of returning veterans directly affected the community in a way that the death of an employee of a private military company never could. Most Australians have direct and indirect experience of the effects and costs of fighting a war. They have lost someone, have been in the military themselves or they know someone who has. This means that when the Australian government uses military force there is a direct and immediate impact on the social and emotional lives of thousands of Australians. This is why the sentiments expressed on ANZAC day and on other days of remembrance have such rhetorical and emotional power.

But is this direct connection between the community and the military desirable?

Arguably, the impact of Australia's military involvements on the Australian community means that emotions such as grief and anger can be manipulated all too easily to generate uncritical support for the government's policies – and to foment desires for revenge on the enemy. By casting dissenters as traitors or 'un-Australian', rhetoric about 'our boys' can and is used to stifle criticism and debate about the morality and legality of the government's defence policies.

It is true that governments use the relationship between military and community to manipulate the community's sentiments to generate support for defence policies. I am not claiming that the relationship between citizens and the military is always a good. But the fact that governments believe that they need to manipulate public sentiment reveals the flipside of the military–community relationship. A government will try to justify their defence policies to the public precisely because it is the community who will bear the costs of a military action. Once these justifications are in the public domain, two things happen. First, criticism and debate becomes possible and second, the government cannot maintain complete control over the public's perceptions of and attitudes about a war. The sentiments aroused by military action become a double-edged sword that has the potential to undermine as well as bolster the government's justifications for the use of military force.

How does this loss of government control occur? There are at least three interrelated aspects of the literal and symbolic relationship between military and community that undermine governments' attempts to control public perceptions of a war: the impact of casualty figures and images of combat, the experiences of veterans and war memorials.

## The impact of war

### Casualties and images of war

Psychiatrist Robert Jay Lifton argues that casualty lists and photographs can provoke two kinds of responses. They can reinforce the support for a war by appealing to a 'they have not died in vain' rhetoric but they can also provoke doubt about the meaning of a war:

> when you see those pictures now [of soldiers killed in combat], in relation to the Iraq war, they are probably more likely to feed doubts and questions about the war because they quickly lead to the issue of why that death occurred or whether that death should have occurred.[29]

This process occurred in Australia during World War I, when the massive number of Australian casualties – over 60,000 – created intense political and social divisions and caused widespread dissatisfaction with Australia's continued involvement in the war, reaching a peak with heated debate about a referendum on conscription.[30]

More recently, the rising American casualties in the ongoing Iraq war have similarly begun to erode public support for continued American involvement. That the government and media are aware of the potential of casualty lists to undermine public support is evident from the response to an April 2004 episode of Nightline in which presenter Ted Koppel spent forty minutes reading out the names of all the soldiers killed in Iraq and Afghanistan, accompanied by their photographs. The programme's producer defended the program by claiming that reading the names and showing photographs of the dead would

> remind our viewers – whether they agree with the war or not – that beyond the casualty numbers, these men and women are serving in Iraq in our names, and that those who have been killed have names and faces.[31]

The programme caused a great deal of controversy – the company that owns several ABC affiliates refused to air it in several cities and accused the programme of being 'motivated by a political agenda designed to undermine the efforts of the United States in Iraq'.[32] This response to the programme demonstrates recognition of the emotional and political impact that casualty lists and photographs can have on public opinion and support for a war.

Because of the impact of images and casualty lists, the United States government has tried to control the images that enter the public domain, particularly photographs of the coffins of soldiers killed in Iraq. The US government considered the issue important enough to institute a ban against publishing photos of soldiers' coffins, which demonstrates that they are aware of the impact such images can have on public attitudes about a war.[33] The Bush administration argued that the ban would protect the families of the soldiers killed in Iraq, but others argue that the ban is intended to prevent the public from becoming aware of the real costs of the war. A professor at Louisiana State University argued that:

> The image of dead Americans, especially the dead American soldier, is probably the most powerful image of war for Americans.... It's the one that immediately strikes us in the gut, because we hate to see it but we recognize we may need to see it.[34]

A veteran similarly argued that 'I see nothing wrong with showing coffins, especially flag-draped coffins, because it's a reminder of what these people have given up.'[35] Images of war – particularly photographs of the dead – make concrete the impact of war on the community in a way that descriptions of combat cannot do. This concrete emotional impact can be powerful enough to alter support for a war.

### Veterans and war memorials

The experiences and voices of veterans can also generate debate and dissent about the uses of military force. During the Vietnam War, veterans played a crucial role in the anti-war movement in the United States. In *The Turning: A History of Vietnam Veterans Against the War* Andrew Hunt describes the impact of the presence of Vietnam veterans at anti-war rallies: 'Right-wing counter-demonstrators who had screamed at dignitaries leading the march quickly quieted down when they saw signs indicating that among the marchers were veterans.'[36] Because of their direct involvement in the war, Vietnam veterans were 'endowed with a legitimacy in the court of public opinion that few other anti-war activists possessed.'[37] An example of the impact that veterans can have on public debate about a war is evident from the following announcement, a version of which appeared in the *New York Times* signed by Vietnam veterans:

> We believe that the conflict in which the United States is engaged in Vietnam is wrong, unjustifiable and contrary to the principles on which this country was founded. We join the dissent of the millions of Americans against this war. We support our buddies still in Vietnam. We want them home alive. We want them home now.

We want to prevent any other young men from being sent to Vietnam. We want to end the war now. We believe this is the highest form of patriotism.[38]

The impact of this statement would have been considerably lessened if it had not been written and signed by veterans. Reference to 'our buddies still in Vietnam' manages to adopt the rhetoric of military comradeship and subvert it to protest against the war – demonstrating how veterans are uniquely placed to use military rhetoric to undermine the government's justifications for a military action.

Veterans are also often involved in the creation of war memorials and other military commemorations, be they for defeats or victories. It was primarily the veterans who campaigned for a public monument to honour the soldiers who died in Vietnam. The US government originally intended only to have a plaque next to the tomb of the Unknown Soldier that bore the inscription 'Let all know that the United States of America pays tribute to the members of the Armed Forces who answered their country's call.'[39] It was the Veterans' Affairs subcommittee that demanded that direct reference to Vietnam be included.[40] It was also veterans who campaigned for the creation of a specific Vietnam Veterans memorial, a process that ended with the building of the now-famous Vietnam Veterans Memorial Wall where the names of the dead are inscribed on black granite. By including all the names of the soldiers who were killed in the Vietnam War, the designer of the memorial, Maya Lin, 'felt that a memorial should be honest about the reality of war and be for the people who gave their lives'.[41] Contrary to expectations, the Wall evoked intense emotional and political responses in visitors – many visitors left objects including not only flowers but also military items, letters and political statements.

The public's reaction to this memorial demonstrates that war commemorations can be far more than the simple loci of patriotism and national sentimentalism. The meanings of war memorials can be extremely complex and the process of deciding how to commemorate a nation's military history can be very fraught. In 'The Vietnam Veterans Memorial: Commemorating a Difficult Past' Robin Wagner-Pacifici and Barry Schwartz describe how the process of choosing a design for the monument and the Vietnam Memorial Wall itself incorporated dissent about the meaning and justification of the Vietnam War and represented what they call 'A nation's conflicting conceptions of itself and its past'.[42] The response to the Wall demonstrates that war memorials can spark dissent and debate, debate arising at least partly from the recognition of the impact of war on the community. The Wall has become, as Wagner-Pacifici and Schwartz put it, 'a kind of debating forum – a repository of diverse opinions about the very war that occasioned its construction'.[43]

Casualty lists and images of war, the experiences of veterans and the war memorials are just three examples of how the relationship between community and military can provoke debate and dissent about a government's justifications for the use of military force. That governments are aware of the potential impact of the military–community relationship is clear from their attempts to control it. These examples demonstrate how the relationship has the power to undermine that control and generate public debate and protest about government defence policies. The reason why governments need to publicly justify the use of military force – the impact on the community – is the same reason why they cannot completely control how the public will respond to those justifications.

However, someone might object that the reason why people protest against wars is not because it is fellow citizens who are involved but because they believe that the war is unjust. Arguments against defence policies should not have to rely on the experiences of veterans or on images of war. It shouldn't matter who is fighting – we should protest (and many do protest) whenever military force is used for unjust causes. If this is the case, then it is irrelevant whether a private military company or a national military force is used because the grounds for criticism – the justness of the cause – are still present even if the military–community relationship is severed.

In an ideal world, this would be true. I agree that who is doing the fighting should not make any difference to the debate about a war. Rational arguments about the justness of a war should be sufficient to generate debate and dissent about how a state uses military force, whether or not that military force is a national army or a private military company.

But there are two problems with this objection. First, on a pragmatic level it does seem to matter who is doing the fighting. When it is the fellow citizens who are doing the fighting, that emotional and symbolic connection makes a difference to people's attitudes about a war. Being faced with the concrete reality of war changes people's views and provokes dissent in ways that rational argument often fails to do. This is not to say that rational debate and emotive debate are incompatible – they are not – but the point is that the emotional and symbolic impact of the military–community relationship can motivate people who are untouched by or uninterested in rational debate. If the relationship is severed, it is likely that fewer people will be affected enough to debate the justness of the government's defence policies and this would significantly lessen the reach and impact of anti-war protests.

Second, the issue at hand is not just what kinds of protests are most effective but also whether governments will attempt to justify the use of force at all. To see this, consider the two main consequences of severing the connection between the community and the military. First, if private military companies are used governments can maintain far greater control over how the public perceives a war. Veterans would not be coming back into the community, images of the dead and casualty lists – if they were released at all – would not have the same impact as images of dead fellow citizens. Second, because of this increased control and because the community would no longer bear the emotional and social cost of war[44] governments would have little or no incentive to try to win public support for a war or even to publicize their reasons for engaging in military actions. This means that the community would lose access to information that would strengthen rational as well as emotional dissent against a war.

We want governments to feel accountable for how they use military force and maintaining the direct relationship between the community and the military is one way of forcing at least some degree of accountability. It is only because governments feel that it is important to gain public support for defence policies that they publicly try to justify the use of military force. As Michael Walzer argues in *Just and Unjust Wars*:

> Public opinion tends to focus on the concrete reality of war and the moral meaning of killing and being killed. It addresses the questions that ordinary men cannot avoid: should we support the war? Should we fight in it?[45]

Take away the relationship between the community and the military and ordinary people *can* avoid asking themselves whether they should support a war. The 'concrete reality of war' is necessary to generate widespread public debate about a government's defence policies. When communities have direct experience of the 'concrete reality' of war, they are forced to question why and when military force is used. This questioning process is extremely valuable. It is essential that governments are held accountable for defence policies and that they are required to at least attempt to justify decisions to engage in war. If private military companies are used, this questioning process and the need for justification are likely to be lost.

Does this mean that governments should never use private military companies?

## How should private military companies be used?

If, as I have argued above, it is important to maintain the symbolic and literal connection between the military and the community, does this mean that there are no situations in which private military companies may be used? What about states that, while legitimate, do not have an established national military force? Perhaps moralizing the difference between private military companies and national forces leaves newly emergent democracies in a very fragile position – particularly if other states are reluctant to intervene. Given that many states are extremely 'risk averse' when it comes to putting their own troops in danger in peacekeeping or other humanitarian missions, shouldn't fragile states have access to the military force they need to protect themselves and maintain emerging democratic processes?[46] Thomas K. Adams makes this point in 'The New Mercenaries and the Privatisation of Conflict':

> If other nations, individually or collectively, are not going to contribute to multilateral peacekeeping or peacemaking forces, shouldn't a state have a right to hire a force able to keep the peace? It seems distinctly odd, both legally and morally, to argue that a state is somehow required to depend on whatever conscripts it can muster and train them as best it can, rather than obtain expert assistance from outside.[47]

I have two responses to this objection. First, by arguing that national military forces should be retained because of the value of the relationship between military and community, I am not claiming that private military companies have no legitimate role to play. I am arguing that they should not *replace* national military forces.[48] Fragile states should be encouraged to develop a national military force – indeed it seems to me that other states have an obligation to assist the training and development of such a force for newly emergent fragile democracies. But if other states fail in their obligation then private military companies might play an important role in training and protecting a nascent national force. The need for developing states to hire private military companies points to a failure of other states to assist, not to the moral preferability of private military companies. If we accept that private military companies should be regulated and subject to international law, then I see no reason why they could not be used in situations where national military forces were either unable or unwilling to act. However, I do argue that they should not be seen as morally equivalent to a national military force or as replacing the need for a national military force.

Furthermore my argument does not in the least imply that states use their national military forces wisely or well. Indeed, my argument is premised on the assumption that governments often don't use their military forces for just causes – hence the need for debate and dissent about a government's defence policies and the value of maintaining the relationship between military and the community. Arguably, states should be willing to risk the lives of their military personnel for humanitarian reasons to a far greater extent than is now the case. The use of military forces in humanitarian interventions requires a significant shift in how military forces see themselves and in how governments perceive their obligations to other states. But the existence of legitimate uses for private military companies does not alter the fact that it is important to maintain the relationship between the community and the military.

## Conclusion

If we treat private military companies as morally equivalent to national military forces, we fail to recognize the emotional, political and symbolic importance of the literal and symbolic relationship between national military forces and the community. Because it is the community who will bear the emotional costs of war, this relationship forces the government to justify the use of military force to the community. Because members of the military are both members of the community and representative of the community, the government does not have full control over the public's perceptions of and attitudes about a war. Images, casualty statistics and veterans' experiences all strongly affect public opinion about a war; and force people to consider the legitimacy of a particular military action in ways that would not occur if private military companies were used. If the military–community relationship is severed, governments would no longer need to court public support, and the community would lose direct access to the experiences and costs of going to war – experiences that not only affect the emotional support for a war but that are also relevant to rational debate about the justness of a war. Given how often governments use force for morally unjustified causes, the value of public debate about war is something that we need to retain. We lose something morally valuable if we lose the relationship between military and community.

## Notes

1  The connection between community and military could be undermined in other ways, for example, by a government recruiting primarily foreign citizens to serve in the military. Such a situation would create similar problems to those that, I argue, arise from the prospect of using private military companies. I am aware that it is unlikely that private military companies will come to replace national forces. However, by considering the hypothetical possibility we can gain a better understanding of the value of national military forces and the moral differences between these and private military companies.

2  At present there are strong pragmatic reasons for not using private military companies arising from the difficulty in establishing their status under international law and holding them legally accountable for their activities. But serious as these concerns are, they do not represent anything intrinsically problematic about private military companies. Instead, they reflect the failure of the current international legislation to adequately monitor and control the ways in which these companies are used. For a discussion of these issues, see Deon Geldenhuys, 'Non-state Deviants in World Affairs', *Strategic Review for Southern Africa*, 2002, Vol. 24, pp. 1–29 and Thomas K. Adams, 'The New Mercenaries and the Privatisation of Conflict', *Parameters*, 1999, Vol. 29, pp. 103–16. I accept the claim that private military companies need to be regulated (rather than banned outright) in international law and need to be held accountable – or at least as accountable as regular military forces.

3  T. Lynch and A.J. Walsh, 'The Good Mercenary?' *The Journal of Political Philosophy*, 2000, Vol. 8(2), pp. 133–53.

4  Ibid. pp. 136–7.

5 For example, serving military officers are usually not permitted to hold political office. How successful these safeguards are is of course a matter of debate. For the purposes of this chapter, I am assuming they are sufficiently successful in preventing the military from having an undue influence on politics. Certainly in America, Australia and Great Britain the military is well controlled. For a discussion of the relationship between the military and the government, see Lance Betros, 'Political Partisanship and the Military Ethic in America', *Armed Forces and Society*, 2001, Vol. 27, pp. 501–23; Douglas L. Bland, 'A Unified Theory of Civil–Military Relations', *Armed Forces & Society*, 1999, Vol. 26(1), pp. 525–40 and Peter D. Feaver, 'The Civil-Military Problematique: Huntington, Janowitz, and the Question of Civilian Control', *Armed Forces and Society*, 1996, Vol. 23, pp. 149–78.

6 Col. Anthony Hartle, *Moral Issues in Military Decision Making*, First Edition, Lawrence, KS: University Press of Kansas, 1989, p. 21.

7 Lynch and Walsh, 'The Good Mercenary?', p. 140.

8 This section derives from material that appears in chapter 3 of my book *Torture and the Military Profession*, Houndmills, Basingstoke: Palgrave-MacMillan, forthcoming in November 2007.

9 In traditional Just War Theory, this right is usually considered to be either reducible to or analogous to the individual's right to self-defence. However, David Rodin, *War and Self-defense*, Oxford: Oxford University Press, 2002, raises serious problems with both these ways of grounding the right to national defence. He argues that

> A war of national-defence is not just a lot of people exercising the right to self-defence at the same time in an organized fashion. Nor is it the state exercising the right of defence on behalf of its citizens. For the state can claim the right to defend itself, when none of its citizens is under imminent threat, and it can claim this right even if it thereby puts its citizens under greater threat than if no defence were mounted.
>
> (p. 140)

For the purposes of this chapter I will not enter into the debate on how to ground the right to national defence; instead I will assume that such a right (however derived) does exist although, as I argue above, it can be forfeited.

10 David Luban, 'Just War and Human Rights', *Philosophy & Public Affairs*, 1980, Vol. 9, pp. 160–81 and 168.

11 Ibid., p. 168.

12 Ibid., p. 168.

13 Michael Walzer, *Just and Unjust Wars: A Moral Argument with Historical Illustrations*, Third Edition, New York: Basic Books, 2000, p. 54.

14 Michael Walzer, 'The Moral Standing of States: A Response to Four Critics', *Philosophy and Public Affairs*, 1980, Vol. 9, p. 214.

15 Ibid., p. 214.

16 Ibid., p. 214.

17 Walzer, *Just and Unjust Wars*, p. 90.

18 Defining the term 'common life' is not straightforward – indeed it is difficult to define it in such a way that it grounds the right to state sovereignty and national defence as analogous to the right to self-defence. Rodin discusses three possible ways of defining common life so that it counts as a moral good that can justify national defence: the argument from the value of political association, the argument from the value of common lives, and the argument from the value of communal integrity and self-determination. See Rodin, *War and Self-defense*, pp. 141–62. However, he notes that each of these arguments

faces problems. For example, it is difficult to establish an objective value in a community that can be recognized outside the community and thereby ground an internationally recognized right to national defence (ibid., pp. 152–3).

19 Stefan Sarvas, 'Professional Soldiers and Politics: A Case of Central and Eastern Europe', *Armed Forces and Society*, 1999, Vol. 26, p. 103.

20 Unless one wants to claim that there is intrinsic moral value in states that is independent from how they treat their citizens. I find such a claim very unconvincing. If states have value, it must lie in the kind of life they encourage or permit their citizens to live.

21 I wish to thank the helpful comments and suggestions I received when I presented this chapter at the Private Military Companies and Global Civil Society: Ethics, Theory and Practice Conference, South Africa and at the Centre for Applied Philosophy and Public Ethics seminar series.

22 Adams, 'The New Mercenaries and the Privatisation of Conflict', p. 114.

23 Although it need not be incompatible with such willingness.

24 This means that even in cases where the members of a national military force are not citizens, they are still symbolically representative of the community. A parallel may be found in the composition of sporting teams. In many cases, the members of a national sporting team may not be from the nation they represent yet they are part of a team that symbolically represents the nation. However, in national military forces in most Western countries the proportion of military personnel who are also from the country in question is likely to be much than the proportion of sportspersons who are from the country they represent. Furthermore, given the importance that I assign to maintaining the physical connection between community and military, it would follow from my argument that national military forces should continue to consist primarily of citizens of the nation. The reasons I give for preferring national military forces over private military companies would also provide reasons for limiting recruitment to citizens or permanent residents of a nation. Thanks to Andrew Alexandra for drawing my attention to the comparison with sporting teams.

25 Note that commemorating the symbolic and literal relationship between military and community does not assume that military personnel are in fact motivated by that relationship when fighting. We honour fallen military personnel not because we think they were motivated by love of country (many probably weren't) but because they represented all of us.

26 I am being agnostic as to whether such narratives truthfully reflect a nation's history. In many cases it is probable that they do not.

27 Charles Bean, quoted in Major General P. R. Phillips, 'ANZAC Values – the Path Traveled and the Way Forward', *Australian Defence Force Journal*, 2001, Vol. 146, p. 71. The American War of Independence has played a similar role in American historical narratives.

28 Mark Forbes, 'Day to Reflect with Pride: Howard; ANZAC Day,' *The Age*, 25 April 2005.

29 Robert Jay Lifton, quoted in Jess Talbert, 'Naming the Dead: Casualty Lists, Memorials and National Grief', Dart Centre for Journalism and Trauma. Accessed 8 July 2005 at www.dartcenter.org/articles/special_features/memorials.html, accessed 10 October 2007.

30 Major Helen Doyle, 'Australian World War I Casualties: Social Impacts,' *Australian Defence Force Journal*, 2004, Vol. 165, pp. 24–34.

31 Lisa de Moraes, 'On "Nightline", a Grim Sweeps Roll Call', 28 April 2004, www.washingtonpost.com/ac2/wp-dyn?pagename=article&contentId=A48102–2004Apr27&notFound=true, accessed on 7 July 2005.

32 'Nightline's Casualty List Muted by Stations', *The Daily News* 30 April 2004, www.tdn.com/articles/2004/04/30/nation_world/news02.prt, accessed on 7 July 2005.
33 Photos of dead soldiers' coffins were also banned during World War I and World War II. During the Vietnam War journalists and photographers were permitted greater freedom in what they could publish. The ban was reinstated during the first Gulf war in 1991. Ray Rivera, 'Images of War Dead a Sensitive Subject', *Seattle Times*, http://seattletimes.nwsource.com/html/nationworld/2001909526_coffinside22m.html, accessed on 21 June 2005.
34 Ibid.
35 Ibid.
36 Andrew E. Hunt, *The Turning: A History of Vietnam Veterans against the War*, New York, New York University Press, 1999, p. 11.
37 Ibid., p. 192.
38 'Vietnam Veterans' Voice', unpublished statement by Jan Barry, c.1967, quoted in ibid., p. 14.
39 Robin Wagner-Pacifici and Barry Schwartz, 'The Vietnam Veterans Memorial: Commemorating a Difficult Past,' *The American Journal of Sociology*, 1991, Vol. 97, p. 385.
40 Ibid., p. 385.
41 Ibid., p. 400.
42 Ibid., p. 1.
43 Ibid., p. 405. There has been similar debate about Holocaust memorials in Germany. For a discussion of the ongoing debate on this issue, see Robert G. Moeller, 'War Stories: The Search for a Usable Past in the Federal Republic of Germany', *The American Historical Review*, 1996, Vol. 101, pp. 1008–48.
44 The community would still bear the financial cost but that might arguably be less than maintaining a national force given that there would be no need to fund pensions for veterans, and no need to bear the costs of a standing army.
45 Walzer, *Just and Unjust Wars*, p. 64.
46 Geldenhuys, 'Non-State Deviants in World Affairs', p. 21.
47 Adams, 'The New Mercenaries and the Privatisation of Conflict', p.112.
48 It follows from my argument that national military forces should aim to recruit primarily citizens (or at least permanent residents) of the community. If a military force was representative of the nation in the sense of controlled solely by the government of the nation, but consisted primarily of foreign military personnel, then the literal connection between community and military would be lost even if the symbolic relationship still existed.

# 16 Interface ethics

## Military forces and private military companies

*Asa Kasher*

The purpose of the present chapter is to point out the ethical problems that emerge where actions are performed at one and the same time and one and the same place by members of two organizations, namely a military force (MF) of a democratic state and a private military company (PMC) that operates within the civil society of the same democratic state. Instances of outsourcing involve such an organizational interface.[1]

Circumstances of such a nature form an organizational interface that is, in a sense, of the simplest kind. Different and more difficult ethical problems would arise in circumstances that involve an interface between an MF of one democratic state and a PMC that operates from another democratic state, or between an MF of a democratic state and a PMC that operates on the behalf of a non-democratic state.[2]

Our discussion will be made from the point of view of the MF involved in the interface under consideration.[3] We will discuss the problems such an MF faces when in that interface and some solutions thereof. The following assumptions will be made about the MF:

1   The MF includes a variety of units that can be involved in an interface with some PMC, ones that carry out a variety of missions, have members of different ranks and various professions and levels of professionalism. Moreover, people in MF uniform can find themselves in an interface with people in a PMC outfit not only in combat but also in a previous stage of deployment and even in some stage of instruction.
2   The MF manifests in its activities a certain set of values and principles which form its organizational ethics. Those values and principles are shared by all members of the MF, though people who belong to units of certain types or are of certain ranks can have additional values and principles that characterize special roles they play within the MF.
3   The MF has a formally established set of values and principles, which we dub the 'military ethics' of the force.

Finally, our discussion will be conceptual in nature. We are not going to discuss in detail any historical case of an interface. We will briefly outline a conception of 'military ethics' in general, show some relationships between typical values and principles of military ethics and certain traits of PMCs, discuss the emerging ethical problems and suggest a possible solution.

## Military ethics in general

Any ethics is a conception of proper behaviour in particular circumstances of activity. Thus, professional ethics in general is a conception of proper behaviour under circumstances of professional activity. Ethics of a certain profession, be it law, command or engineering, is a conception of the proper behaviour under circumstances of activities of persons *qua* lawyers, commanders or engineers, respectively. Similarly, ethics of a certain organization – military, academic or industrial – is a conception of proper behaviour *qua* members of that organization.

A conception of proper behaviour within the framework of a certain profession in a certain society rests on three sub-conceptions of professional ethics (PE) as follows:[4]

PE-1 a conception of being a professional in general;
PE-2 a conception of being of that particular profession and
PE-3 a conception of being a member of the particular society.

A conception of what constitutes the ethics for proper behaviour within the framework of a certain organization in a certain society will rest on similar sub-conceptions. In the case of the organizational ethics of an MF (MOE) of a democratic society it will be premised on the following three sub-conceptions:

MOE-1 a conception of being a member of an organization in general;
MOE-2 a conception of being a member of a military organization of a
　　　state and
MOE-3 a conception of being a member of the citizenry of a democratic state.

Note that the organizational ethics of a PMC, which is a conception of proper behaviour within the framework of its activity, shares with the organizational ethics of an MF of a democratic state conception (MOE-1), since both an MF of a state and a PMC are organizations. If a PMC operates within the framework of a democratic society, its organizational ethics shares conception (MOE-3) with that of the MF of a democratic state, or at least major parts thereof, if the PMC operates in one democratic regime and the MF is of another democratic state that has a different democratic regime. Naturally, conception (MOE-2), which constitutes the organizational identity of the MF of a democratic state as such, is not expected to be shared by the conception of the PMC as to its organizational identity. Although some components of those two organizational identities can be common to both, since both carry out activities of a military nature, a conspicuous distinction between the two is that between an organ of the executive branch of a democratic state and between a profit-oriented private company. Some of the ethical problems we are going to encounter under interface conditions stem from the major difference between a governmental agency and a private company.

We turn now to a brief presentation of the conceptions that constitute an organizational ethics of an MF of a democratic state.

The notion of being a professional has been portrayed on different levels. One level is that of the societal features of a profession, such as the operation of some institutions of formal instruction and licensing. However, one can become aware of such societal features of being a professional without by that having gained an adequate understanding of what is a profession. Hence, a philosophical portrayal is required that would show the 'deep' framework of concepts underlying the 'surface' cluster of features. For the present purposes we simply assume that the underlying conceptual framework of being a member of a profession in general involves (1) having a systematic body of knowledge; (2) having an effective proficiency in solving problems of a typical nature ('a tool box'); (3) being committed to permanent advancement of those knowledge and proficiency; (4) having an understanding of a 'local' nature of the tools and methods of the 'tool box' and (5) having an understanding of a 'global' nature, that of the nature and identity of the profession in general.[5]

The notion of being a member of an organization is here treated in a similar way. We assume that the underlying conceptual framework of being a member of an organization in general involves (1) being a member of a coordinated goal-directed activity group; (2) being a member of a rule-governed activity group, where every major component of the activity, whether individual or collective, is specified by the rules or by a decision-making body or method specified by the rules; (3) holding a position in a distribution of authority and responsibility among all members of the group and (4) having an understanding of a 'global' nature, that of the goal and of the values embodied in the rules that govern the collective activity of the group

On the background of those conceptions of being a professional and being a member of an organization in general, the next conception included in the organizational ethics of an MF of a democratic state is that of the self-identity of a person in uniform as a member of a certain profession within the framework of a certain organization. We assume that the combatants form a professional community within the MF the uniform of which they wear and so do the commanders within that MF. Those professions can be characterized by appropriate sets of core values which give rise to principles of conduct. Here, for example, is the set of core values included in the 1994 Israeli Defence Forces (IDF) Code of

Ethics.[6] They constitute a conception of what it means to be a combatant within the framework of the IDF, but they can also be used in developing a conception of what it means to be a member of the IDF, whether combatant or not. The differences between combatants and non-combatants is not reflected in the set of core values itself, but rather in the derivative principles of conduct that involve different circumstances of military activity.

IDF values were specified in that Code of Ethics to be (when ordered according to the Hebrew alphabetical order): Perseverance (Courage), Responsibility, Reliability, Setting a Personal Example, Human Life, Purity of Arms (Restraint of Force), Professionalism, Discipline, Loyalty, Being a Representative and Comradeship. We will return to some of those values for a detailed discussion when we consider interface circumstances where not all agents operate with those values in mind or in ethics.

Note that those core values are not all of the same nature. For example, the values of Loyalty and Perseverance reflect the mission of the IDF and the goal of military activity, the values of Professionalism, Discipline and Setting a Personal Example are instrumental, in the sense that they have been found to be necessary for effective military activity, and the values of Human Life and Purity of Arms are moral constraints imposed in a democratic state on military activity. Such distinctions may turn out to be of practical significance when we consider the ethical problems that emerge under interface conditions.

Finally, an MF of a democratic state, which consists of citizens of a democratic society, needs a conception of democracy in general and the special nature of the democratic regime in which it serves as an agency. For the present purposes we take it for granted that a conception of democracy in general involves a conception of human dignity and its practical protection. We assume that such a conception involves four principles of proper conduct: (1) The distinction between human beings and everything else on earth, including objects and animals, ought to be reflected in practice; (2) The distinction is between human beings *qua* human beings and all the rest, and not between different kinds of human being; (3) Basic human liberties should be protected in practice, in a fair way and (4) Restrictions may be imposed on basic human liberties only if necessary for the protection of human liberties of all and only in a fair way. Such a conception is embodied in the constitutional structure of every democratic regime, which protects, in a fair way, all basic human rights.

A conception of military ethics of an MF of a democratic state includes as sub-conceptions of all the aforementioned conceptions. On the background of this conception of proper behaviour of military professionals within a military organization, we turn now to an analysis of the ethical problems that emerge under interface conditions. First, we discuss a couple of examples of the interface ethical problems that involve the assumed conception of being a professional. Second, we discuss the interface ethical problems that involve military values, and finally we discuss the interface ethical problems that involve the democratic conception of human dignity protection.

## Being a professional: ethical problems of interface

The ethical problems that emerge under interface conditions, from the point of view of being a professional in the MF involved, are problems of sharing professional elements with the PMC that takes part in the interface. A major example would be the ethical problem of sharing lessons drawn from combat experience.

Consider a military operation that was carried out by professionals of both an MF of a democratic state and a PMC. The assumed conception of being a professional requires local understanding, which is tantamount to being able to answer all 'why' questions arising out of and with respect to one's actions. When a group of members of an MF and members of a PMC carry out a coordinated collective action, the professionals who participated in the operation have been required to understand not only their own, individual actions but also to a certain extent their fellows' actions. After the mission has been accomplished, all the participants are expected to draw lessons from the operation, on grounds of a professional analysis of it and for the sake of professional improvement. Such a professional analysis will emerge from a debriefing activity in which all the professionals, both of the MF and the PMC, have to participate. The natural result of such a debriefing activity is improvement lessons that are shared by professionals of both organizations who participated in the operation and the debriefing, and later by both organizations.

Here are two ethical problems that emerge. First, a problem of trust. Debriefing is a procedure that rests on the assumption that participants are absolutely reliable when they tell their fellows what they did and what happened to them during the operation. Absolute reliability includes absolute openness. Participants are committed to a full-fledged disclosure of what they experienced. Such norms of honesty pertain to an internal MF debriefing and most probably to an internal PMC debriefing. However, would an MF officer be justified in assuming that those norms prevail when he is leading a debriefing in which members of both the MF and the PMC actively participate? Members of a PMC may well be committed by contract to avoid disclosure of information about the PMC, even under interface conditions, even if members of the PMC hold crucial data about the operation in which they took part together with members of the MF.

Second, a problem of the distribution of new knowledge. To see the problem, consider the following conditions: Unit Alpha of the MF has just operated with members of PMC One. Unit Beta of the same MF is about to carry out similar missions with members of PMC Two. Now, a combatant commander *qua* professional within the MF is under an ethical obligation to share lessons drawn from one's recent experience with his fellow combatant commanders who are about to carry our similar missions. Should lessons drawn by Alpha officers together with members of PMC One be shared with officers of Beta who are going to operate together with members of PMC Two, possibly a competitor of PMC One? Put differently, does the fact that lessons drawn by Alpha officers involve internal knowledge about PMC One impose any restriction on the extent to which those lessons are shared with Beta officers?

We will return to a suggested solution of such ethical problems in a later section, after additional ethical problems are presented.

## Professional identity: ethical problems of interface

Apparently, values that are essential elements of military ethics can genuinely appear in a PMC code of ethics and be manifest in the behaviour of its members. However, when we compare values of an MF with those of a PMC, we should clarify the distinction between following similar principles on different grounds. Both an MF and a PMC are goal-directed activity groups, but the goals of the former are usually radically different from those of the latter and consequently the nature of commitment expected from people in the MF uniform to the military ethics of the MF, its values and principles is usually different from that expected from members of a profit-oriented PMC. In order to gain a grasp of the distinction, let us consider the poles of the spectrum of possible commitments: On the one hand we have wholehearted commitment to national security, while on the other hand we have to deal with the matter of compliance with contractual obligations. We do not assume that the attitude among people in the uniform of MF is always at the former pole, nor do we assume that the attitude among members of PMCs is always at the latter pole, but we do assume that on the average attitudes of people in an MF uniform will be closer to the former pole while those of members of profit-oriented PMCs will be closer to the latter one.

Consider the value of Responsibility, first when it is one of the foci of a person's wholehearted commitment to national security, and then when it is the subject matter of a clause in a person's contractual obligation to perform certain actions.[7] The former attitude will naturally give rise to an informally maximalist interpretation of the duty to search for apt opportunities of shouldering responsibility, while the latter attitude will possibly give rise to a formally minimalist interpretation of the duty to comply with contractual obligations. Such a distinction seems natural when we compare the group of people whose benefit is the ultimate goal of an MF of a democratic state, namely the citizens of the state, with the group of people whose benefit is the ultimate goal of a profit-oriented PMC, namely its share holders. The same distinction is revealed when we compare the natural depiction of a case where a person commits an act of desertion, during one group's coordinated attempts to accomplish its mission. Whereas desertion of an MF unit facing an enemy force would be regarded, from the point of view of the MF, as a form of betrayal, desertion of a PMC group facing an enemy force would be regarded, from the point of view of PMC, as a breach of contract.

Next, consider the value of Human Life.[8] Within the framework of a democratic state, the military ethics of any of its MFs has to manifest an appropriate respect for the human dignity of its members from which an appropriate form of protection of their life follows. To be sure, such an attitude applies to people in uniform who have volunteered to be career combatants. Given the conception of human dignity we briefly presented in a previous section, it is a fundamental moral obligation of a democratic state to respect the life of its combatants. A state complies with that obligation in a variety of ways: (1) A democratic state should have a firm justification for being actively involved in a war, which always means sending at least some of its combatants to act under conditions that jeopardize their life; (2) An MF of a democratic state should always attempt to minimize casualties among its troops, when operations are planned and when they are performed; (3) A democratic state should provide its MFs with equipment of types that are meant to protect their life during combat; (4) An MF of a democratic state should avoid any significant jeopardy to the lives of people in uniform, when required activities are not of the crucial types of facing enemy forces or trying to rescue human life.[9]

Indeed, an MF of a democratic state acts within a certain budgetary framework. It is always possible to imagine a larger budget spent on better personal or on crew's life-protecting equipment, but such a possibility does not give sufficient grounds for a policy that would prefer distribution of a better personal or crew's life-protection equipment over, say, deployment of more sophisticated artillery batteries that might deter the enemy from attacking the troops. However (5) expenditure policies that would prefer production and distribution of life-protection equipment of a lower quality, when high-quality life-protection equipment can be presently produced, distributed and used, would be unjustified in a democratic state if strictly budgetary in nature.

Now, neither of the moral obligations from (1) to (5) above of a democratic state and its MF is a requirement that would be taken by every PMC to self-evidently bind it. For example, nothing in the very idea of a PMC would restrain it from operating, and thereby jeopardizing the life of its members, in a way different from the one a democratic regime should pursue. Similarly, a PMC can be imagined making decisions with respect to possible purchase and distribution of personal life-protection equipment, for example, on grounds of actuarial considerations raised in case casualties are suffered. Such distinctions reflect yet another form of the distinction between maximalist and minimalist attitudes, this time, however, not on the part of individuals but rather on the part of their deeply different organizations.

Third, consider the value of Restraint of Force, or 'Purity of Arms' in the language of the IDF Code of Ethics. Within the moral framework of a democratic state, protection of human dignity is required not only when citizens have to be protected, but as has been briefly mentioned earlier, protection of human dignity is required whenever human beings are encountered, circumstances of a military operation not excluded. The most familiar examples of Restraint of Force are probably the principles that govern proper treatment of Prisoners of War [POWs] and those that impose military operations, within the context of an international armed conflict, a distinction between treatment of combatants and protection of non-combatants.[10]

On numerous occasions, following principles of Restraint of Force means making more efforts, spending more time and money, even taking more risks in accomplishing missions in a proper way.[11] MFs of a democratic state are expected to take all the required steps to keep use of military force restrained within the confines of a system of human dignity protection as set out by the constitutional principles, ethical values and legal regulations that take into account both domestic and international law in matters of warfare. Causing collateral damage, under conditions of military necessity, by an MF of a democratic state, using ammunition of an old, imprecise type, for budgetary reasons, where much less collateral damage could have been caused by using ammunition of a better type, should be regarded as being unjustified on moral, ethical and legal grounds.

A PMC, which is a profit-oriented organization, even if expected to comply with legal obligations to treat POWs properly, cannot be expected to minimize collateral damage when a serious attempt to do it would involve a significant additional expenditure. Whenever there is a significant gap between the legal 'threshold' and the ethical 'shelf', raising the standards of activity from being above the 'threshold' to being above the 'shelf' may correlate with rising expenditure. Under such conditions, a profit-oriented PMC is naturally expected to act slightly above the legal 'threshold' even if it is much below the moral and ethical 'shelf' of a democratic regime. The principle of proportionality, which requires that collateral damage be minimized, is a possible example of that gap, where PMCs will invoke the laws in justification of the behaviour that would be unethical for an MF of a democratic state.

Similar observations apply to the military value of Discipline. Any reasonable conception of military Discipline will include a conception of Obedience. However, a practice of obedience forms a legal 'threshold', where Obedience, in a full-fledged sense of the term, forms the much higher, ethical 'shelf'. Whereas Obedience is manifest in a practice of following orders, Discipline involves mutual relationships between troops and their commanders of understanding each other's predicament, of trust, both professional and personal, in each other's intentions and abilities, and of wholehearted identification with each other. Again, where the ethical 'shelf' of Discipline is expected to be manifest in mutual relationships of people in an MF of a democratic state and their commanders, it is the 'threshold' of Obedience that is expected between members of PMCs and their superiors and subordinates.[12]

Finally, we consider a component of the military value of Comradeship. The value itself can be expressed in terms of a principle, namely, 'if your fellow combatant faces a military problem he cannot solve on his own, then it thereby becomes a problem you have to solve in his help.' The IDF principle 'Thou shall not desert a wounded fellow in a battle field' is a derivative of that Comradeship principle. Note that undertaking the mission of solving one's fellow combatant's problem will involve jeopardizing one's own life. Hence, a conception of Selfless Service is a component of an adequate conception of Comradeship. (It is, indeed, a component of other conceptions of certain military values, such as Loyalty, as well.)

Since Comradeship in the aforementioned sense is a necessary condition for unit cohesion, which in turn is a necessary condition for effectiveness in combat, it follows that Selfless Service is a necessary condition for effectiveness in accomplishing missions and gaining victory. These conceptual and psychological relationships between the military values of Comradeship and Selfless Service and between military effectiveness hold for both MFs and PMCs. However, while people in an MF uniform are expected to be wholeheartedly committed to their fellow citizen's national security, and therefore also to Comradeship and Selfless Service, members of PMCs are expected to be rather reluctant to commit themselves to life-jeopardizing Comradeship, where the ultimate goal served by Selfless Service is that of the share holders of the profit-oriented PMC that employs them. Here, we do not cast any doubt on the possibility that emotional relationships may develop among members of some small units of PMCs, to the extent that members will jeopardize their life in order to rescues their fellow members. However, on our understanding of the nature of Comradeship, the duty a combatant has to perform in support of a fellow combatant, under circumstances of need, does not depend on previously entrenched emotional relationships. The major gap between commitment to Comradeship in MFs and PMCs follows from the difference in the nature of the two kinds of organization, not a difference in the personality traits of members thereof.

So far we have outlined significant differences between military ethics of an MF of a democratic state and that of a profit-oriented PMC. The ethical problems that arise, from the point of view of such an MF, when it operates together with a PMC are all of the same kind. When people in an MF uniform act together with members of a PMC, what happens at the interface of the military ethics of the MF and the organizational ethics of the PMC is that the two ethical systems of the MF and the PMC influence the members of other. Values of the military ethics of the MF get changed under the informal pressure of an interactive collaboration between the MF and the PMC. The natural change that is expected to take place is that of pushing the standards of MF activity from the vicinity of the ethical 'shelf' towards the usually lower standards at the vicinity of the legal 'threshold'. This is a negative influence. The ethical interface problems are here problems of the natural danger of the ethical standards of the MF becoming lower as a result of open cooperation with a PMC.

## Human dignity protection: ethical problems of interface

We have already discussed expected differences between the military ethics of an MF and the organizational ethics of a PMC, when we discussed in the previous section the values of Human Life and Restraint of Force.[13]

## The outsourcing interface

A common form of interface between an MF and a PMC is that of outsourcing, where a privatization of a certain element of the activity of the MF of the state has taken place. For the sake of our discussion of some ethical problems of the interface of MFs and PMCs in general, we would like to draw a distinction between two types of outsourcing. We dub them 'opaque outsourcing' and 'transparent outsourcing'. The distinction is, again, drawn from the point of view of the MF under interface conditions. When people in an MF uniform, are exposed just to the product of a PMC and not to the organizational ethics of the process of production, it is an opaque outsourcing, or more generally, an opaque interface. An air force pilot who flies, say, a helicopter produced by a certain private company, acts under opaque interface conditions, since he is familiar with the helicopter, but not with the ethics of the helicopter production plant or concern. However, a soldier whose logistic caravan is being secured by a PMC (or rather a private security company, a PSC), is exposed to the organizational ethics of the accompanying PSC, to the extent it is manifested in the behaviour of members of that PSC. This is an example of a transparent outsourcing, or more generally, of a transparent interface.

The ethical importance of the distinction between opaque and transparent outsourcing, or interface in general, is clear. Whereas an opaque interface does not involve a channel of ethical influence on the people in the MF uniform, since they are exposed just to a product of the related PMC, each kind of transparent interface does involve such a channel, the existence of which is expected to have a negative ethical effect within the MF under conditions of interface.

Although the present opaque–transparent distinction is simple and can undoubtedly be much improved, it can serve us in formulating a preliminary principle for interface between MFs of a democratic state and PMCs in particular and private outsourcing companies in general: Interface Principle (IP) 'Opaque interface should be permissible, while transparent interface should be forbidden.' Such a principle solves all the aforementioned ethical problems. We take it that every alternative MF–PMC interface principle will take the form of a refinement of the present principle (IP).

Here are some practical consequences of (IP):

- Outsourcing of arms or facility production can be of high technological standard and opaque and therefore permissible.
- Outsourcing strategic advice can be of high professional standards and opaque and therefore permissible.
- Outsourcing training can be of the required technical standards and opaque in some kinds of technical instruction and therefore permissible, but can be problematic in value-laden kinds of training and therefore possibly forbidden. Generally speaking, the more similar a training situation is to real combat conditions, the more ethically problematic it can become to resort to outsourcing.
- Outsourcing logistics in combat support is ethically problematic due to probable problems of Perseverance.
- Finally, outsourcing combat as well as sensitive intelligence gathering (and other 'inherently governmental functions') should be regarded as being strictly forbidden because of the variety of ethical problems of interface discussed earlier as well as for a variety of other reasons.[14]

In conclusion, it seems advisable, from the point of view of the military ethics of an MF of a democratic state, to require that whatever involves a probable and significant gap between military ethics of an MF of a democratic state and the organizational ethics of a profit-oriented PMC should remain an inherently governmental function, performed by an MF of the state under no transparent interface conditions.

## Acknowledgement

This chapter is an extended version of part of a paper delivered during the PMCs, States and Global Civil Society Conference, Drakensberg, KwaZulu-Natal, South Africa, July 2005. I am grateful to participants in the conference for their helpful comments on the lecture.

# Notes

1 For useful general discussions, see Peter W. Singer, *Corporate Warriors: The Rise of the Privatized Military Industry*, Ithaca, NY: Cornell University Press, 2003; and Alan Bryden and Marina Caparini (eds), *Private Actors and Security Governance*, Zurich and Berlin: Lit Verlag, 2006.

2 Additional types of interface include circumstances of cooperation between MFs of different states in war, humanitarian intervention or peace keeping. Interface of any of these types is beyond the scope of the present paper.

3 Another interesting point of view would be that of governance. See Alan Bryden, 'Approaching the Privatization of Security from a Security Governance Perspective' in Alan Bryden and Marina Caparini (eds), *Private Actors and Security Governance*, pp. 3–19 and Marina Caparini, 'Applying a Security Governance Perspective to the Privatization of Security', in the same volume at pp. 263–82.

4 See Asa Kasher, 'Professional Ethics and Collective Professional Autonomy', *Ethical Perspectives*, 2005, Vol. 12(1), pp. 67–98 for an elucidation.

5 See ibid. for a discussion.

6 See Asa Kasher, *Military Ethics*, Tel Aviv: MOD Publishing House, 1996, in Hebrew.

7 At this point a possible objection would be natural, namely that unlike career officers and NCOs who are usually taken to be committed to national security, conscripts and people on reserve duties find themselves in these positions on grounds of a binding law. However, such a description of the position of conscripts and reservists is wrong. Their military ethics involves a commitment to national security, beyond adherence to the rule of law.

8 Although the IDF Code of Ethics couches this value in terms of the sanctity of human life, the value manifests the attitude of a democracy to the life of its citizens and not any religious stance. Life is usually a necessary condition for being able to exercise human and civil rights and participate in collective decision-making procedures.

9 Condition (d) is a principle of the 1994 IDF Code of Ethics. Condition (b) is included in the formal definition of the value. See Kasher, *Military Ethics* for an elaboration.

10 See, for example, Yoram Dinstein, *The Conduct of Hostilities under the Law of International Armed Conflict*, Third Edition, Cambridge: Cambridge University Press, 2004.

11 See Asa Kasher and Amos Yadlin, 'Military Ethics of Fighting Terror: An Israeli Perspective', *Journal of Military Ethics*, 2005, Vol. 4(1), pp. 3–32 for an application of the principle in military ethics of fighting terrorism.

12 See Asa Kasher, 'Between Obedience and Discipline: Between Law and Ethics', *Professional Ethics*, 2002, Vol. 10(2–4), pp. 97–122 for an elaboration.

13 Some common types of interface give rise to additional problems that have moral aspects within a democratic state, such as public scrutiny of security becoming more difficult when parts of the activity take place within the closed confines of PMCs. For a recent discussion on this issue, see Shane, Scott and Nixon, Ron, 'In Washington, Contractors Take on Biggest Role Ever', *The New York Times*, 4 February 2007.

14 See Singer, *Corporate Warriors: The Rise of the Privatized Military Industry*, ch. 14, for example.

# 17 The new model soldier and civil–military relations

*Elke Krahmann*

Nearly 25,000 private military contractors were estimated to operate in Iraq in 2005. Many earned between $100,000 and $200,000 per year – up to ten times more than their colleagues in the national armed or police forces with whom they received their training and worked for many years.[1] At the same time national armed forces in the United States and other industrialized countries have been suffering from a shortage of resources and manpower induced by cutbacks after the end of the Cold War.[2] The interventions in Afghanistan and Iraq have lowered morale even further as armed forces personnel have to go through repeated rotations and the service of soldiers at the end of their careers has been extended involuntarily. As a consequence, national soldiers have been leaving the armed forces in droves.[3]

The origins of this paradoxical development are typically linked to the transformation of the international security environment after the Cold War. Initially the decreased threat of a superpower confrontation with the Soviet Union led to substantive reductions in defence budgets and armed forces personnel within the transatlantic region. Less than one decade later, the perceived rise of 'new' threats such as global terrorism, civil conflicts and state failure has increased demands on the armed forces to a level unknown since the 1970s.[4]

However, whereas governments in North America and Europe were able to portray the Cold War as an essential threat to national security, they find themselves less able to convince both citizens and soldiers of the need to engage in international interventions and peacekeeping missions abroad. The need for an expansion of the armed forces appears to be obvious if the current level of international engagement is to continue, but governments are at a loss over how to achieve it.[5] On the one hand, the reintroduction of conscription in countries such as the United States or the United Kingdom appears to be out of the question because many of the new security risks do not pose a direct military threat to their homelands.[6] Although civil wars such as in the former Yugoslavia and the development of nuclear capabilities in Iran and North Korea have been obvious global security concerns, there has been a widespread consensus that these threats are highly unlikely to lead to attacks on United States or European territory. On the other hand, European countries which have maintained sizeable armed forces due to the continuation of national conscription have found it difficult to justify the use of draftees in overseas missions.

Shifting to private military forces appears to be the best solution for both problems. In the case of the United States and the United Kingdom, private military contractors can help to relieve the overstretch of national armed forces created by multiple simultaneous interventions. In the case of Europe, private military forces promise a resolution of the growing international demand for more than financial contributions to overseas peacekeeping and the increasing military ambitions of continental governments in the absence of public support and suitable military structures and capabilities.

But the use of private military forces also has a number of drawbacks. In particular the costs of private military contractors have been rising as companies compete for qualified personnel in the wake of major interventions such as Kosovo, Afghanistan and Iraq. Moreover, while national soldiers can be compelled to perform their service where and when the government determines, private contractors are free to choose their area of operation and, to a degree, to name their price. Finally, there are the dual questions of accountability of private military contractors to the general public and their control?

A growing number of studies have examined these issues.[7] However, the existing literature has so far failed to consider the proliferation of private military contractors in terms of its transformative impact on civil–military relations. Most analyses have been concerned with micro–level issues such as whether contractors are more cost-efficient than uniformed military, how to improve the operational control over private military contractors in the field and how to hold contractors legally accountable for violations of national and international laws. The fundamental political questions which are raised by the growing use of private military contractors for civil–military relations in modern democracies have been neglected.

In response, the aims of this chapter are twofold. First, it analyses the transformation of the military profession in North America and Europe. It argues that studies of the 'postmodern' military are underestimating the extent of this revolution by regarding the proliferation of private military contractors merely as one of the characteristics of postmodern armed forces, rather than their core feature.[8] Second, this chapter seeks to understand the resultant impact on civil–military relations. It examines how the transition from the traditional models of the citizen-soldier and the professional soldier to the private military contractor affects the political foundations of the relationship between the soldier, civil society and the democratic state.

## From citizen-soldier to contractor

The shift from citizen-soldiers to voluntary professional armed forces in the United States and the United Kingdom after the 1960s has received much attention in the literature on civil–military relations. Already before the end of the draft in the United States in 1973, Samuel P. Huntington elaborated in his seminal study *The Soldier and the State* the emergence of the military professional among the officer corps in North America and Europe.[9] The rise of the professional soldier has widely been regarded as a key step towards more efficient, effective and even more accountable armed forces. Charles C. Moskos has in fact suggested that the professional army is the defining characteristic of the late modern nation-state.[10]

However, the citizen-soldier tradition is not (yet) as obsolete as many Anglo-American authors seem to imply.[11] In continental Europe the draft continued to be the dominant mode of national defence until the 1990s. Even following the end of the Cold War some states in Europe have held on to the citizen-soldier ideal. This is not to deny that perceived advantages in terms of military effectiveness and overseas deployability as well as problems with the equality of the draft after the massive reduction of standing armies at the end of the Cold War have led many European countries to replace their conscript armies with all-volunteer forces. Belgium (1994), the Netherlands (1996), France (2001), Spain (2001), Portugal (2003), Hungary (2004) and Slovenia (2004) have already phased out the draft; while the Czech Republic, Italy, Romania and Slovenia plan to do so in the near future.[12] Nevertheless, important European states have maintained their commitment to the citizen-soldier tradition, including Austria, Denmark, Germany, Greece, Norway, Poland, Sweden, Switzerland and Turkey.[13] In spite of the obvious drawbacks of military conscription, they consider the citizen-soldier as fundamental to their understanding of legitimate armed forces.

At the same time as North America and Europe have been divided over the merits and demerits of the citizen-soldier over the professional, a new model soldier appears to have been emerging: the military contractor who works for a private company that provides military and military support services for profit, but is employed by states for homeland defence and international interventions. Although an increasing number of studies have pointed out the proliferation of the 'new mercenaries' in the post-Cold War era,[14] little has been said about the extent to which governments in the transatlantic region are outsourcing national defence to private companies. As a consequence, the characteristics and self-understanding of the private military contractor have not been examined as a new model of 'soldier'. The assumption is either that only civilian and support tasks are contracted out, whereas the so-called core functions remain with the armed forces, or that private military contractors are 'mercenaries' without any professional standards. The former suggests that private military contractors are civilians and not soldiers; the latter implies that they form a distinct category outside legitimate civil–military relations.

Both assumptions are outdated. Over the past two decades the range of military core functions which must not be contracted out has progressively declined. Thus in post-war Iraq, private military contractors not only carried weapons, but also engaged in fighting with local insurgents. In the United States and the United Kingdom armed forces the shift from the professional soldier to the military contractor has been the most extensive,[15] but other countries such as Canada are also following their example. Moreover, the private military companies registered in North America and Europe assert that they have nothing in common with mercenaries. They are corporate entities with clear standards of vetting, training and operation. In fact, as Doug Brooks and Matan Chorev point out in this volume, some companies have their own codes of ethics and are pressing for a voluntary self-regulation of the industry in order to drive out the 'cowboys'.[16] Moreover, the new military entrepreneur offers a much broader range of military and military support services than the traditional mercenary who used to be hired for combat. Due to the differentiation of military functions and the growing role of technologies, the private military contractor is as often sitting at a computer as he or she is carrying arms.

The following examines the characteristics of the citizen-soldier, the professional and the contractor as ideal types. It focuses on four aspects: the relationship between the soldier and the state, the motivation and identity of the soldier, and the connection between political and military roles.

## The citizen-soldier

The origins of the citizen-soldier tradition have variously been attributed to ancient Greece,[17] to republican Rome[18] or to the American and French revolutions.[19] It prescribes that soldiers should be citizens, and that citizens should be soldiers. In fact, in North America and Europe citizenship rights, in particular the right to vote, were extended in line with military service.

Although common by the twentieth century, there was initially no direct link between citizen-soldier and universal conscription. In particular in Anglo-American countries the ideal of the citizen-soldier was that of the volunteer. The United States and the United Kingdom believed in small standing armies and reliance on local militias which required few personnel. Even during war, the governments of both countries preferred to call on their citizens to volunteer for military service. Mass conscription was not adopted in the United States and the United Kingdom until World War I.[20] It was justified by the direct threat to the national homeland which arose from new military technologies, such as airplanes and submarines. Peacetime conscription was first introduced in the United States in 1940 following the beginning of World War II in Europe.[21]

Several characteristics shape the citizen-soldier model. The first and most important characteristic is the link between citizenship and military service.[22] Under the terms of a real or imagined social contract between the citizen and the state, the state protects its citizens, while the citizen serves in defence of the country.[23] Under what conditions and in what form this service can be required has varied historically as well as among countries.[24] In Anglo-American countries the ideal prevailed that national military service would only be entered into voluntarily. However, the obligation of the citizen in a national emergency was always implicit. The permissive security environment of the United States and the United Kingdom, both isolated from invasion by their 'island' status, lessened the threat of such an emergency.[25] It changed when technological advances increased the vulnerability of both countries. World Wars I and II justified mass conscription because of the scale of the conflict and the immediacy of the threat to their homelands. In the United States, the Korean and Vietnam Wars were subsequently used to justify the decision not to return to peacetime non-conscription as had been the case after the end of World War I. However, as will be discussed in more detail below, they also eventually led to the introduction of all-volunteer forces.[26] Only in continental Europe, the threat of an invasion by the Warsaw Pact was able to legitimize the continuation of the universal draft until the end of the Cold War.

The second characteristic of the citizen-soldier is the lack of a professional identity. As Eliot A. Cohen argues: 'the true citizen-soldier's identity is fundamentally civilian. [. . .] His participation in military life is temporary and provisional.'[27] The civilian identity of the citizen-soldier is particularly visible in the case of local militias, but with the rise of modernity it became collectivized at the level of the state in the form of universal conscription. Accordingly, when the citizen-soldier engages in combat, his or her motivation is essentially self-defence.[28] As the modern citizen only obtains public rights through the existence of the state, the defence of the state becomes the defence of his or her citizenship.

The third characteristic is the merger of social, political and military roles within the concept of the citizen-soldier. The citizen-soldier does not have to sever his or her linkages with family and friends in order to develop a new collective identity as a professional and to shift his or her primary commitment to a military unit. Neither is the citizen-soldier required to abstain from political engagement. In fact, he or she is encouraged to do so because political activity is understood to be one of the hallmarks of good citizenship alongside military service.

## The professional

Although the military professional as ideal type had its origins in the officer corps of the nineteenth century,[29] the shift from conscript to all-volunteer forces in the United Kingdom in 1962 and the United States in

1973 can be credited with the maturation of the model. In the United States, this transformation has widely been attributed to the Vietnam War which undermined public belief in the legitimacy and equitability of universal conscription and, with it, public support for the citizen-soldier model.[30] Similarly, in Europe the recent shift towards professional armed forces has been linked to the increased demand for international operations and the problems of drafting only a proportion of all eligible citizens due to the reduction in national armed forces after the end of the Cold War.

The characteristics of the professional soldier model have been most extensively analysed by Samuel Huntington. In particular, Huntington identifies three features of the professional soldier: a politically neutral sense of duty to the state, military expertise and a professional identity.[31] Morris Janowitz finds similar elements which he calls 'personal fealty', 'the pursuit of glory', 'gentlemanly conduct' and 'brotherhood'.[32]

The most important feature which distinguishes the professional soldier model from the citizen-soldier is the sense of duty to the state or constitution as an abstract entity and the related requirement of political neutrality.[33] At the time of Huntington's and Janowitz's studies the self-image of the professional soldier and, in particular, of the officer was one of dedication and self-sacrifice for the nation: 'They believe that they, as the "standard bearers," embody virtues which transcend "crass commercialism".'[34] Sam C. Sarkesian *et al.* agree: 'Generally, the professional is not motivated by financial gain but by patriotism and service to society.'[35] In spite of the rise of 'postmodern' values such as individualism and consumerism since the 1980s, and despite the emergence of what Charles Moskos has termed an 'occupational' view of the military profession,[36] these sentiments can still be found among the all-volunteer forces in the United States.[37] Contemporary recruitment campaigns might focus on individual objectives and gains such as receiving an education, adventure and being able to see the world. But the ideals of patriotism and service to the nation continue to play an important role for those who join the armed forces and, if they are no longer a primary reason for signing up, they are instilled into professional soldiers during years of service. Moreover, patriotism comes to the fore when a state is engaged in a conflict. Thus a 2003 survey of male-enlistment motivation in the United States found that 'doing something for our country' outranked all other reasons, whereas in 2001 it had only been a secondary factor.[38]

In addition, Sarkesian *et al.* recommend that

> a degree of separation (psychological distance) must be maintained between US society and the military profession to ensure military capability and combat effectiveness. [. . .] The political–military dynamics resulting from the role of the profession in politics should ensure nonpoliticization of the profession.[39]

Although numerous scholars have pointed out that the assumption that military advice can ever be politically neutral is misguided,[40] the ideal persists. Political neutrality is a guiding norm for the Anglo-American system of public service as opposed to alternative traditions, such as in Germany, which embraces political engagement both within its armed forces and civil service.[41] Moreover, the ideal can be observed in the critique of openly political statements or affiliation by professional soldiers, especially of leading generals in the United States.[42]

A second characteristic of the professional soldier is the development of military expertise through extended schooling and training. Unlike Huntington who equates a profession with a vocation,[43] Janowitz regards military expertise as the defining aspect of the professional soldier. According to him, a professional, 'as a result of prolonged training, acquires a skill which enables him to render specialized service'.[44] While the distinctiveness of the skills required by the professional soldier appears to have been exaggerated and, in any case, has been declining with the growing use of civilian technologies and emphasis on technical know-how in contemporary warfare, basic combat training remains a central and distinguishing element of the military profession.[45]

The final feature of the professional soldier is the development of a distinct identity as a profession.[46] There are a number of characteristics which separate a profession from a 'mere' occupation. These include lengthy formal training, professional standards and an occupational consciousness. Most importantly, a profession is 'based upon altruistic service' and sanctioned by society as 'morally praise-worthy and ... [due] high esteem, respect, confidence, prestige and, not infrequently, privilege'.[47] Professionalism is crucial because of the unique expertise of the military in the use of armed force and its potential for abuse. As Don Snider and Gayle Watkins argue:

> The high degree of expertise found in professions requires relative autonomy in the application and adaptation of their expert knowledge. [...] However, in return for this limited autonomy, the American society expects the profession to police itself, exhibiting a high degree of behavioural control through social structures such as education, selection processes, character inculcation, and ethical codes.[48]

In the United States, professionalism has traditionally been achieved by separating the armed forces from broader society, by education and indoctrination, and an emphasis on combat as the distinctive feature of the military to promote a common identity and sense of purpose.[49] In 2001 Abrams and Bacevich observed that the requirement for a professional ethos was as strong as ever: The 'era of high-tech warfare has not obviated the need for a traditional combat ethos – the mix of physical and mental toughness, discipline, raw courage, and willingness to sacrifice that was the hallmark of the effective militaries in the wars of the 20th century.'[50]

## The contractor

Charles Moskos was perhaps the first scholar to identify the beginnings of the emergence of the military contractor. In the mid-1980s he observed among professional soldiers in the United States the rise of an 'occupational' view of the military profession. Moskos argued that volunteers were joining the armed forces because of self-interest rather than patriotism with increasing consideration given to financial rewards.[51] Nevertheless, the institutional and normative system of the all-volunteer forces remained largely unaffected by these changes and thus did the model of the professional soldier.

The true emergence of the modern military entrepreneur has been more due to changes in policy than military self-understanding. Specifically, government outsourcing of an increasing range of military and military-support functions to private companies has created a growing demand for military contractors during the past two decades. In the United Kingdom, the outsourcing of military services began with the privatization of the national armaments industries under Margaret Thatcher. However, it quickly progressed under Tony Blair to include nearly all types of military services short of combat, ranging from military logistics to training.[52] The United States was initially slower to outsource military services to private contractors, however, it has now overtaken the United Kingdom in terms of the scope and the number of functions provided by private military entrepreneurs. The United States was also the first country to expand the use of private military contractors in international interventions such as in the former Yugoslavia, Afghanistan and Iraq.[53]

The operation in Iraq has been singled out by the media and academics as an illustration of rise of the military contractor.[54] While in the first Gulf War only one in a hundred military personnel was a private contractor, in Iraq the proportion has increased to one to one.[55] In August 2007, the US Department of Defence alone employed about 127,000 private military contractors alongside 145,000 US troops.[56] The majority of these contractors have been working in military support functors such as logistics and transport. However, an estimated 25,000 contractors have provided armed services such as personnel, transport and site protection.[57] As a result, private military contractors provided a larger contingent than the United Kingdom which had 8,500 troops in Iraq; in fact, military contractors were the second largest contingent after the US armed forces.

Although there appears to be a fine line between the professional soldiers in an all-volunteer force who view their occupation as a job and their colleagues who think in terms of vocation, there are several features which clearly distinguish the military contractor from the professional soldier.

The first is the disconnect between military service and duty to the state. As Sarkesian *et al.* argue '[t]he primary distinctive feature of the military profession is "ultimate liability," the willingness to give one's life as part of the professional ethos. Also, its sole client is the state.'[58] The military contractor does not recognize this ultimate liability. Whereas the professional soldier voluntarily swears allegiance to the state or the constitution, the military entrepreneur is not bound to anybody but him or herself.[59] The lack of contractor liability is recognized by the United States and the United Kingdom governments who admit that there is no legal basis for enforcing contractual obligations on deployed operations, especially if private military companies fear for the lives of their employees. The UK Ministry of Defence thus writes: 'Under current legislation, the Military Commander cannot insist that the Contractor or its personnel remain in theatre against their will.'[60] Indeed, several contractors withdrew from the UK operation TELIC in Iraq because of the security risk.[61] In the United States, some basis for forcing military entrepreneurs to fulfil their contracts in theatre can be found in the Uniform Code of Military Justice (UCMJ), but only in a Congressionally declared war. Even in war, some authors doubt whether the current interpretation of the US Constitution would permit the enforcement of contractual obligations to the military.[62] During the first Gulf War a primary US contractor thus left the operations theatre because of concerns about missile attacks.[63]

The second characteristic distinguishing the military contractor from the professional soldier is profit motivation. While the military professional typically ranks patriotism higher than financial rewards in his or her motivation to join the armed forces,[64] the military contractor has no qualms about the primacy of monetary gain in his or her choice of employment. Although many private military contractors in Iraq also claim other motives such as trying to help[65] and fighting for democracy and freedom,[66] they admit that the key reason for their being in the region is the high wages they can earn as military contractors.[67] As one US citizen recruited by Halliburton for one of the notoriously dangerous truck driver positions in Iraq puts it: 'I look at it from a business perspective. When you're talking a possible $1,000 a day tax free, it's real attractive.'[68]

National patriotism as a motivation is further undermined by the fact that most private military contractors are neither working for nor in their home countries. In Iraq private military employees come from a wide variety of nations with a growing number of contractors recruited from developing countries such as Columbia, Chile, Fiji, Nepal and the Philippines or from Eastern European states such as Croatia, Bosnia, Bulgaria and Ukraine.[69] Nationality is irrelevant for the military contractor. Most private military companies are happy to recruit anybody who has the necessary expertise. As a consequence, there is an alienation of political and military roles played by the military contractor. The citizenship of the military entrepreneur has little impact on who gains his or her service. In return, the political actions of the military contractor have no influence on his or her employer. The military function of the military contractor is commodified and completely separated from his or her political person.

Finally, the military contractor lacks a distinct professional and collective identity. Due to the differentiation between military and military-support functions in contemporary warfare, private military contractors are typically specialists with a particular technical expertise. Whereas the professional soldier is primarily categorized in terms of rank, the private military contractor is trained, hired and paid for his or her special skill. The military contractor is a technician who provides a particular function from managing base camps to flying unmanned spy planes. Many private military contractors do not even have basic military training.

In addition, military contractors do not develop a collective group identity. Most private military contractors are hired through short-term contracts of two to six months and by different firms at a time. In fact, as speed of deployment is one of their main advantages, private military companies generally operate through lists of potential employees who are called up if and when their skills are required. As a consequence, contractors are typically thrown together with others for a particular operation with little training and preparation. The mixing of different nationalities and backgrounds also inhibits the formation of a collective identity. Some companies offering armed security services therefore recruit from certain nations, occupations and even sections of national armed forces in order to improve unit cohesion.

## The transformation of civil–military relations

The preceding analysis illustrates that the increasing employment of private military contractors does not merely fill shortages created by the cutback of national armed forces after the end of the Cold War. It introduces a new model of soldier (Table 17.1). This new model of soldier

*Table 17.1* Three ideal models of soldier

| Characteristics | Citizen-Soldier | Professional | Contractor |
| --- | --- | --- | --- |
| Relation with the State | Reciprocal obligation | Duty | None |
| Motivation | Self-defence | Patriotism | Profit |
| Identity | Individual-civilian | Collective-professional | Individual-professional |
| Roles | Combination of political and military roles | Separation of political and military roles | Alienation of political and military roles |

raises a number of questions about the composition and character of national armed forces today. More importantly, it has serious implications for civil–military relations. This section examines how the use of private military contractors poses fundamental political challenges for the democratic control over the legitimate use of violence by undermining the established civil–military structures of accountability and control.

According to Sarkesian *et al.*, 'civil–military relations encompass the political relationships among the professional officers [sic] corps, the leaders of the nations, and the military and the society it serves.'[70] In democratic societies civil–military relations are particularly sensitive because of four problems. The first is the 'power of the military establishment'; the second is 'maintaining discipline and good order' of the armed forces; the third is how to ensure public control of the military, but also of the government which wields it; and the fourth is the government's dependency on the military's expertise.[71]

The principles and institutions employed by democratic states to address these problems vary historically and geographically.[72] They are closely related to a state's model of soldier. States which predominantly subscribe to the citizen–soldier model favour the integration of the armed forces with society and the political system to facilitate public accountability and control. Conversely, states which have adopted the professional soldier model tend to advocate the separation of the armed forces from the political process and independent professional standards as principal means for controlling the military.[73] Since many contemporary democracies maintain a mixture of both citizen-soldiers and professional soldiers in their national armed and reserve forces, this division is less clear cut in practice. Moreover, there has been a convergence of norms and institutions which are regarded as fundamental for democratic civil–military relations among democracies in Europe and North America due to international military collaboration and integration.[74]

In particular, there is agreement on the importance of three factors in promoting democratic control over the armed forces and the legitimate use of violence. The first is institutional structures which establish the primacy of civilian authority over the military. The second is the support of and adherence to democratic norms among the armed forces. The third is the relations between the armed forces and civil society.[75]

Institutional structures play a crucial role in shaping democratic civil–military relations. Fundamental are clear channels of political and legal responsibility enshrined in the constitution, national laws and armed forces regulations which subordinate the military to democratically elected governments and the rule of law.[76] As Bland argues: 'Every action and decision of the civil authority and the military must be based on national laws specifically delineating, and, where appropriate, limiting the powers of each.'[77] Specifically, the military because of its monopoly over large scale means of violence must be sworn to 'diligently discharge their duties according to the law and...make this pledge to the civil authority (i.e. the head of state or the constitution) and not to any military leader or institution.'[78] Moreover, both the government and the military must be made accountable to the electorate through independent parliamentary or congressional scrutiny and public audit.[79]

Formal institutions, however, are not sufficient to ensure democratic control over those who wield armed force for the state. Since the military can easily abuse its control over public means of violence, it is in fact the voluntary submission of the armed forces to civilian rule that preserves democratic government.[80] The principles and norms which guide military behaviour are therefore equally, if not more, important for the maintenance of democratic control over the armed forces.[81] Foremost among these norms is the principle of civilian control which is embodied in the democratic political structures, guidelines and decisions with which the military is confronted on a daily basis.[82] According to Bland, 'civil–military relations in mature liberal democracies stand on the willing obedience of officers to civil authority not because officers always respect the idea of the civil authority, but because they value above all else a liberal democracy.'[83] Submission to civilian leadership is complemented by commitment to the rule of law and a set of professional standards, such as honour and duty, which reinforce the former.[84]

Finally, as Jessica Wolfendale argues in this volume, democratic control and accountability are facilitated through the closeness of the military to the society that it serves.[85] The integration of the military with civil society is typically measured through the composition of the armed forces and their representativeness in terms of gender, race, class or political and social norms and preferences.[86] In addition, closeness includes the familiarity of civil society, in particular of politicians, with military life through conscript experiences or military service in international conflicts.[87] High levels of mutual interpenetration and a common identity are regarded as supportive of democratic civil–military relations because they increase the commitment of the armed forces to the defence of their society, ensure that the military shares societal norms and beliefs, and facilitate support for government policies.

The model of the private military contractor undermines these historically established means of democratic control in a number of ways and thus requires a revision of traditional civil–military relations.[88] With regard to institutional structures, most democracies are woefully unprepared for the proliferation of private contractors in national and international military operations. Based on laws and regulations dating back to the beginning of the twentieth century, private military contractors continue to be defined as 'civilians accompanying the force', that is, they are considered as civilians under national and international laws and political structures.[89] In terms of civil–military relations, this means that private military contractors operate outside established military chains of command and political lines of accountability. Although private military contractors are employed in functions which were previously provided by soldiers, the mere fact that these positions are now filled by civilians seems to justify that they are not subject to the same levels of political and public control as their uniformed colleagues. Albeit private military contractors are increasingly sharing or taking control over collective means of violence such as the use of small arms for base guarding and embassy security, predator drones, aircraft and missile technology, they are exempt from military laws and regulations and, where they are included under Status of Armed Forces Agreements (SOFA), they are also beyond prosecution in the countries in which they are operating.

In addition, existing democratic institutions have not been designed for ensuring the public accountability of private military contractors. Audit agencies such as the Government Accountability Office in the United States and the National Audit Office in the United Kingdom are able to report on the cost and conduct of private military contractors in single instances, but their investigations are hampered by the complexity of contracts, the lack of centralized information regarding military outsourcing and the scale of defence privatization. Parliamentary, congressional or media oversight is even more limited because of these factors and the confidentiality claimed by many private military companies in their dealings with governments in order to limit the dissemination of information to potential competitor firms. Even where private military companies are found to be in breach of government contracts or policies, they can only be held accountable in legal, but not in political terms. Companies which have been accused of misconduct or defrauding the US government in the recent intervention in Iraq, have frequently suffered no consequences beyond having to repay the government where it could be verified that they had overcharged the armed forces. In fact, most of the companies which have been involved in fraud have been awarded new government contracts irrespective of their past records due to a lack of competition for larger projects.

The problem that current institutional structures are not designed to ensure the democratic control and accountability of private military contractors is exacerbated by the fact that private contractors are in theory more likely to behave in ways that undermine democratic civil–military relations because they do not share the values of citizen or professional soldiers. Foremost, as has been outlined in the first section, private military contractors do not recognize their duty to the state and the constitution as the core principle underlying their actions. In fact, they may have no moral commitment to defending democracy or the state that hires them. Many companies have no qualms about working for dictatorial governments or withdrawing their services if the risks become too high. The value of democratic patriotism is replaced by profit. Private military contractors also lack collective professional standards which would establish democratic beliefs and principles as the basis for their contracts and operations. Whereas a significant part of the training of citizen-soldiers and professional soldiers is dedicated to instilling democratic norms into the beliefs and mindsets of the members of the armed forces, democratic values are considered irrelevant for private military contractors.

Finally, the alienation between political and professional identities in the private military contractor model undermines the integration of the military with the society that they serve. Although some authors have argued that the influx of private technical specialists contributes to a civilianization of the armed forces and greater representativeness,[90] there is little empirical evidence for this assertion. Most positions that are outsourced to private military contractors require little technical expertise, such as military base guarding or logistical support, and primarily draw employees from skilled, but not university-educated backgrounds. The use of private military contractors thus reinforces rather than weakens current trends in the recruitment of professional soldiers which indicates a disproportionate intake among the lower to middle and working classes as well as the minority sections of society.[91] The gap between UK and US civil societies and their armed forces becomes even greater in the international interventions where the majority of private military contractors are foreign nationals. Since many of these contractors are drawn from developing countries, they are unlikely to share the political, social or cultural values of the states that they are working and, in some cases, fighting for. In reverse, society and political leaders are less concerned about the loss of human lives among foreign and private military contractors than among national citizen-soldiers or professional soldiers. Moreover, private military contractors do not receive the same level of government or societal support as their uniformed colleagues if they are wounded or killed 'in action' or suffer from post-traumatic stress disorders.

## Conclusion

The proliferation of private military contractors in contemporary national and international security policy is more than just one aspect of the 'postmodern' military. It indicates the emergence of a new model of the soldier and a fundamental transformation of civil–military relations. A number of experts of civil–military relations have noted this challenge, but so far little research has been conducted on it. This chapter has made a first attempt to define the nature of the 'new model soldier' and the ways in which it undermines existing models for the democratic control of the armed forces. Specifically, this chapter has argued that the private military contractor model operates outside historically established institutional and legal structures that seek to safeguard democratic civilian control and accountability. Private military contractors are currently working in a vacuum in national and international law which makes it difficult to hold them both politically and legally accountable. Existing institutional weaknesses are aggravated by the divergent norms and standards embraced by and applied to private military contractors, albeit many work in positions previously occupied by military personnel. Finally, democratic civil–military relations are challenged by the increasing distance between civil society and the members of the armed forces through the hiring of foreign nationals for international interventions.

Several interlinked conclusions can be drawn from this preliminary analysis. First, the objective to improve political and legal oversight over private military contractors is not merely a necessity if private military contractors can be shown to act contrary to established political and legal norms. Ensuring political control and accountability over the publicly sanctioned use of armed force is a fundamental aspect of civil–military relations within the democratic state. Second, recent United States and United Kingdom attempts to clarify the position of private military contractors as 'civilians accompanying the force' are a step in the wrong direction because they fail to recognize private military contractors as a new type of soldier. They increasingly operate in military functions and represent an integral part of the postmodern military. Third, the degree to which we might need to rethink civil–military relations in contemporary democratic societies might be much greater than has so far been realized. It is surely possible and desirable to modify current political and legal institutions in order to improve the oversight and accountability of private military contractors employed by national armed forces. However, as has been argued above, formal institutions are not sufficient to ensure the democratic behaviour of those who wield the state's monopoly on violence; dedication to the democratic ideal, duty to the nation, professionalism and the intermeshing of the military with civil society are even more important. How the latter can be achieved or what could replace them is still an open question.

## Notes

1 The Associated Press, 'Many Elite Soldiers Leave for Better Pay', 21 July 2004.
2 Christopher Dandeker, 'The United Kingdom: The Overstretched Military', in Charles C. Moskos, John Allen Williams and David R. Segal (eds), *The Postmodern Military*, Oxford: Oxford University Press, 2000, p. 33.
3 CTV.ca News, 'Canada Losing JTF2 Soldiers to Mercenaries: NDP', 21 November 2006; Ann Scott Tyson, 'Military Offers Special Perks in Bid to Retain Special Forces', *Christian Science Monitor*, 21 January 2005.
4 Stan Crock, Thomas F. Armistead, Anthony Bianco and Stephanie Anderson Forest, 'Outsourcing War', *Business Week*, Issue 3849, 15 September 2003, pp. 68–78.
5 Timothy Edmunds, 'What Are Armed Forces for? The Changing Nature of Military Roles in Europe', *International Affairs*, 2006, Vol. 82(6), pp. 1059–76.

6 E. Abrams and A. Bacevich, 'A Symposium on Citizenship and Military Service', *Parameters*, Summer 2001, Vol. 31(2), pp. 18–22.

7 Deborah Avant, *The Market for Force: The Consequences of Privatizing Security*, Cambridge: Cambridge University Press, 2005; Robert Mandel, *Armies Without States: The Privatization of Security*, Boulder, CO: Rienner, 2002; Peter W. Singer, *Corporate Warriors: The Rise of the Privatized Military Industry*, Ithaca, NY: Cornell University Press, 2003.

8 See Table 2.1 – Charles C. Moskos, 'Toward a Postmodern Military: The United States as a Paradigm' in Charles C. Moskos, John Allen Williams and David R. Segal (eds), *The Postmodern Military*, Oxford: Oxford University Press, 2000, p. 15.

9 Samuel P. Huntington, *The Soldier and the State. The Theory and Politics of Civil–Military Relations*, Cambridge, MA: Belknap Press of Harvard University Press, 1957.

10 Moskos 'Toward a Postmodern Military: The United States as a Paradigm'.

11 Morris Janowitz, for instance, proclaims the end of mass conscription in NATO as early as 1972. See Morris Janowitz, 'Strategic Dimensions of an All Volunteer Force' in Sam C. Sarkesian (ed.) *The Military–Industrial Complex. A Reassessment*, London: Sage, 1972, p. 127.

12 Cindy Williams, 'From Conscripts to Volunteers. NATO's Transitions to All-Volunteer Forces', *The Naval War College Review*, 2005, Vol. 58(1), pp. 35–62.

13 Christopher Jehn and Zachary Selden, 'The End of Conscription in Europe?', *Contemporary Economic Policy*, April 2002, Vol. 20(2), pp. 93–100 and 94; Henning Sørensen, 'Conscription in Scandinavia during the Last Quarter Century: Developments and Arguments', *Armed Forces & Society*, 2000, Vol. 26(2), pp. 313–34.

14 Mandel, *Armies without States: The Privatization of Security*; Singer *Corporate Warriors: The Rise of the Privatized Military Industry*.

15 A Markusen,. 'The Case against Privatizing National Security', *Governance*, 2003, Vol. 16(4), pp. 471–501; Elke Krahmann, 'Controlling Private Military Companies in the UK and Germany: Between Partnership and Regulation', *European Security*, 2005, Vol. 13(2), pp. 277–95, also as presented to the International Studies Association Annual Convention, 2003, www.isanet.org/portlandarchive.html#, accessed on 12 October 2006.

16 See Chapter 8 in this volume by Doug Brooks and Matan Chorev.

17 R. Claire Snyder, 'The Citizen–Soldier Tradition and Gender Integration of the U.S. Military', *Armed Forces & Society*, 2003, Vol. 29(2), pp. 185–204.

18 April Carter, 'Liberalism and the Obligation to Military Service', *Political Studies*, 1998, Vol. 46(1), p. 70

19 Morris Janowitz, 'The All-Volunteer Military as a "Sociopolitical" Problem', *Social Problems*, 1974, Vol. 22(3), p. 434; Peter Karsten, 'The U.S. Citizen–Soldier's Past, Present, and Likely Future', *Parameters*, Summer 2001, Vol. 31(2), pp. 61–73.

20 Margaret Levi, 'The Institution of Conscription', *Social Science History*, 1996, Vol. 20(1), pp. 133–67.

21 Karsten, 'The U.S. Citizen–Soldier's Past, Present, and Likely Future'.

22 Eliot A. Cohen, 'Twilight of the Citizen–Soldier', *Parameters*, 2001, Vol. 31(2), pp. 23–8.

23 Karsten, 'The U.S. Citizen–Soldier's Past, Present, and Likely Future', p.62; Kestnbaum, Meyer 'Citizenship and Compulsory Military Service: The Revolutionary Origins of Conscription in the United States', *Armed Forces & Society*, 2000, Vol. 27(1), p. 7.

24 Kestnbaum, 'Citizenship and Compulsory Military Service: The Revolutionary Origins of Conscription in the United States', p. 8.

25 Janowitz , *All-Volunteer Military*, p. 434.
26 Ibid., p. 435.
27 Cohen, 'Twilight of the Citizen–Soldier', p. 24.
28 Herrera speaks of 'self-governance'. See Richardo A. Herrera, 'Self-Governance and the American Citizen as Soldier, 1775–1861', *The Journal of Military History*, January 201, Vol. 65(1), p. 21.
29 Huntington, *The Soldier and the State. The Theory and Politics of Civil–Military Relations*, pp. 30–58.
30 James Burk, 'The Military Obligation of Citizens since Vietnam,' *Parameters,* Summer 2002, Vol. 31(2), pp. 48–60.
31 Huntington, *The Soldier and the State*.
32 Morris Janowitz, *The Professional Soldier. A Social and Political Portrait,* New York: Free Press, 1960.
33 Huntington, *The Soldier and the State*, pp. 8–18.
34 Janowitz, *Professional Soldier*, pp. 228.
35 Sam C. Sarkesian, John Allen Williams and Fred B. Bryant, *Soldiers, Society, and National Security*, Boulder, CO: Lynne Rienner, 1995, p. 13.
36 Mosokos cited in Sarkesian, John Allen Williams and Fred B. Bryant, *Soldiers, Society, and National Security*, p. 14.
37 James Burk, 'Patriotism and the All-Volunteer Force', *Journal of Political and Military Sociology*, Fall 1984, Vol. 12, pp. 229–41.
38 John Eighmey, 'Why Do Youth Enlist? Identification of Underlying Themes', *Armed Forces & Society*, 2006, Vol. 32(2), pp. 307–28.
39 Sarkesian, John Allen Williams and Fred B. Bryant, *Soldiers, Society, and National Security*, p. 2.
40 Bengt Abrahamsson, *Military Professionalization and Political Power*, Beverly Hills, CA: Sage, 1972; Janowitz, *Professional Soldier*, p. 13.
41 Janowitz, *Strategic Dimensions*, p. 156.
42 Sarkesian, John Allen Williams and Fred B. Bryant, *Soldiers, Society, and National Security*, p. 139.
43 Huntington, *The Soldier and the State*, p. 11.
44 Janowitz, *Professional Soldier*, p. 5.
45 Sarkesian, John Allen Williams and Fred B. Bryant, *Soldiers, Society, and National Security*, p. 8, p. 15.
46 Hew Strachan, 'The Civil–Military "Gap" in Britain', *The Journal of Strategic Studies*, June 2003, Vol. 26(2), pp. 47–8.
47 Downes, C.J. 'To Be or Not to Be a Profession: The Military Case', *Defense Analysis*, 1985, Vol. 1(3), pp. 147–8.
48 Don M. Snider and Gayle L. Watkins, 'The Future of Army Professionalism: A Need for Renewal and Redefinition', *Parameters*, 2000, Vol. 30(3), pp. 5–20.
49 Janowitz, *All-Volunteer Military*, p. 439.
50 Abrams and Bacevich, 'A Symposium on Citizenship and Military Service', pp. 18–22.
51 Charles C. Moskos, 'What Ails the All-Volunteer Force: An Institutional Perspective', *Parameters*, 2001, Vol. 31(2), pp. 29–47; see also Sarkesian, John Allen Williams and Fred B. Bryant, *Soldiers, Society, and National Security*, p. 14.
52 Krahmann, 'Controlling Private Military Companies in the UK and Germany: Between Partnership and Regulation'.
53 Christopher Spearin, 'American Hegemony Incorporated: The Importance and Implications of Military Contractors in Iraq', *Contemporary Security Policy,* 2003, Vol. 24(3), pp. 26–47.
54 David Isenberg, 'A Fistful of Contractors: The Case for a Pragmatic Assessment of Private Military Companies in Iraq', British American Security Information Council, September 2004.

55 Spearin, 'American Hegemony Incorporated: The Importance and Implications of Military Contractors in Iraq', p. 28. Others estimate the number in the Gulf War closer to one in fifty. See Deborah Avant, 'The Privatization of Security and Change in the Control of Force', *International Studies Perspectives*, 2004, Vol. 5, pp. 153–7.

56 Statement of Chairman Marty Meehan, Subcommittee on Oversight and Investigations, Hearing re: the Use of Contractors in Training, Equipping, and Sustaining the Iraqi Security Forces, US House of Representatives, House Armed Services Committee, 25 April 2007.

57 Government Accountability Office (GAO), *Rebuilding Iraq: Actions Needed to Improve Use of Private Security Providers*, GAO-05-737, Washington, DC: GAO, 2005, p. 8.

58 Sarkesian, John Allen Williams and Fred B. Bryant, *Soldiers, Society, and National Security*, p. 15.

59 Stan Crock, Thomas F. Armistead, Anthony Bianco, Stephanie Anderson Forest, 'Outsourcing War', *Business Week*, Issue 3849, 15 September 2003, pp. 68–78.

60 MoD Defence Contracts Bulletin, 'Contractors on Deployed Operations', 9 April 2003, p.26. Available at: www.contracts.mod.uk, accessed on 25 October 2007.

61 National Audit Office, *Ministry of Defence: Operation TELIC – United Kingdom Military Operations in Iraq*, HC 60 Session 2003–2004, London: The Stationary Office, 2003, p. 21.

62 Frank Camm and Victoria A. Greenfield, *How Should the Army Use Contractors on the Battlefield? Assessing Comparative Risk in Sourcing Decisions*, Santa Monica, CA: RAND, 2005, p. 154.

63 Lieutenant Commander Stephen P. Ferris and David M. Keithly, 'Outsourcing the Sinews of War: Contractor Logistics', *Military Review*, 2001, Vol. LXXXI(5), p. 76.

64 Burk, 'Patriotism and the All-Volunteer Force'.

65 Andrew Jacobs and Simon Romero, 'U.S. Workers, Lured by Money and Idealism, Face Iraqi Reality', *New York Times*, 14 April 2004; Ariana Eunjung Cha and Jackie Spinner, 'Some U.S. Workers Say the Risk Is Too Great', *Washington Post*, 15 April 2004.

66 Manuel Roig-Franzia, 'Ohioan Gung-Ho, Despite Dangers', *Washington Post*, 2 April 2004.

67 Sheila McNulty, 'Come to Hell with Halliburton – The Pay's Good', *Financial Times*, 14 June 2004; Clare Murphy, 'Iraq's Mercenaries: Riches for Risks', *BBC News Online*, 1 April 2004.

68 Andrew Jacobs and Simon Romero, 'U.S. Workers, lured by Money and Idealism, Face Iraqi Reality', *New York Times*, 14 April 2004, available at: http://query.nytimes.com/gst/fullpage.html?res=9D0DE3D6163BF937A2575 7C0A9629C8B63, last accessed 11 October 2007.

69 Jonathan Franklin, 'US Contractor Recruits Guards for Iraq in Chile', *Guardian*, 5 March 2004; Sinno Efron, 'Iraq: Worry Grows as Foreigners Flock to Risky Jobs', *Los Angeles Times*, 30 July 2005.

70 Sarkesian, John Allen Williams and Fred B. Bryant, *Soldiers, Society, and National Security*, p. 133.

71 Douglas L. Bland, 'A Unified Theory of Civil–Military Relations', *Armed Forces & Society*, 1999, Vol. 26(1), p. 13.

72 Anthony Forster, *Armed Forces and Society in Europe*, Basingstoke: Palgrave, 2006, p. 20.

73 Huntington, *The Soldier and the State*, pp. 83–4; Bland, 'A Unified Theory of Civil–Military Relations', p. 14.

74 Forster, *Armed Forces and Society in Europe*, p. 4
75 Sarkesian, John Allen Williams and Fred B. Bryant, *Soldiers, Society, and National Security*, p. 137.
76 Bland, 'A Unified Theory of Civil–Military Relations', p. 534.
77 Ibid, p. 532.
78 Ibid, p. 533.
79 Ibid, p. 532.
80 Richard H. Kohn, 'How Democracies Control the Military', *Journal of Democracy* 1997, Vol. 8(4), pp. 140–53.
81 Bland, 'A Unified Theory of Civil–Military Relations', p. 525.
82 Peter Feaver cited in ibid, p. 528.
83 Ibid, p. 529.
84 Morris Janowitz cited in ibid, p. 528; Kohn, 'How Democracies Control the Military', p. 147.
85 See Chapter 15 in this book by Jessica Wolfendale. See also Sarkesian, John Allen Williams and Fred B. Bryant, *Soldiers, Society, and National Security*, p. 137; Snider and Watkins, 'The Future of Army Professionalism: A Need for Renewal and Redefinition'.
86 Ole R. Holsti, 'A Widening Gap between the U.S. Military and Civilian Society? Some Evidence, 1976–1996', *International Security*, 1998, Vol. 23(3), pp.5–42; Peter D. Feaver and Richard H. Kohn (eds), *Soldiers and Civilians. The Civil–Military Gap and American National Security*, Cambridge, MA: MIT Press, 2001.
87 Sarkesian, John Allen Williams and Fred B. Bryant, *Soldiers, Society, and National Security*, pp. 136–7.
88 James Burk, 'Theories of Democratic Civil–Military Relations', *Armed Forces & Society*, Fall 2002, Vol. 29(1), pp. 17–18.
89 US Headquarters Department of the Army, *Contractors on the Battlefield*, FM 3–100.21, January 2003.
90 Charles C. Moskos, John Allen Williams and David R. Segal, 'Armed Forces after the Cold War', in Moskos op. cit., pp. 1–13.
91 David M. Halbfinger and Steven A. Holmes, 'Military Mirrors Working-class America,' *New York Times*, 30 March 2003.

# Select bibliography

Avant, Deborah, *The Market for Force: The Consequences of Privatizing Security*, Cambridge: Cambridge University Press, 2005.
——'Privatizing Military Training', *Foreign Policy In Focus*, Vol. 7(6), May 2002, available at www.fpif.org/pdf/vol7/06ifmiltrain.pdf, accessed 11 October 2007.
Bryden, Alan and Caparini, Marina (eds), *Private Actors and Security Governance*, Zurich and Berlin: Lit Verlag, 2006.
Chesterman, Simon and Lehnardt, Chia (eds), *From Mercenaries to Market: The Rise and Regulation of Private Military Companies*, Oxford: Oxford University Press, 2007.
Coady, C.A.J. (Tony), 'Mercenary Morality', in Antony G.D. Bradney (ed.), *International Law and Armed Conflict (Archiv für Rechts- und Sozialphilosophie, Beiheft 46)*, 1992, Stuttgart: Franz Steiner Verlag, pp. 55–69.
Donald, Dominick, 'After the Bubble; British Private Security Companies after Iraq', Whitehall Paper No. 65, London: RUSI, 2006.
International Review of the Red Cross, Issue on Private Military Companies, No. 863, September 2006. Available at: www.icrc.org/Web/Eng/siteeng0.nsf/htmlall/section_review_2006_863?OpenDocument, accessed 10 October 2007.
Isenberg, David, *A Fistful of Contractors: The Case for a Pragmatic Assessment of Private Military Companies in Iraq*, British American Security Information Council, 2004.
Kaldor, Mary, *New and Old Wars: Organized Violence in a Global Era*, Cambridge: Polity Press, 1999.
Leander, Anna, 'The Market for Force and Public Security: The Destabilizing Consequences of Private Military Companies', *Journal of Peace Research*, 2005, Vol. 42(5), pp. 605–22.
Lynch, Tony and Walsh, Adrian J., 'The Good Mercenary?', *The Journal of Political Philosophy*, 2000, Vol. 8(2), pp. 133–53.
Mandel, Robert, *Armies without States: The Privatization of Security*, Boulder, CO: Rienner, 2002.
Mills, Greg and Stremlau, John (eds), *The Privatization of Security in Africa*, Johannesburg: The South African Institute of International Affairs, 1999.
Musah, Abdel-Fatau and Fayemi, Kayode (eds), *Mercenaries: An African Security Dilemma*, London: Pluto, 2000.
Oakeshott Michael, *Hobbes on Civil Association*, Berkely: University of California Press, 1975.

Percy, Sarah, 'Regulating the Private Security Industry', Adelphi Paper 384, London: Routledge for International Institute for Strategic Studies, 2006.

Schreier, Fred and Caparini, Marina, 'Law, Practice and Governance of Private Military and Security Companies', Occasional Paper No. 6, Geneva: Geneva Centre for the Democratic Control of the Armed Forces, March 2005.

Shearer, David, 'Private Armies and Military Intervention', Adelphi Paper 316, International Institute for Strategic Studies, Oxford: Oxford University Press, 1998.

Singer, Peter W., *Corporate Warriors: The Rise of the Privatized Military Industry*, Ithaca, NY: Cornell University Press, 2003.

—— 'War, Profits, and the Vacuum of Law: Privatized Military Firms and International Law', *Columbia Journal of Transnational Law*, 2004, Vol. 42(2), pp. 521–49.

—— 'Outsourcing War', *Foreign Affairs*, March/April 2005, Vol. 84(22), pp. 119–32.

US Government Accountability Office (GAO), 'Rebuilding Iraq: Actions Needed to Improve Use of Private Security Providers', GAO-05-737, Washington, DC: GAO, 2005.

Walzer, Michael, *Just and Unjust Wars: A Moral Argument with Historical Illustrations*, 3rd Edition, United States of America: Basic Books, 2000.

# Index

Guantanamo Bay 184
Gulf War 121
gun culture 64
Gurr, T.R. 61

*Hamdan v. Rumsfeld* (2006) 177–8
Hampson, F.J. 3, 19–20
Hardy, T. 57
Hinduism 64–5
history, military 223–5
Hoare, M. 21, 22, 24, 25, 26–7, 30, 32
honourable soldiers 62–6
Host Country Nationals (HCNs) 119
human dignity 244
humanitarian catastrophes 9–10
humanitarian interventions 39, 59–60,
   210–12; *see also* peacekeeping
   operations
human life, value of 241
human rights violations 82, 220
human security 205–6, 206–7
Huntington, S. 249, 252
Hussein, S. 35

images of war 225–6, 228–9
indigenous populations 20
indirect rule 52
instrumental dependence 95, 96
insurance, international security 98–9
Intelligence and Security Command
   (INSCOM) 135
intelligence market, changes in 138–40
intelligence services, private provision
   of 10, 131–41
interface ethics 235–45
International Commission on
   Intervention and State
   Sovereignty 206
International Committee of the Red
   Cross (ICRC) 159
International Criminal Court 197
international humanitarian law (IHL)
   11; mercenaries and 160–2;
   responsibilities under 165–9; status
   of staff of PMSCs under 160–5;
   violations of 159–60
international interventions:
   accountability and 197–8;
   authorization of 199–200; increases
   in 193, 197; *see also* humanitarian
   interventions; peacekeeping
   operations
international non-governmental
   organizations (INGOs) 145–6

International Peace Operations
   Association (IPOA) 7, 79–80,
   125–6, 207
international political environment
   208–9
international security insurance 98–9
International Traffic in Arms
   Regulations (ITAR) 126
Iraq 14; casualties in 226; lack of legal
   constraints in 81–2; PMSCs in 19,
   78, 79, 81–2, 91, 119, 127, 173–4,
   209–10; regulation of PMSCs in
   172–3
Islam 66

Jackson, G. 63–4
Japan 63
*jihad* 66
*jus ad bellum* considerations 56, 66–7
*jus in bello* considerations 56–7,
   58, 59, 67
*Just and Unjust Wars* (Walzer) 3
Just War Theory 6, 34–5, 56–7, 61,
   66–8, 68, 220

Kasher, A. 13, 235
Kinsey, C. 7–8, 70
Kosovo 96
Krahmann, E. 14, 247
Kuwait 35

Leander, A. 123–4
lean state 194
legal constraints 64, 81–2
legitimacy 2, 30–1, 209–10, 220
Liberia 120–1, 146, 148–52, 155
Lifton, R.J. 225
local communities 76
Local Nationals (LNs) 119
logistics and support companies
   (LSCs) 118
loyalty 21
Luban, D. 219–20
lucrepaths 34, 37
Lynch, T. 218

Machiavelli, N. 33, 36, 40, 110
market forces 97–8, 107–8
market power 107
market pressures 205
market regulation 108–9
Marx, K. 50
materialism 7
Mattis, J.N. 63